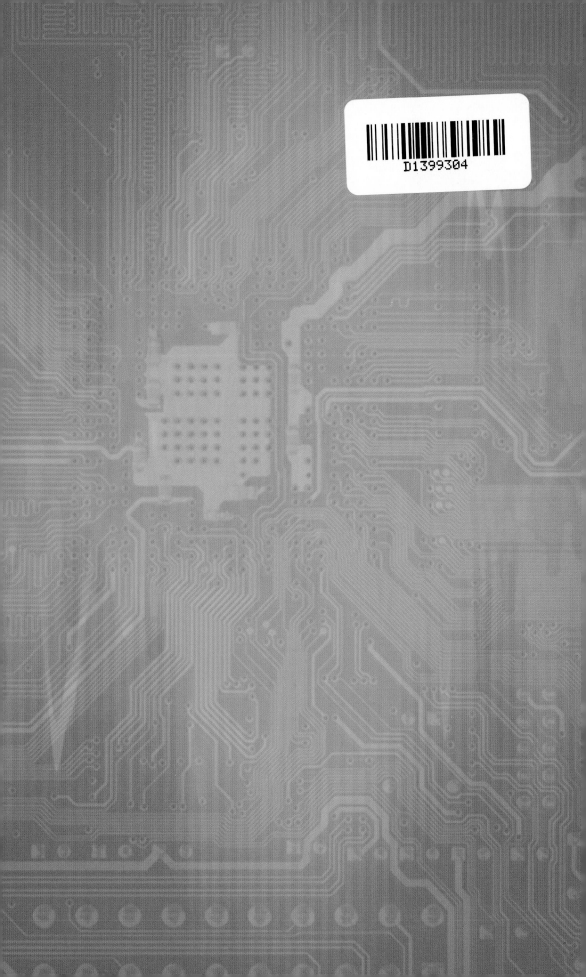

D1399304

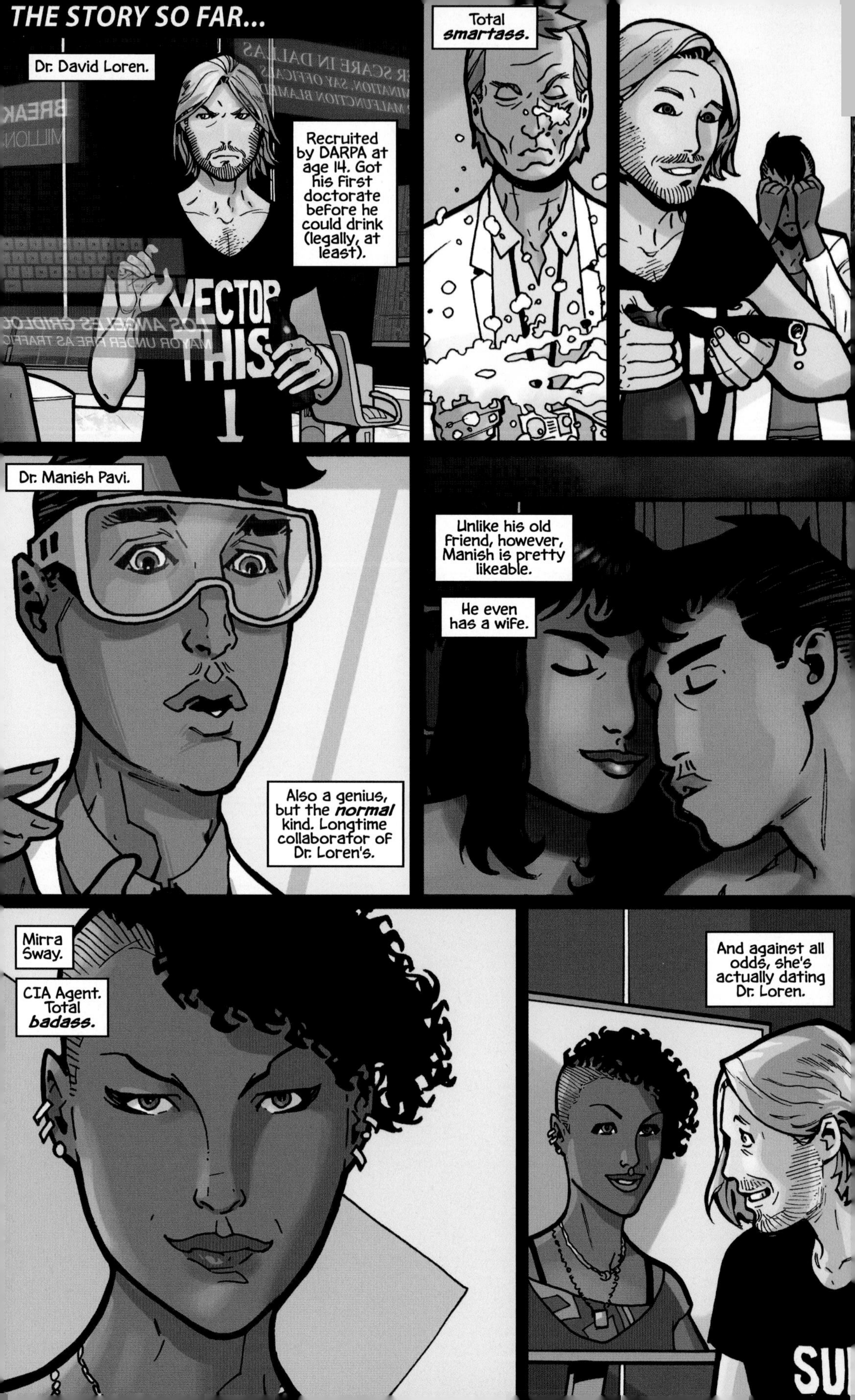
THE STORY SO FAR...
Dr. David Loren.
Recruited by DARPA at age 14. Got his first doctorate before he could drink (legally, at least).
VECTOR THIS
Total smartass.
Dr. Manish Pavi.
Also a genius, but the normal kind. Longtime collaborator of Dr. Loren's.
Unlike his old friend, however, Manish is pretty likeable.
He even has a wife.
Mirra Sway.
CIA Agent. Total badass.
And against all odds, she's actually dating Dr. Loren.

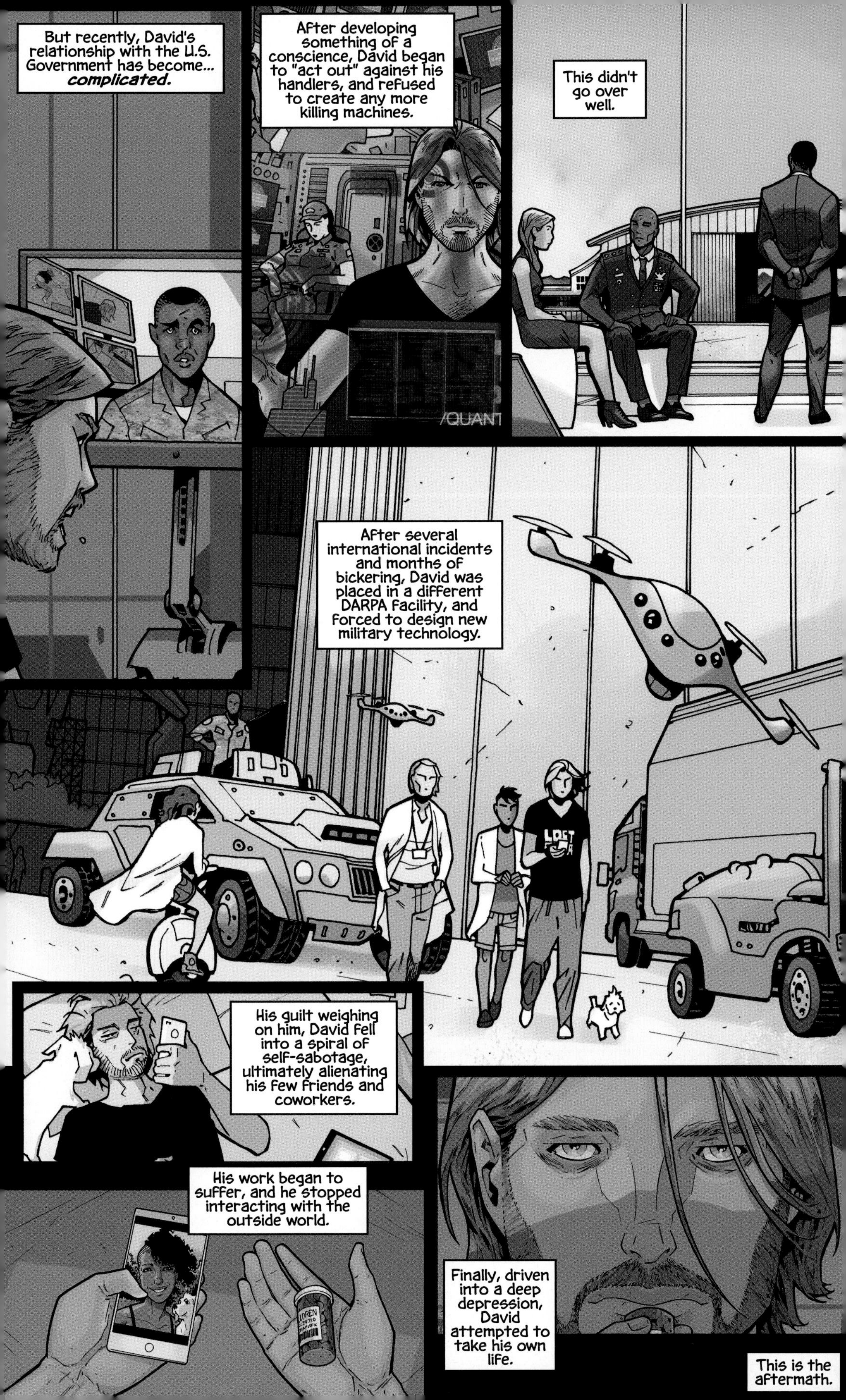
But recently, David's relationship with the U.S. Government has become... *complicated.*
After developing something of a conscience, David began to "act out" against his handlers, and refused to create any more killing machines.
/QUANT
This didn't go over well.
After several international incidents and months of bickering, David was placed in a different DARPA facility, and forced to design new military technology.
LOST
His guilt weighing on him, David fell into a spiral of self-sabotage, ultimately alienating his few friends and coworkers.
His work began to suffer, and he stopped interacting with the outside world.
LOREN
Finally, driven into a deep depression, David attempted to take his own life.
This is the aftermath.

CHAPTER ONE

THINK TANK

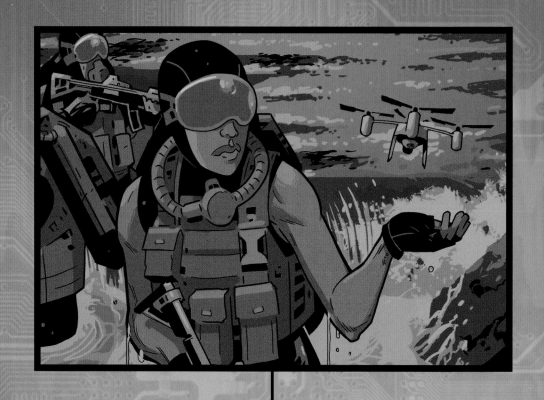

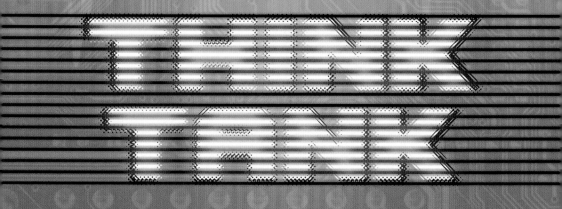

" *Man is the cruelest animal.*"

– Friedrich Nietzsche

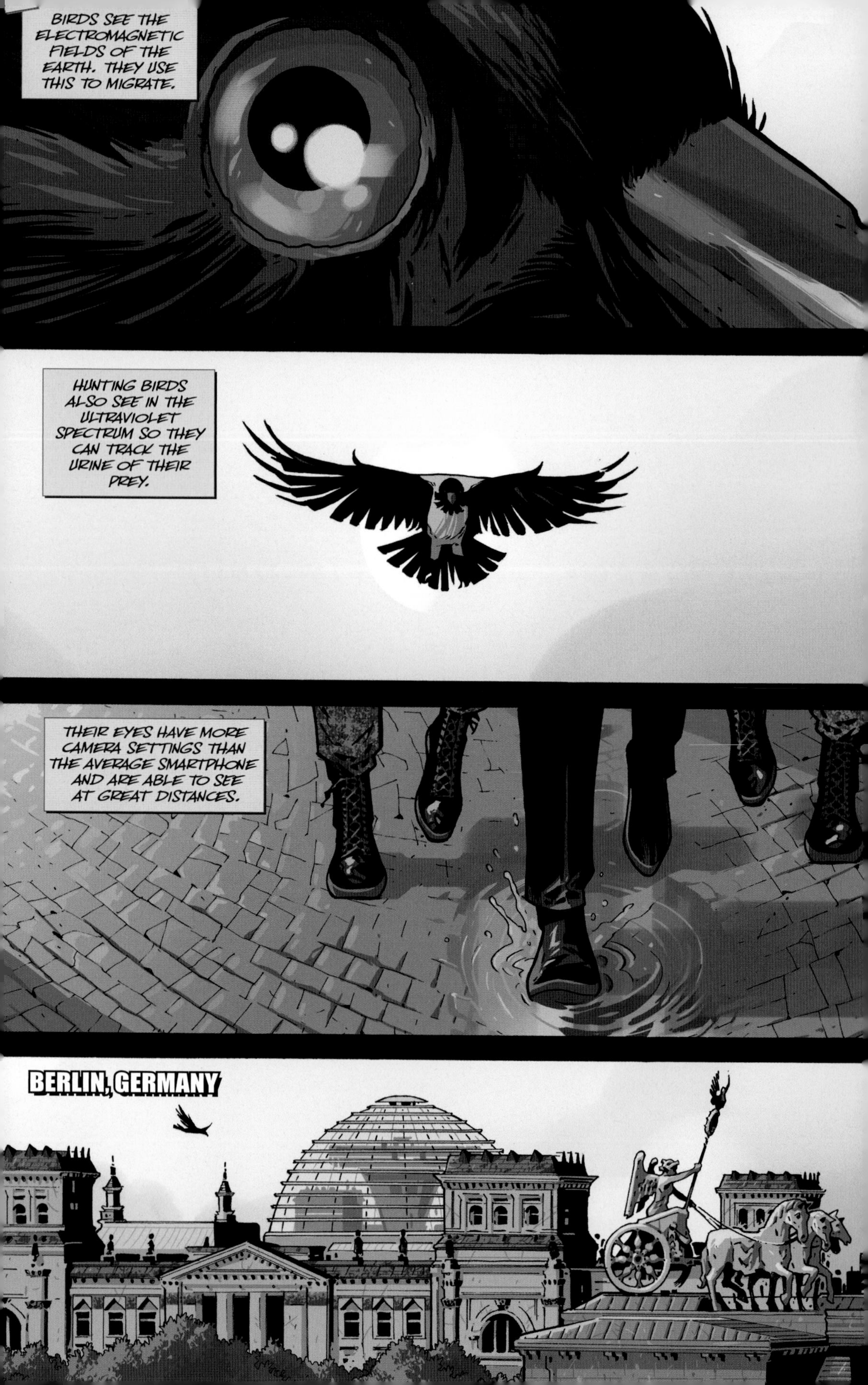
BIRDS SEE THE ELECTROMAGNETIC FIELDS OF THE EARTH. THEY USE THIS TO MIGRATE.
HUNTING BIRDS ALSO SEE IN THE ULTRAVIOLET SPECTRUM SO THEY CAN TRACK THE URINE OF THEIR PREY.
THEIR EYES HAVE MORE CAMERA SETTINGS THAN THE AVERAGE SMARTPHONE AND ARE ABLE TO SEE AT GREAT DISTANCES.
BERLIN, GERMANY

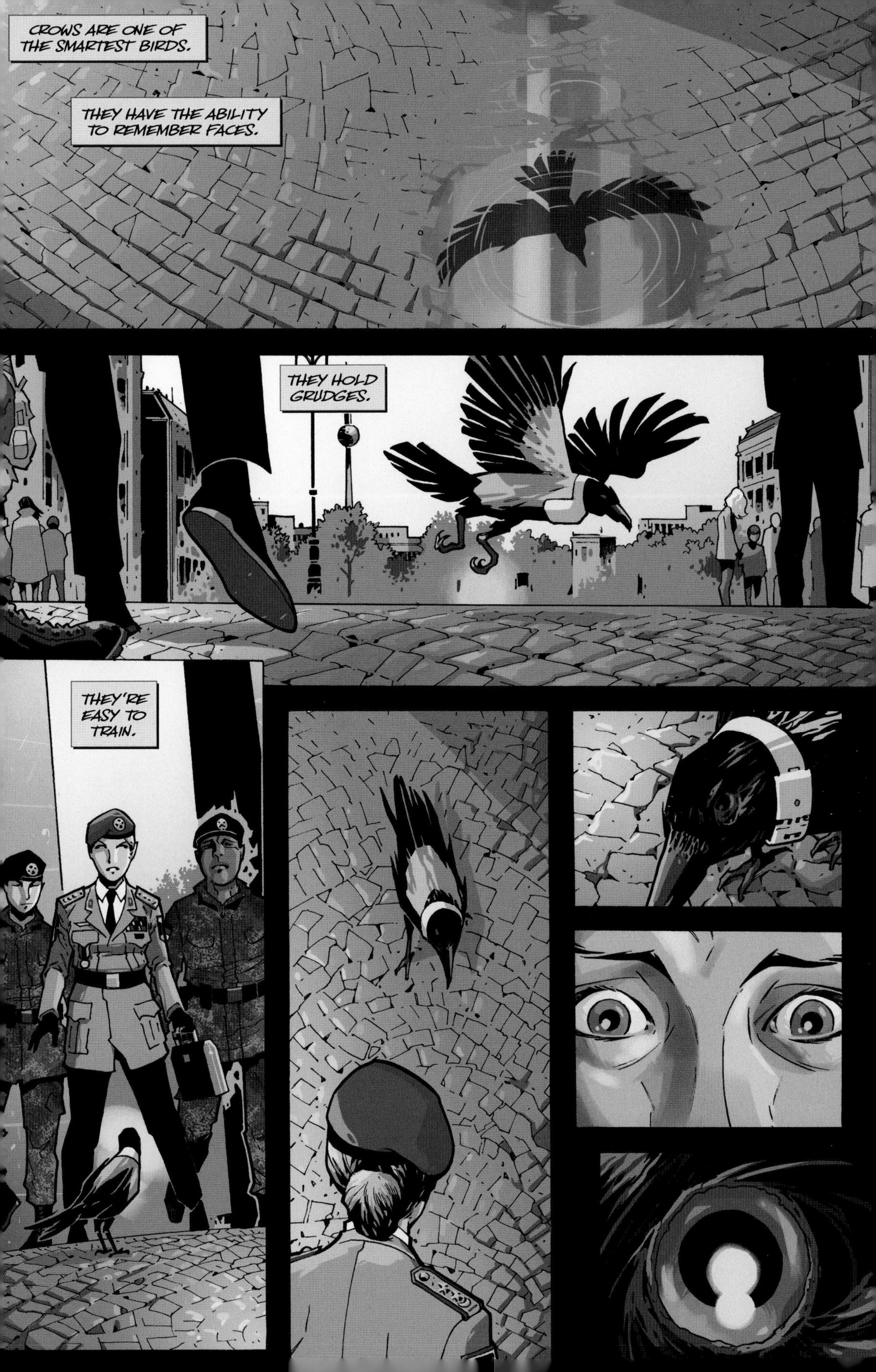
CROWS ARE ONE OF THE SMARTEST BIRDS.
THEY HAVE THE ABILITY TO REMEMBER FACES.
THEY HOLD GRUDGES.
THEY'RE EASY TO TRAIN.

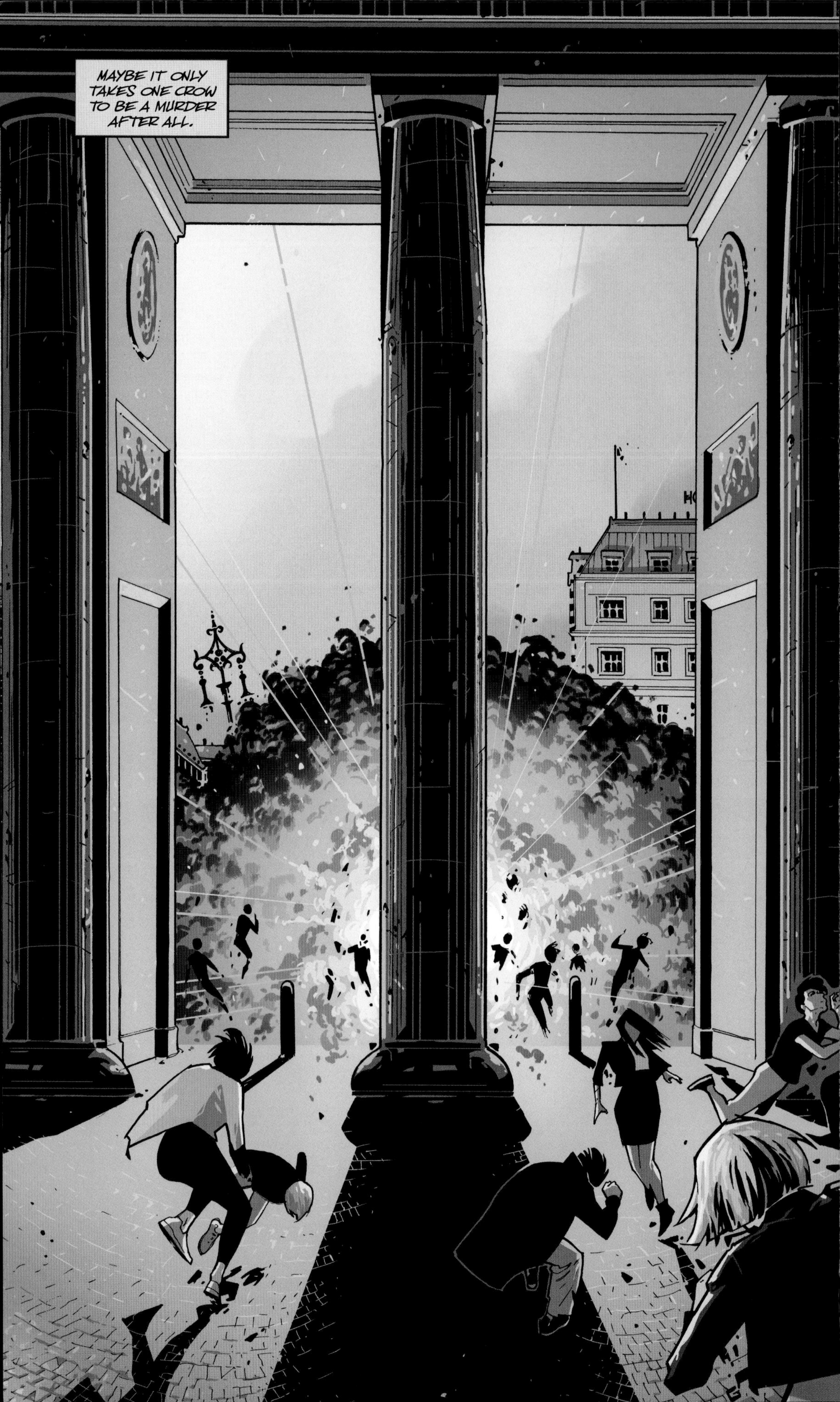
MAYBE IT ONLY TAKES ONE CROW TO BE A MURDER AFTER ALL.

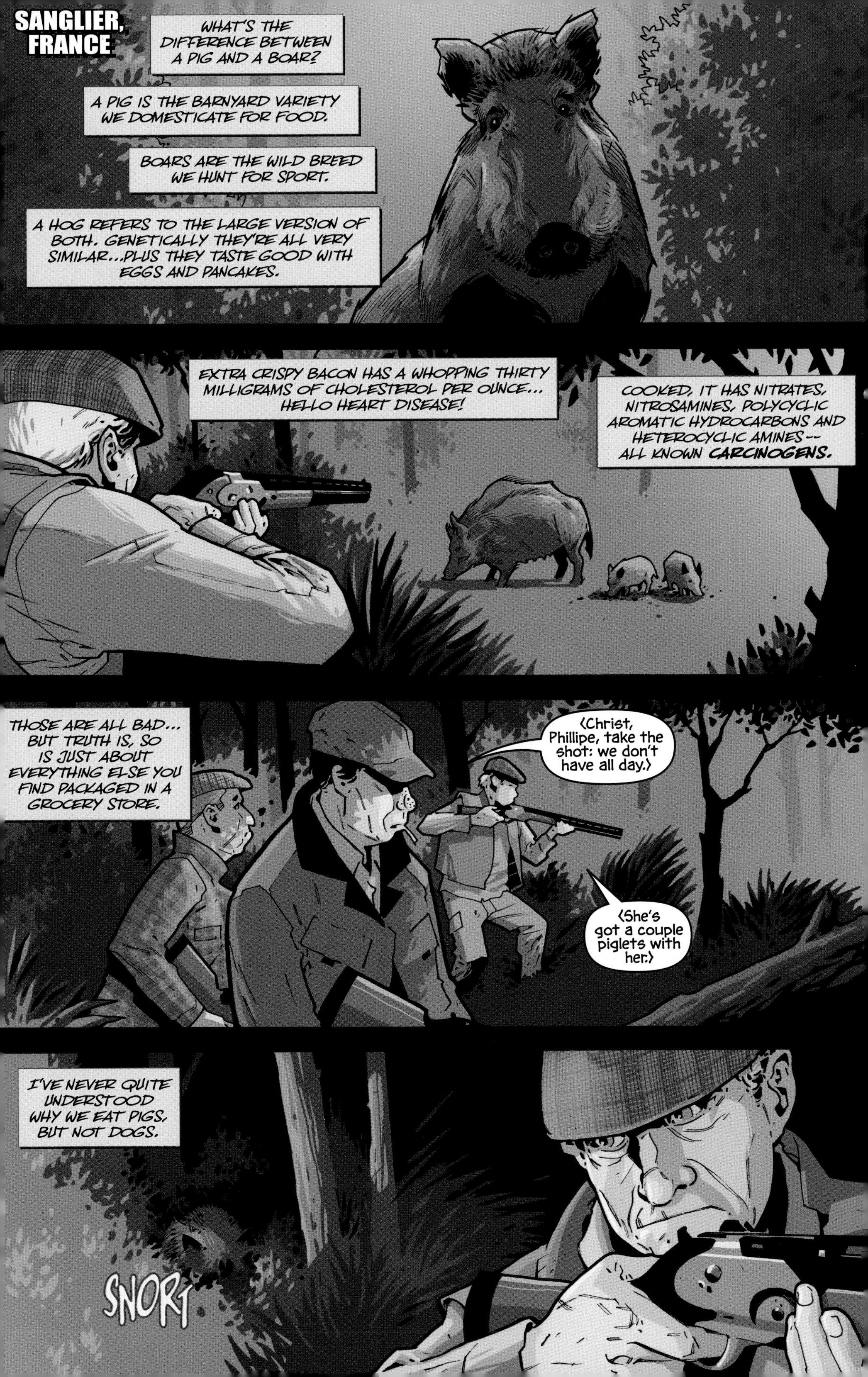
SANGLIER, FRANCE
WHAT'S THE DIFFERENCE BETWEEN A PIG AND A BOAR?
A PIG IS THE BARNYARD VARIETY WE DOMESTICATE FOR FOOD.
BOARS ARE THE WILD BREED WE HUNT FOR SPORT.
A HOG REFERS TO THE LARGE VERSION OF BOTH. GENETICALLY THEY'RE ALL VERY SIMILAR...PLUS THEY TASTE GOOD WITH EGGS AND PANCAKES.
EXTRA CRISPY BACON HAS A WHOPPING THIRTY MILLIGRAMS OF CHOLESTEROL PER OUNCE... HELLO HEART DISEASE!
COOKED, IT HAS NITRATES, NITROSAMINES, POLYCYCLIC AROMATIC HYDROCARBONS AND HETEROCYCLIC AMINES-- ALL KNOWN CARCINOGENS.
THOSE ARE ALL BAD... BUT TRUTH IS, SO IS JUST ABOUT EVERYTHING ELSE YOU FIND PACKAGED IN A GROCERY STORE.
‹Christ, Phillipe, take the shot: we don't have all day.›
‹She's got a couple piglets with her.›
I'VE NEVER QUITE UNDERSTOOD WHY WE EAT PIGS, BUT NOT DOGS.
SNORT

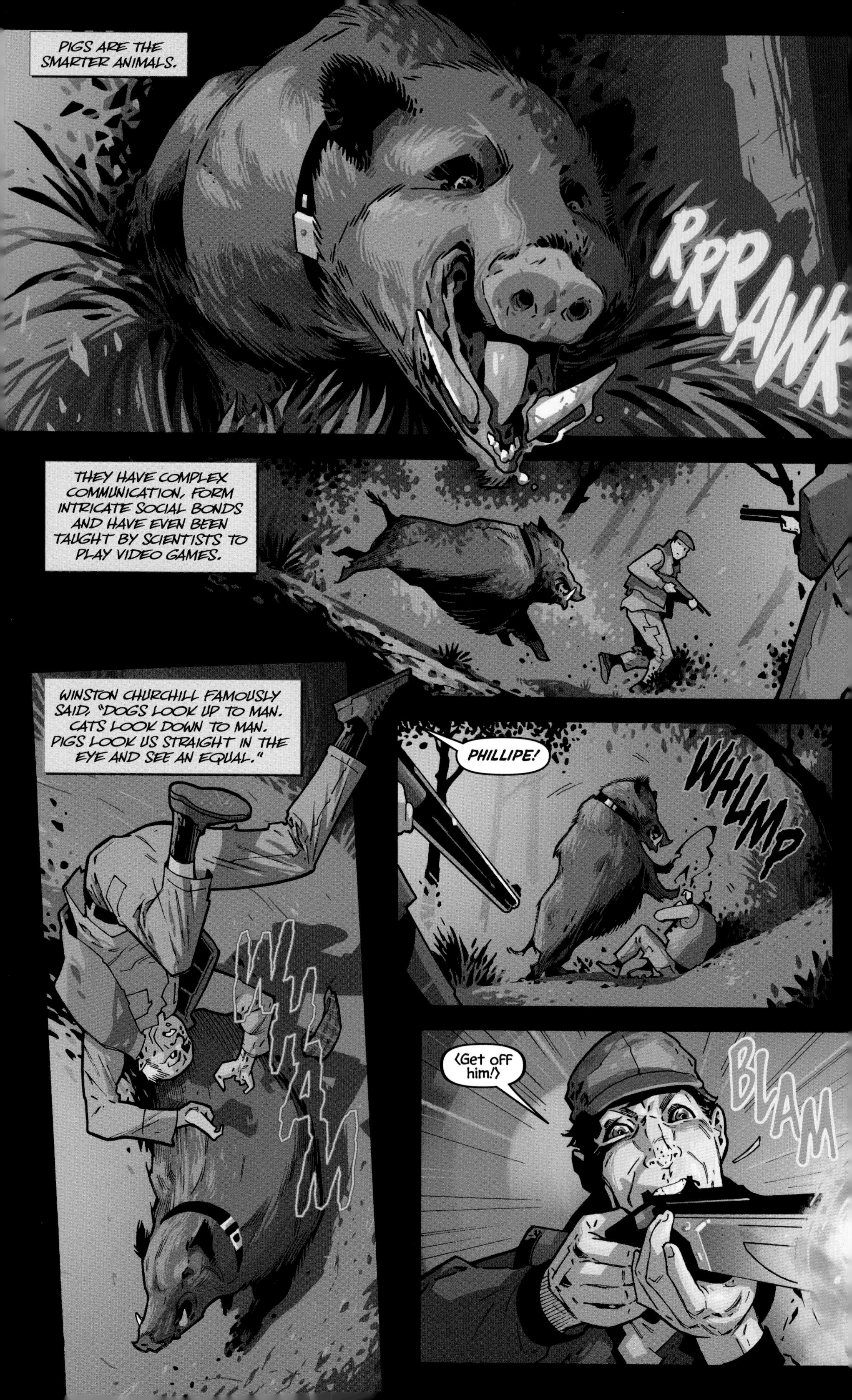
PIGS ARE THE SMARTER ANIMALS.
RRRAWR
THEY HAVE COMPLEX COMMUNICATION, FORM INTRICATE SOCIAL BONDS AND HAVE EVEN BEEN TAUGHT BY SCIENTISTS TO PLAY VIDEO GAMES.
WINSTON CHURCHILL FAMOUSLY SAID, "DOGS LOOK UP TO MAN. CATS LOOK DOWN TO MAN. PIGS LOOK US STRAIGHT IN THE EYE AND SEE AN EQUAL."
WHAM
PHILLIPE!
WHUMP
‹Get off him!›
BLAM

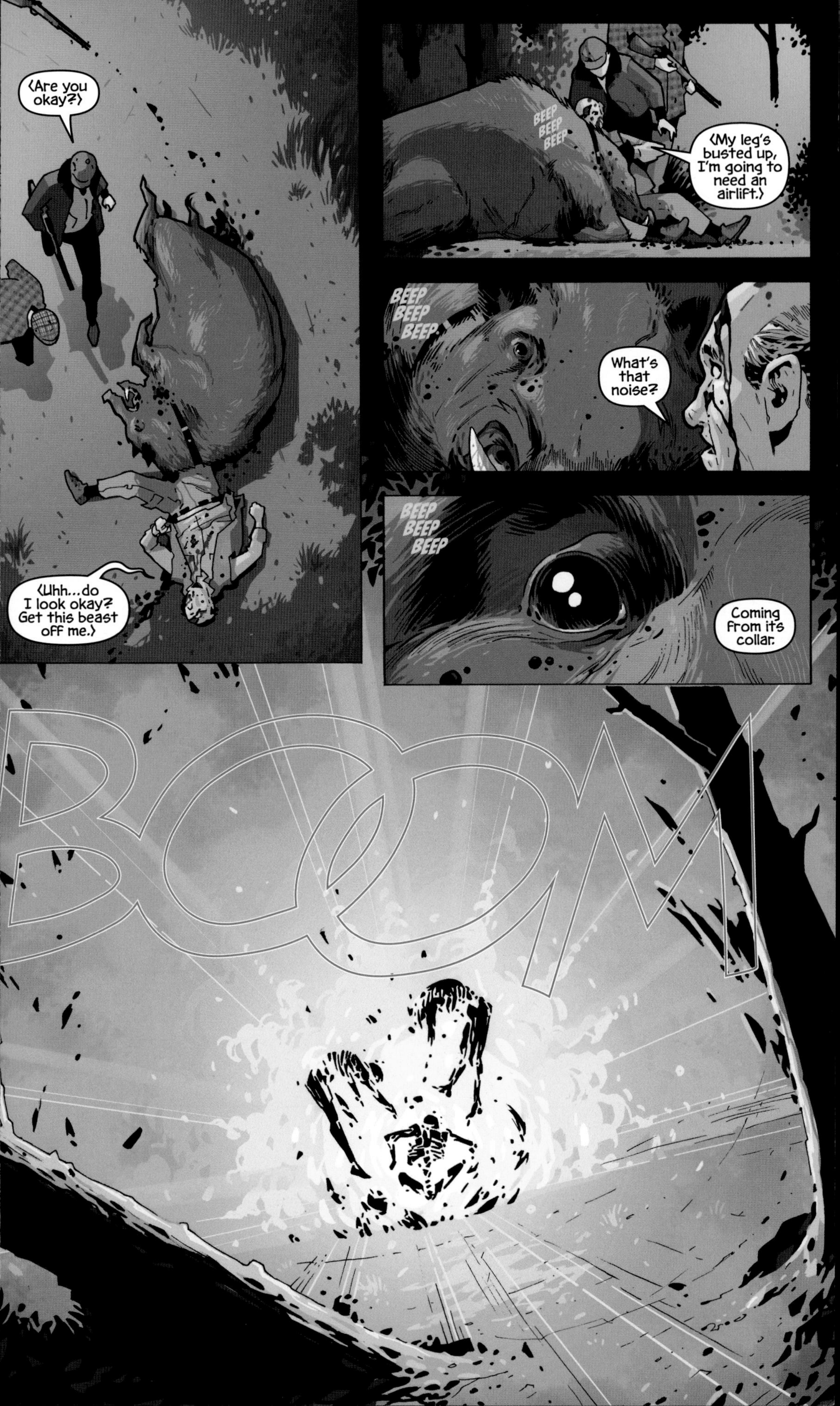

‹Are you okay?›
‹Uhh...do I look okay? Get this beast off me.›
BEEP BEEP BEEP
‹My leg's busted up, I'm going to need an airlift.›
BEEP BEEP BEEP
What's that noise?
BEEP BEEP BEEP
Coming from its collar.
BOOM

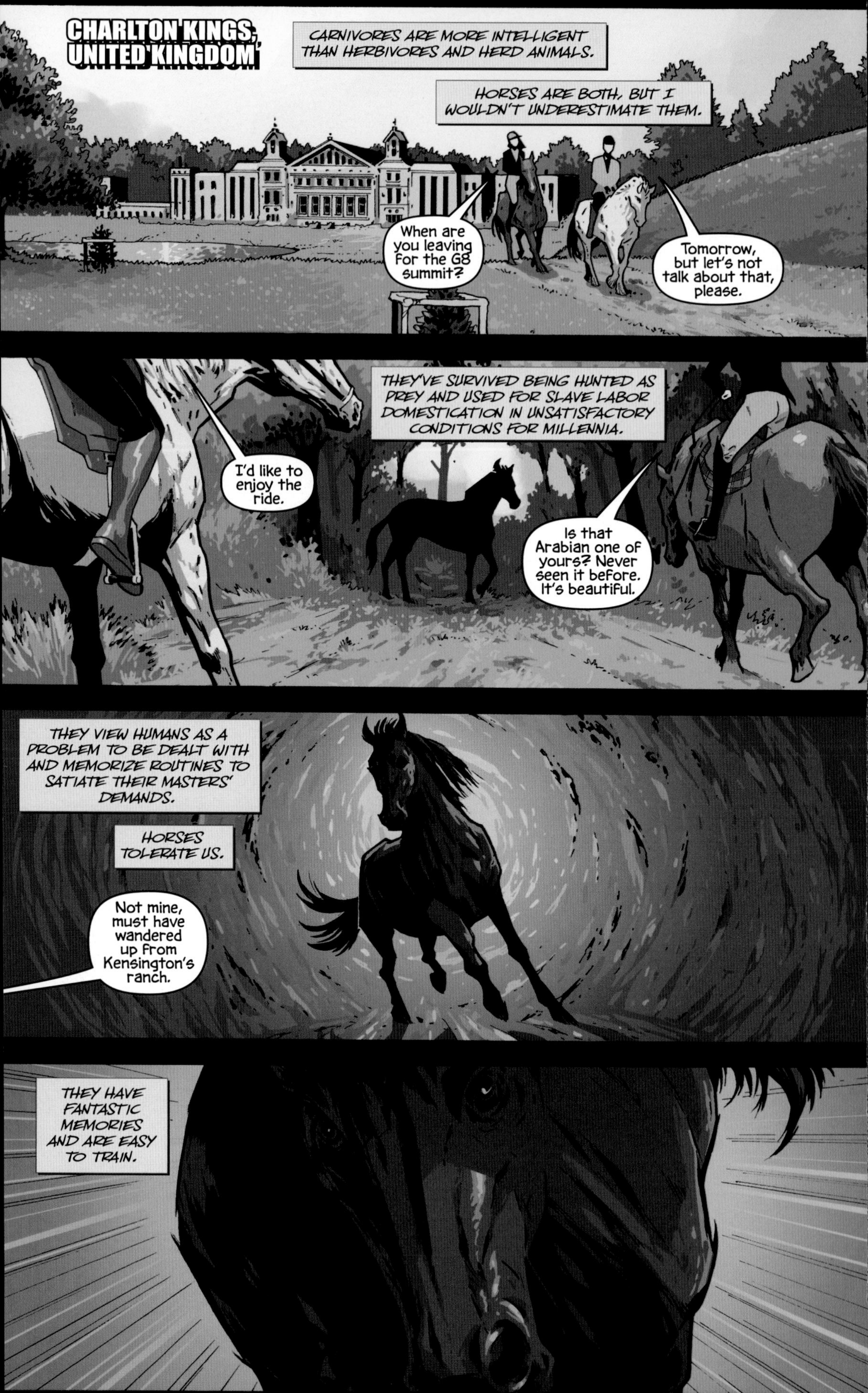
CHARLTON KINGS, UNITED KINGDOM
CARNIVORES ARE MORE INTELLIGENT THAN HERBIVORES AND HERD ANIMALS.
HORSES ARE BOTH, BUT I WOULDN'T UNDERESTIMATE THEM.
When are you leaving for the G8 summit?
Tomorrow, but let's not talk about that, please.
THEY'VE SURVIVED BEING HUNTED AS PREY AND USED FOR SLAVE LABOR DOMESTICATION IN UNSATISFACTORY CONDITIONS FOR MILLENNIA.
I'd like to enjoy the ride.
Is that Arabian one of yours? Never seen it before. It's beautiful.
THEY VIEW HUMANS AS A PROBLEM TO BE DEALT WITH AND MEMORIZE ROUTINES TO SATIATE THEIR MASTERS' DEMANDS.
HORSES TOLERATE US.
Not mine, must have wandered up from Kensington's ranch.
THEY HAVE FANTASTIC MEMORIES AND ARE EASY TO TRAIN.

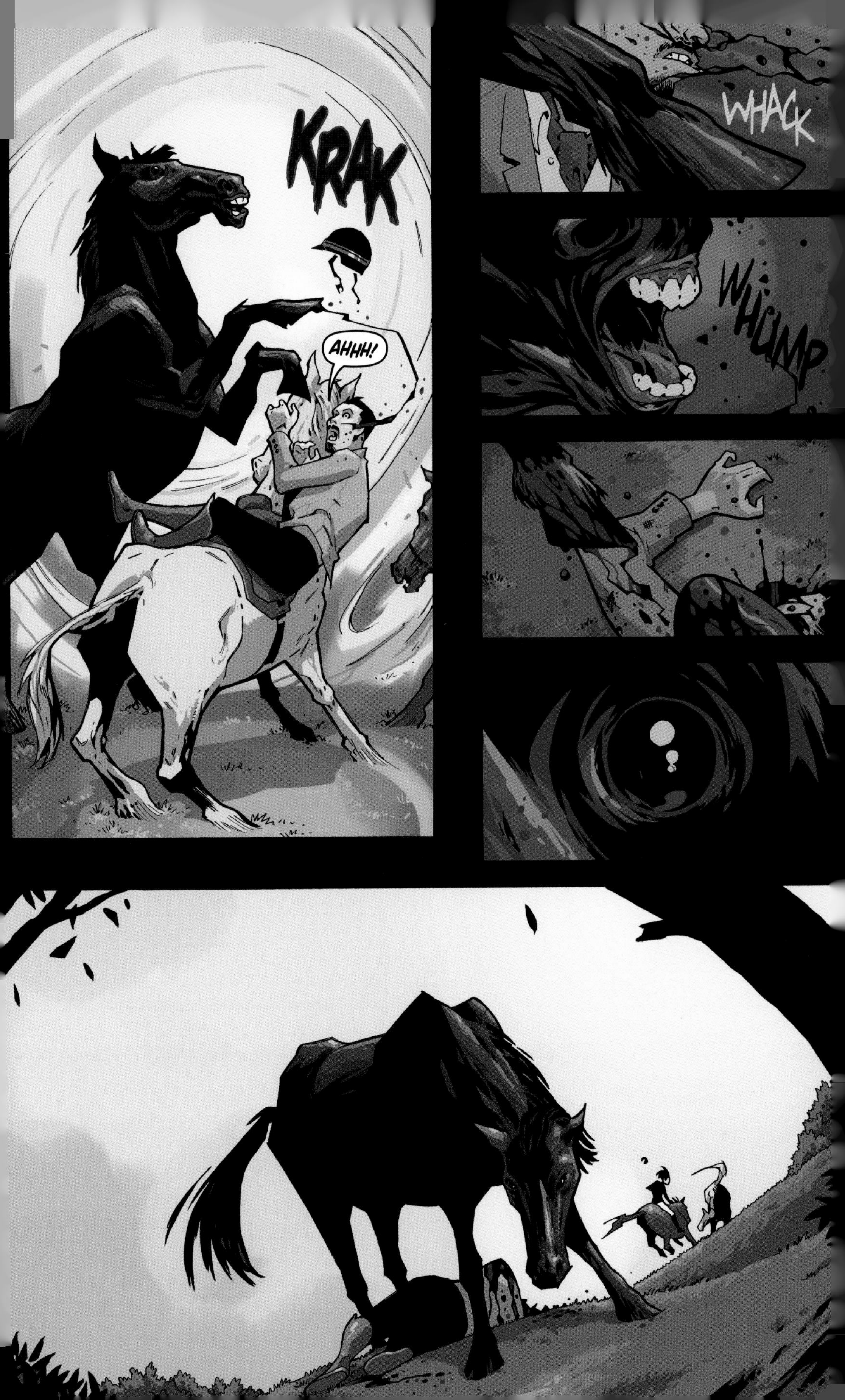
KRAK
AHHH!
WHACK
WHUMP

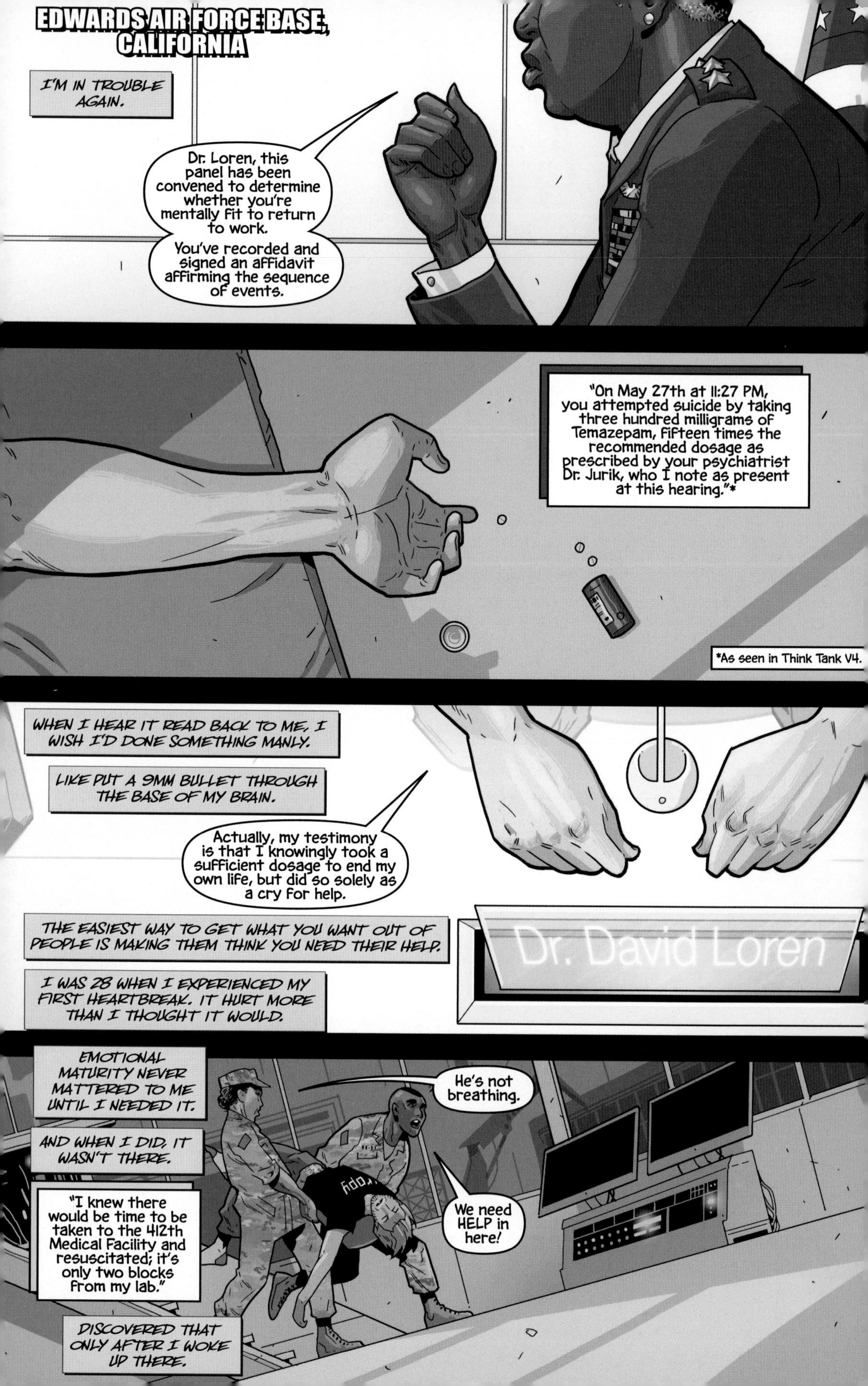

EDWARDS AIR FORCE BASE, CALIFORNIA
I'M IN TROUBLE AGAIN.
Dr. Loren, this panel has been convened to determine whether you're mentally fit to return to work.
You've recorded and signed an affidavit affirming the sequence of events.
"On May 27th at 11:27 PM, you attempted suicide by taking three hundred milligrams of Temazepam, fifteen times the recommended dosage as prescribed by your psychiatrist Dr. Jurik, who I note as present at this hearing."*
*As seen in Think Tank V4.
WHEN I HEAR IT READ BACK TO ME, I WISH I'D DONE SOMETHING MANLY.
LIKE PUT A 9MM BULLET THROUGH THE BASE OF MY BRAIN.
Actually, my testimony is that I knowingly took a sufficient dosage to end my own life, but did so solely as a cry for help.
THE EASIEST WAY TO GET WHAT YOU WANT OUT OF PEOPLE IS MAKING THEM THINK YOU NEED THEIR HELP.
Dr. David Loren
I WAS 28 WHEN I EXPERIENCED MY FIRST HEARTBREAK. IT HURT MORE THAN I THOUGHT IT WOULD.
EMOTIONAL MATURITY NEVER MATTERED TO ME UNTIL I NEEDED IT.
He's not breathing.
AND WHEN I DID, IT WASN'T THERE.
"I knew there would be time to be taken to the 412th Medical Facility and resuscitated; it's only two blocks from my lab."
We need HELP in here!
DISCOVERED THAT ONLY AFTER I WOKE UP THERE.

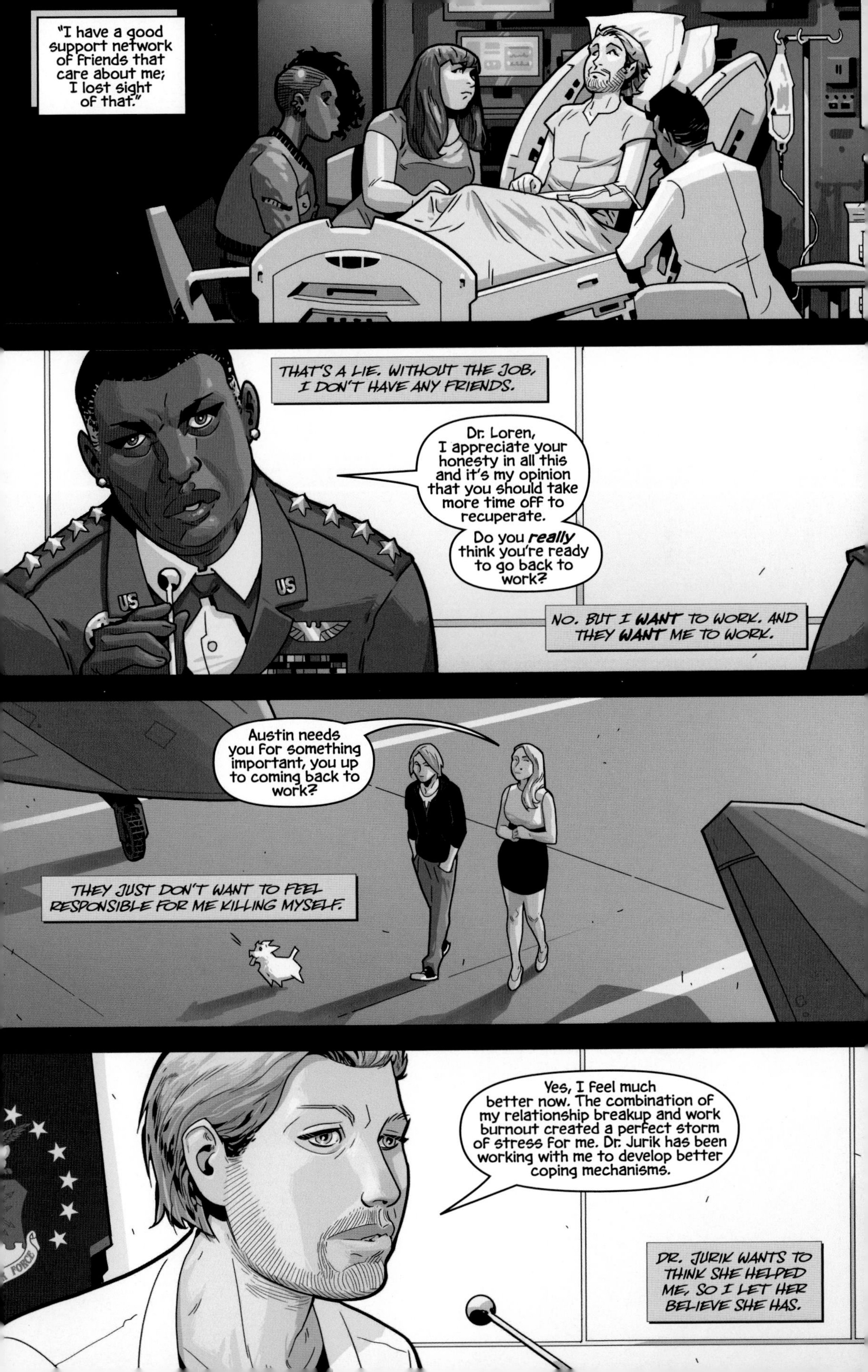
"I have a good support network of friends that care about me; I lost sight of that."
THAT'S A LIE. WITHOUT THE JOB, I DON'T HAVE ANY FRIENDS.
Dr. Loren, I appreciate your honesty in all this and it's my opinion that you should take more time off to recuperate.
Do you ***really*** think you're ready to go back to work?
NO. BUT I **WANT** TO WORK. AND THEY **WANT** ME TO WORK.
Austin needs you for something important, you up to coming back to work?
THEY JUST DON'T WANT TO FEEL RESPONSIBLE FOR ME KILLING MYSELF.
Yes, I feel much better now. The combination of my relationship breakup and work burnout created a perfect storm of stress for me. Dr. Jurik has been working with me to develop better coping mechanisms.
DR. JURIK WANTS TO THINK SHE HELPED ME, SO I LET HER BELIEVE SHE HAS.

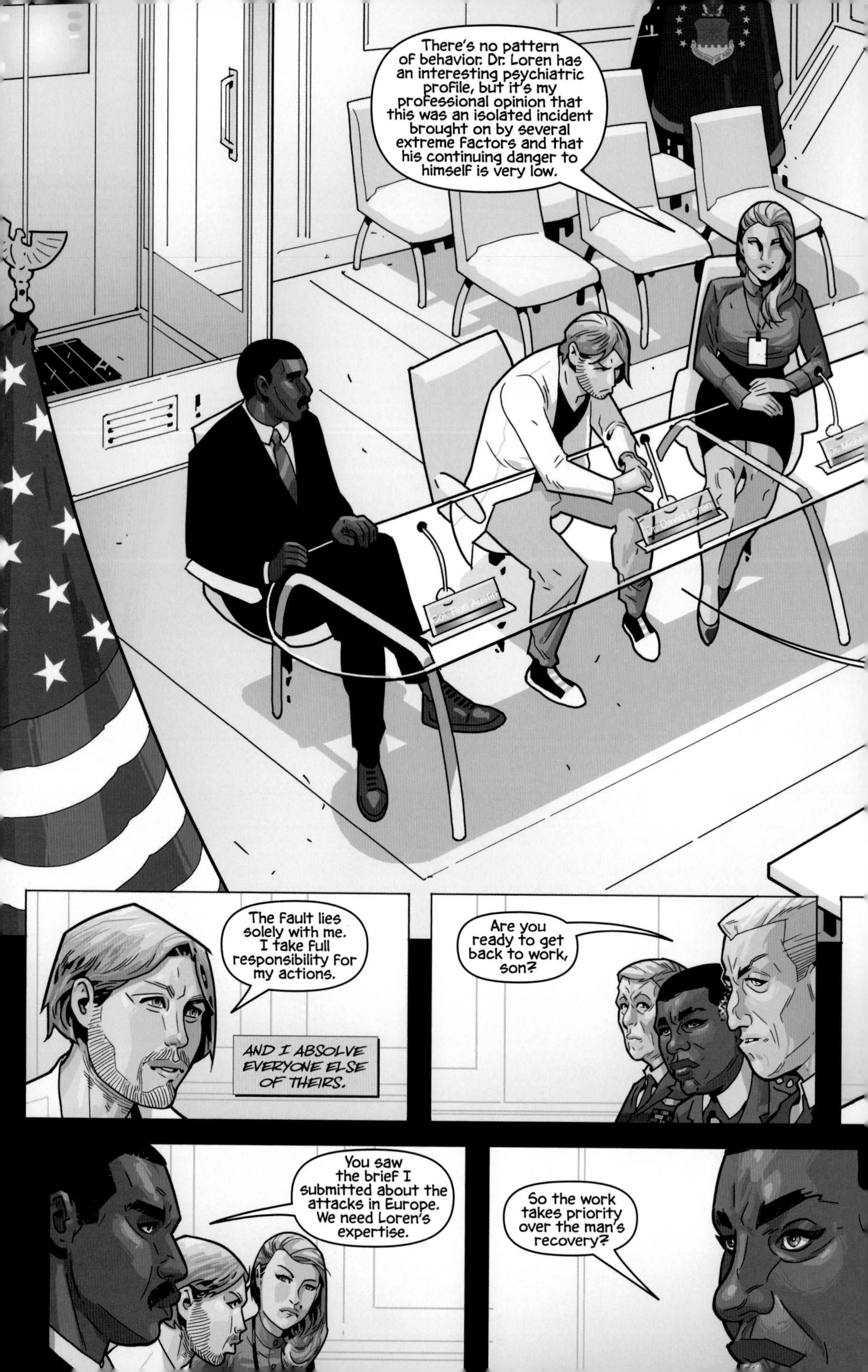
There's no pattern of behavior. Dr. Loren has an interesting psychiatric profile, but it's my professional opinion that this was an isolated incident brought on by several extreme factors and that his continuing danger to himself is very low.
Dr. David Loren
Col. Ron Austin
The fault lies solely with me. I take full responsibility for my actions.
AND I ABSOLVE EVERYONE ELSE OF THEIRS.
Are you ready to get back to work, son?
You saw the brief I submitted about the attacks in Europe. We need Loren's expertise.
So the work takes priority over the man's recovery?

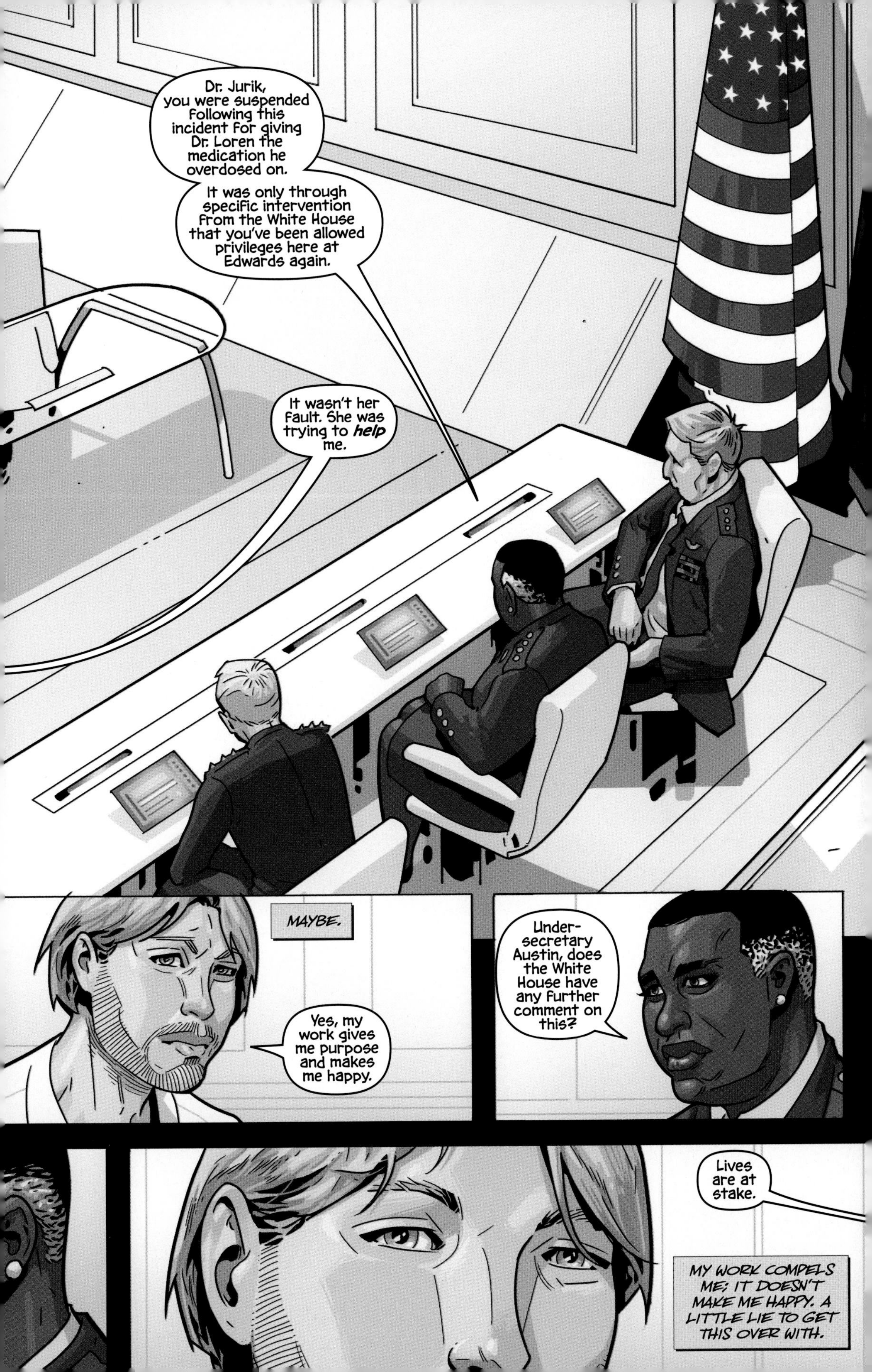

Dr. Jurik, you were suspended following this incident for giving Dr. Loren the medication he overdosed on.
It was only through specific intervention from the White House that you've been allowed privileges here at Edwards again.
It wasn't her fault. She was trying to *help* me.
MAYBE.
Yes, my work gives me purpose and makes me happy.
Under-secretary Austin, does the White House have any further comment on this?
Lives are at stake.
MY WORK COMPELS ME; IT DOESN'T MAKE ME HAPPY. A LITTLE LIE TO GET THIS OVER WITH.

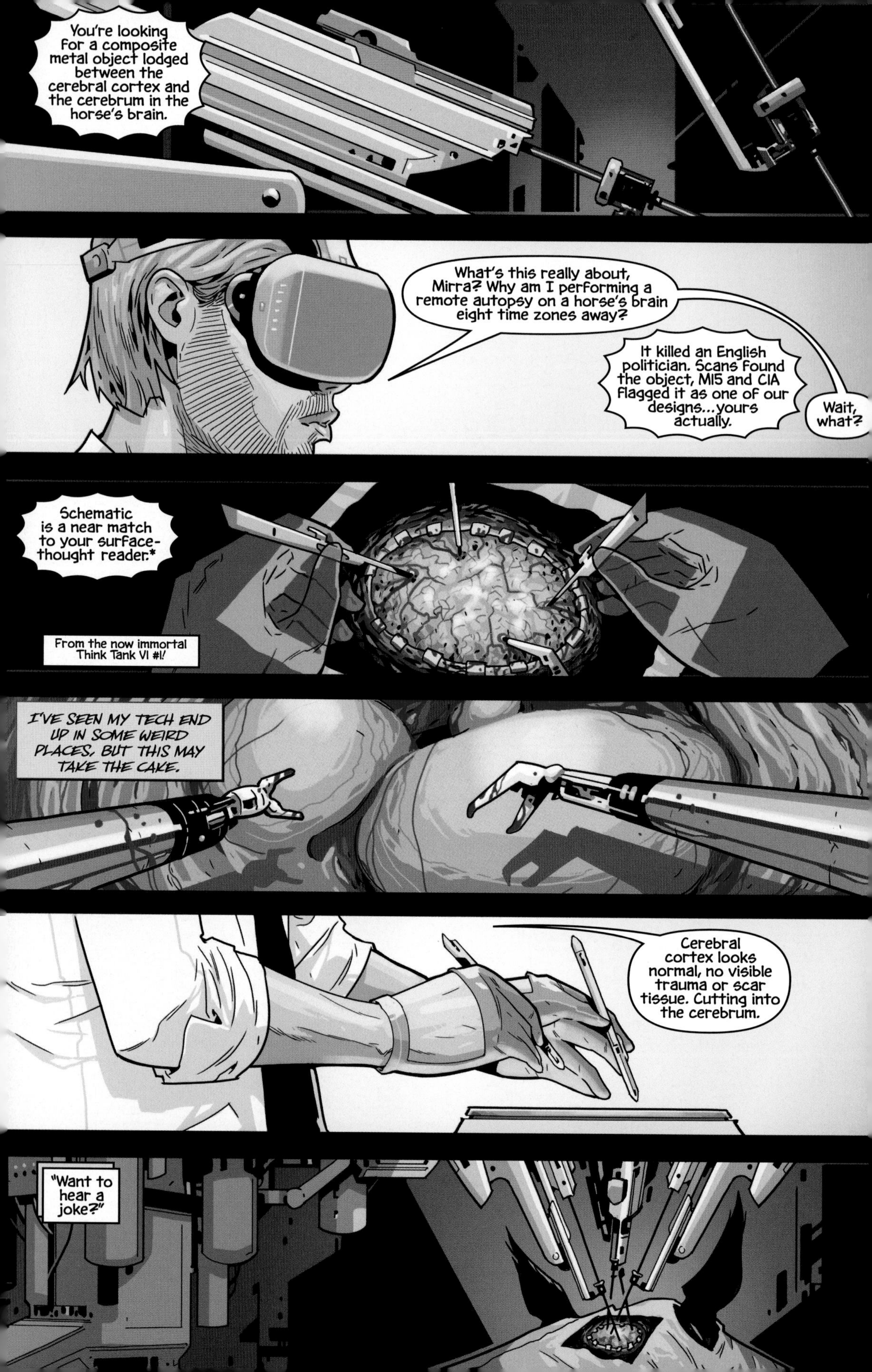
You're looking for a composite metal object lodged between the cerebral cortex and the cerebrum in the horse's brain.
What's this really about, Mirra? Why am I performing a remote autopsy on a horse's brain eight time zones away?
It killed an English politician. Scans found the object, MI5 and CIA flagged it as one of our designs...yours actually.
Wait, what?
Schematic is a near match to your surface-thought reader.*
From the now immortal Think Tank VI #1!
I'VE SEEN MY TECH END UP IN SOME WEIRD PLACES, BUT THIS MAY TAKE THE CAKE.
Cerebral cortex looks normal, no visible trauma or scar tissue. Cutting into the cerebrum.
"Want to hear a joke?"

No.

Did you hear about the horse with the negative altitude?

She always said neigh.

When you told me you loved me, you laughed at my jokes.

That just missed being funny.

David, you promised to not take us back here. Let's focus on the horse.

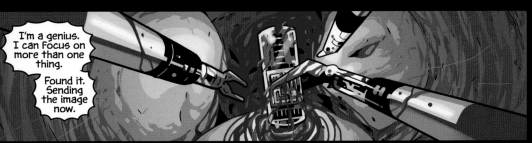

I'm a genius. I can focus on more than one thing.

Found it. Sending the image now.

Holy shit, David, that is your *surface-thought reader*, but they reversed the signal to output...and is that MIT's new light-emitting diode?

Could that be used to control an animal?

Maybe. MIT used the light to control mice...linking it to a reversed reader the user could input simple commands into the animal's brain.

Did Dr. Sejic have access to your research?

Now how about you tell me what's actually going on?

Come with me.

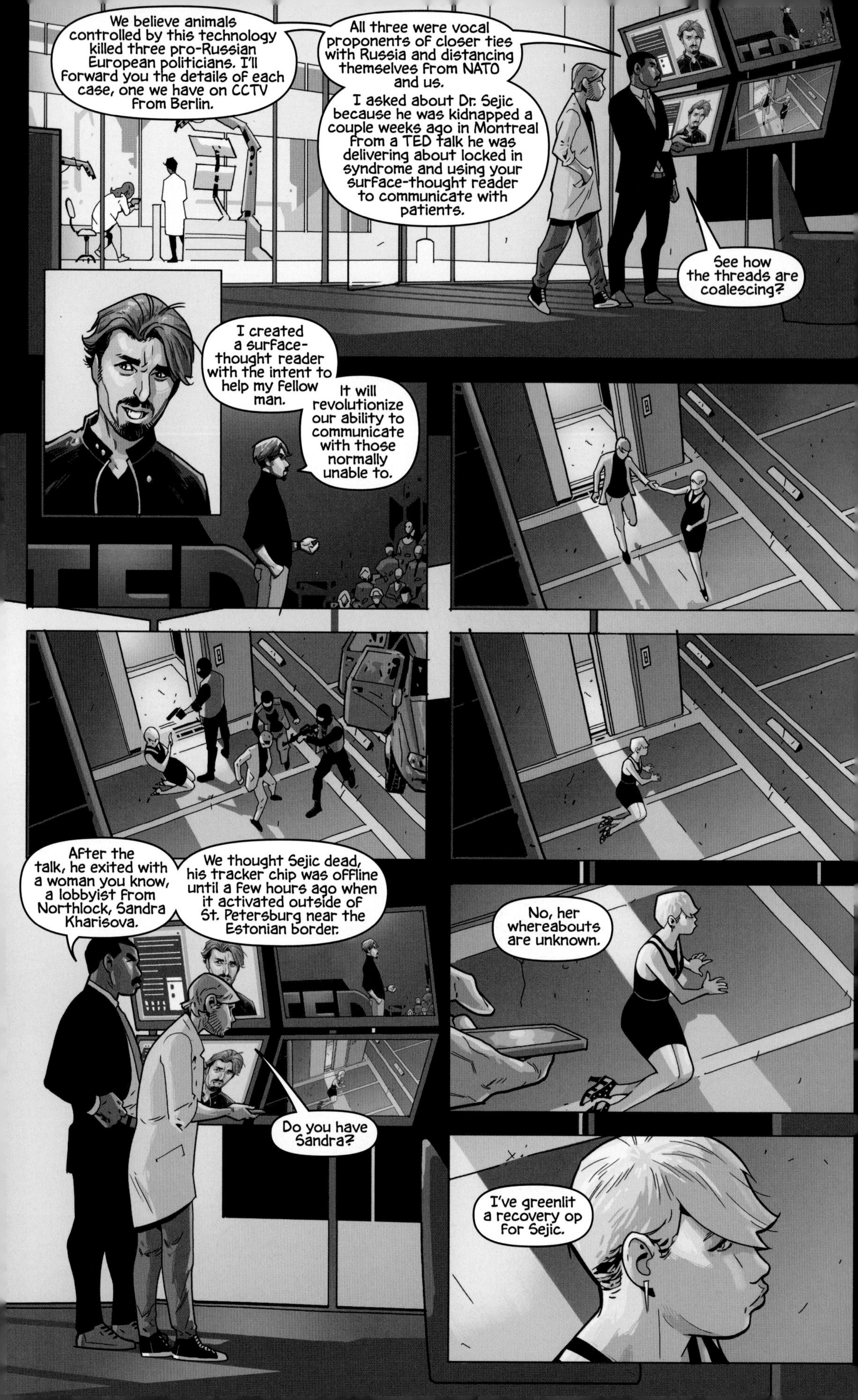

We believe animals controlled by this technology killed three pro-Russian European politicians. I'll forward you the details of each case, one we have on CCTV from Berlin.
All three were vocal proponents of closer ties with Russia and distancing themselves from NATO and us.
I asked about Dr. Sejic because he was kidnapped a couple weeks ago in Montreal from a TED talk he was delivering about locked in syndrome and using your surface-thought reader to communicate with patients.
See how the threads are coalescing?
I created a surface-thought reader with the intent to help my fellow man.
It will revolutionize our ability to communicate with those normally unable to.
After the talk, he exited with a woman you know, a lobbyist from Northlock, Sandra Kharisova.
We thought Sejic dead, his tracker chip was offline until a few hours ago when it activated outside of St. Petersburg near the Estonian border.
Do you have Sandra?
No, her whereabouts are unknown.
I've greenlit a recovery op for Sejic.

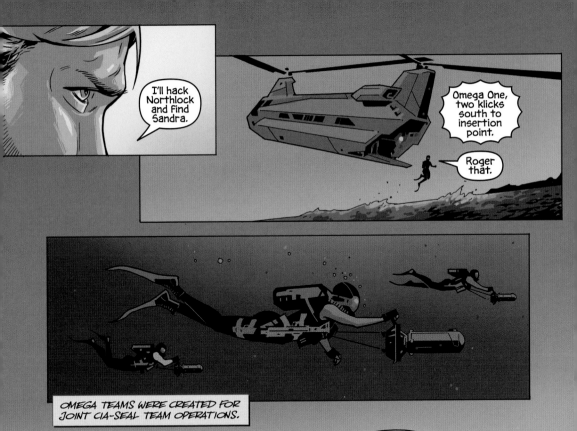

I'll hack Northlock and Find Sandra.

Omega One, two klicks south to insertion point.

Roger that.

OMEGA TEAMS WERE CREATED FOR JOINT CIA-SEAL TEAM OPERATIONS.

Hawk 4 released at insertion one. Eyes live.

You've got twenty minutes until exfiltration.

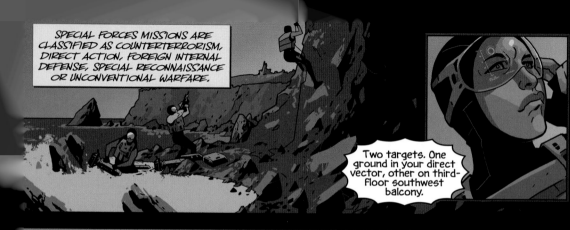

SPECIAL FORCES MISSIONS ARE CLASSIFIED AS COUNTERTERRORISM, DIRECT ACTION, FOREIGN INTERNAL DEFENSE, SPECIAL RECONNAISSANCE OR UNCONVENTIONAL WARFARE.

Two targets. One ground in your direct vector, other on third-floor southwest balcony.

THIS IS A DIRECT ACTION MISSION, A SHORT DURATION STRIKE USED TO SEIZE, CAPTURE, RECOVER OR DESTROY ENEMY WEAPONS AND INFORMATION OR RECOVER DESIGNATED PERSONNEL OR MATERIAL.

POK

POK

ВХОДИТЬ

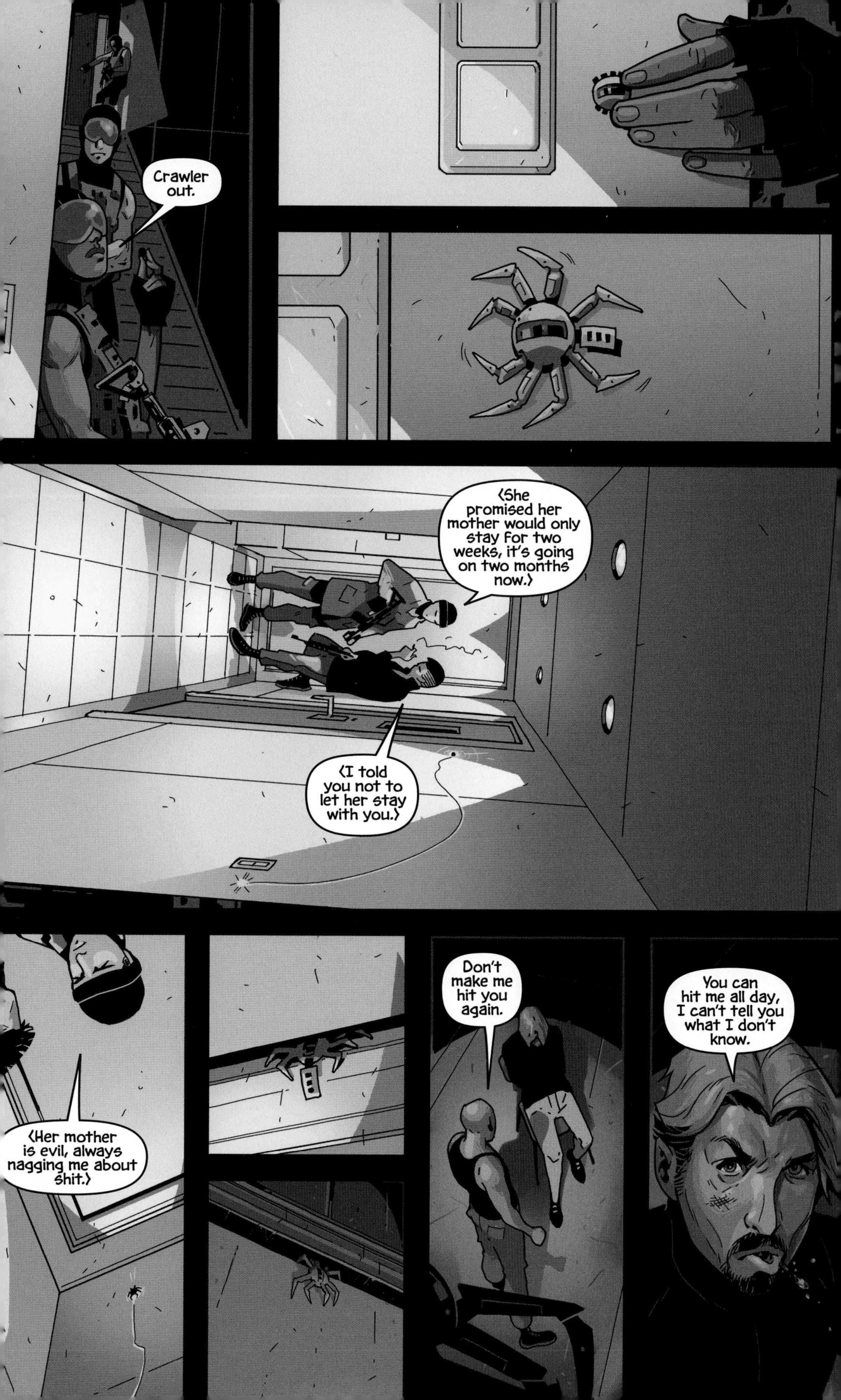

Crawler out.
‹She promised her mother would only stay for two weeks, it's going on two months now.›
‹I told you not to let her stay with you.›
‹Her mother is evil, always nagging me about shit.›
Don't make me hit you again.
You can hit me all day, I can't tell you what I don't know.

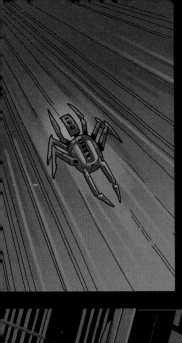

Ahh.

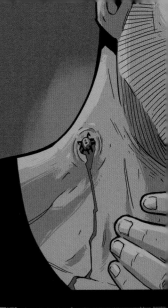

That's a new one.

WHUMP

BLAM
WHAM
THUMP

KRAK

Hello?

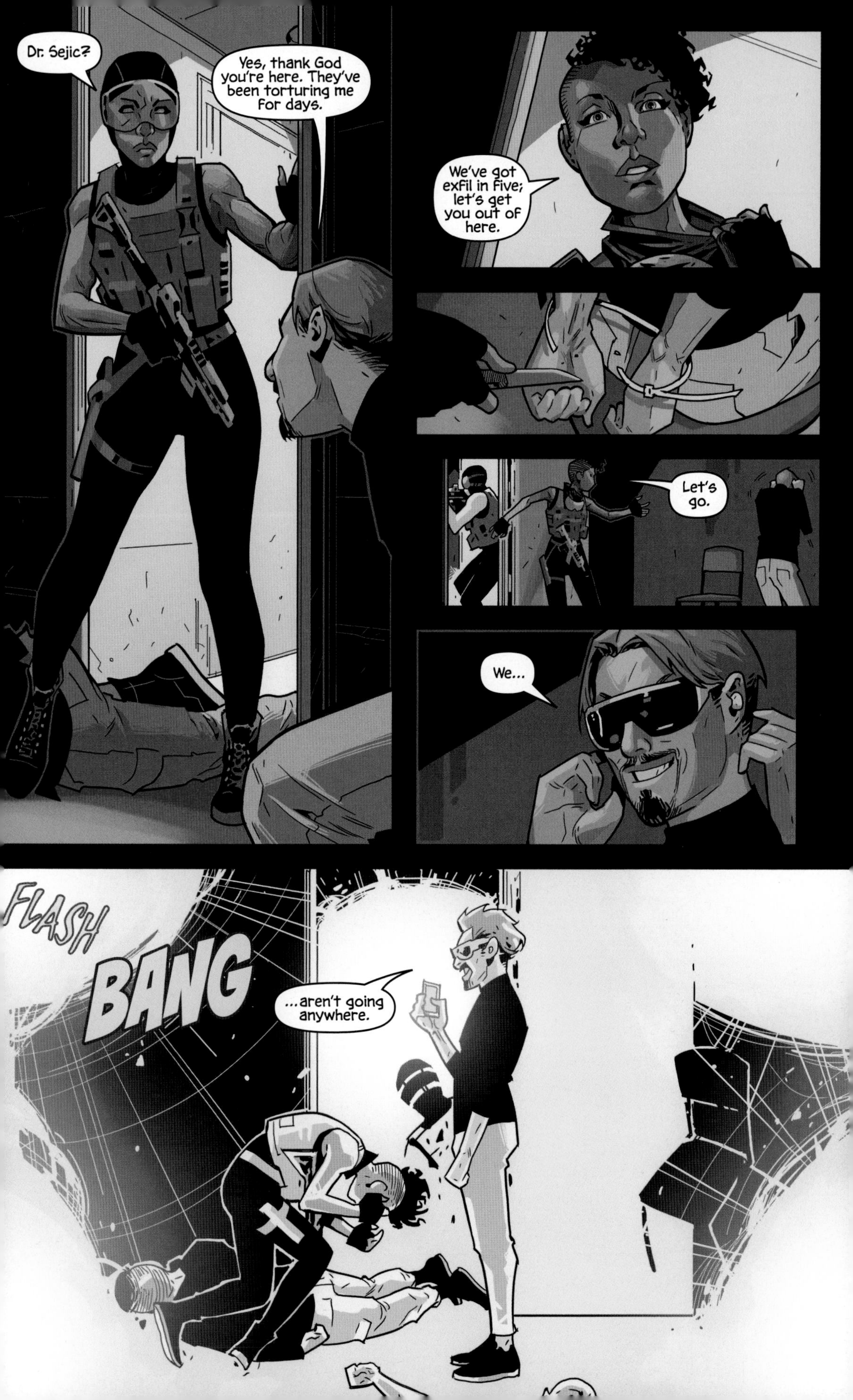
Dr. Sejic?
Yes, thank God you're here. They've been torturing me for days.
We've got exfil in five; let's get you out of here.
Let's go.
We...
FLASH
BANG
...aren't going anywhere.

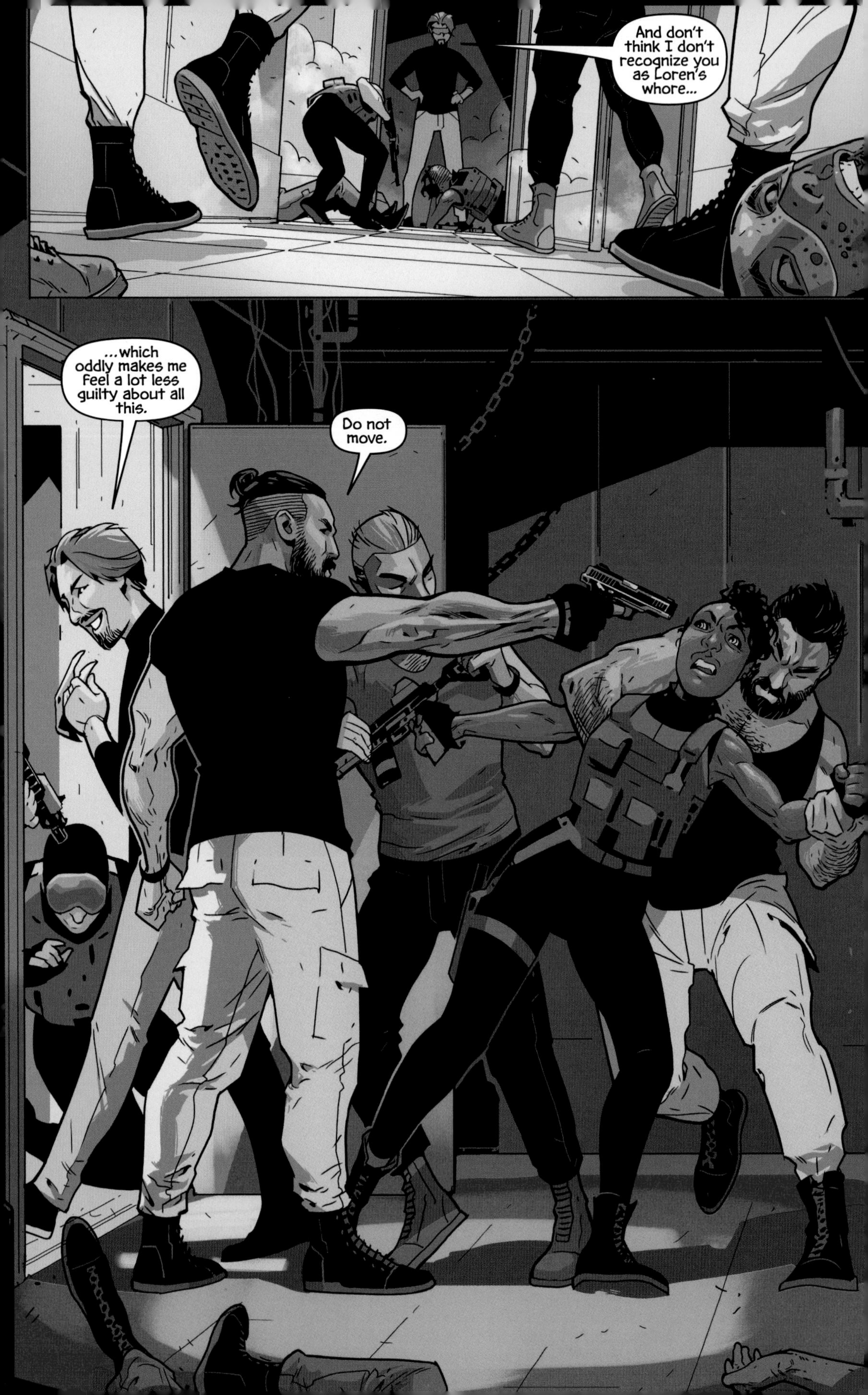
And don't think I don't recognize you as Loren's whore...
...which oddly makes me feel a lot less guilty about all this.
Do not move.

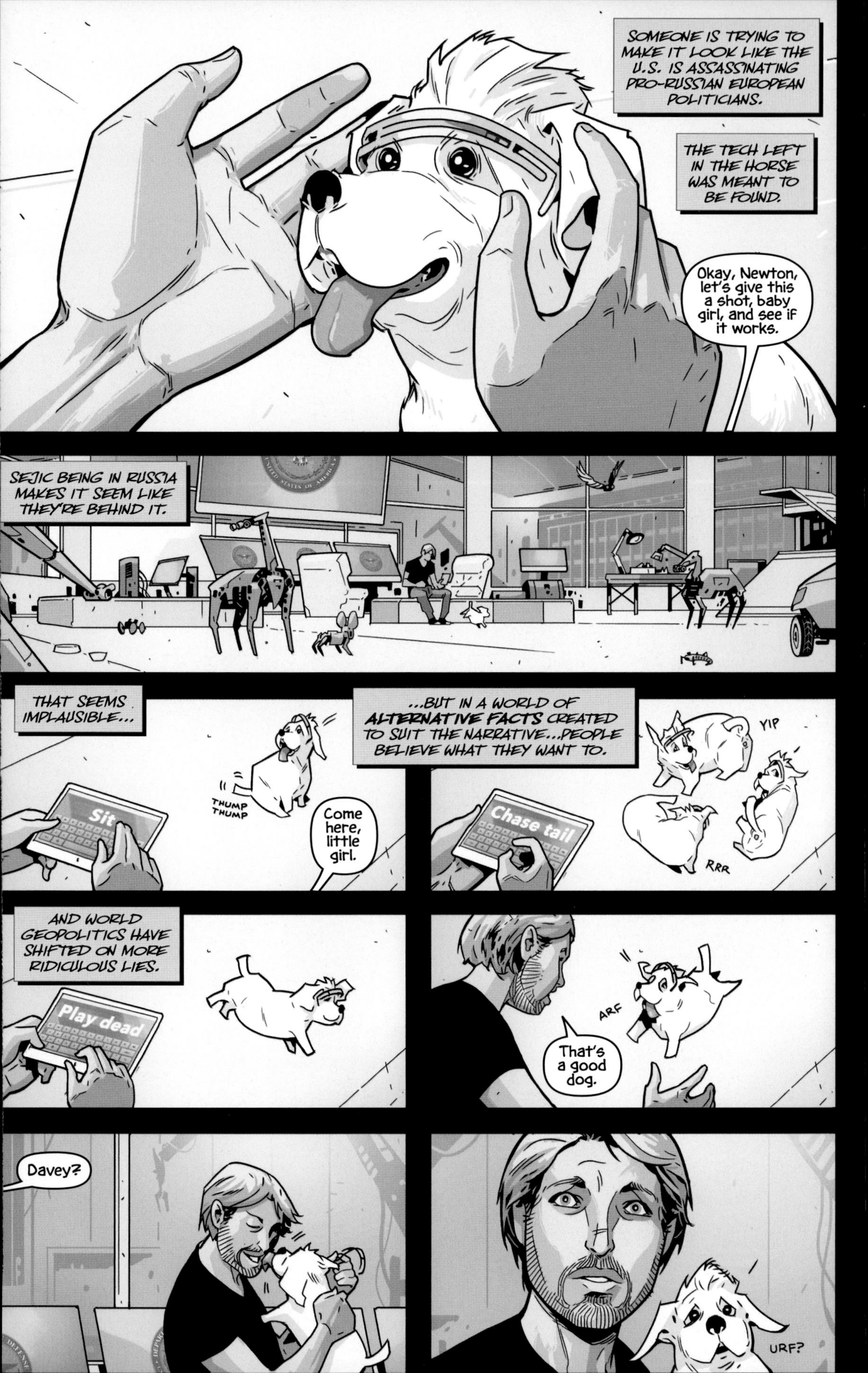
SOMEONE IS TRYING TO MAKE IT LOOK LIKE THE U.S. IS ASSASSINATING PRO-RUSSIAN EUROPEAN POLITICIANS.
THE TECH LEFT IN THE HORSE WAS MEANT TO BE FOUND.
Okay, Newton, let's give this a shot, baby girl, and see if it works.
SEJIC BEING IN RUSSIA MAKES IT SEEM LIKE THEY'RE BEHIND IT.
THAT SEEMS IMPLAUSIBLE...
Sit
THUMP THUMP
Come here, little girl.
...BUT IN A WORLD OF ALTERNATIVE FACTS CREATED TO SUIT THE NARRATIVE...PEOPLE BELIEVE WHAT THEY WANT TO.
Chase tail
YIP
RRR
AND WORLD GEOPOLITICS HAVE SHIFTED ON MORE RIDICULOUS LIES.
Play dead
ARF
That's a good dog.
Davey?
URF?

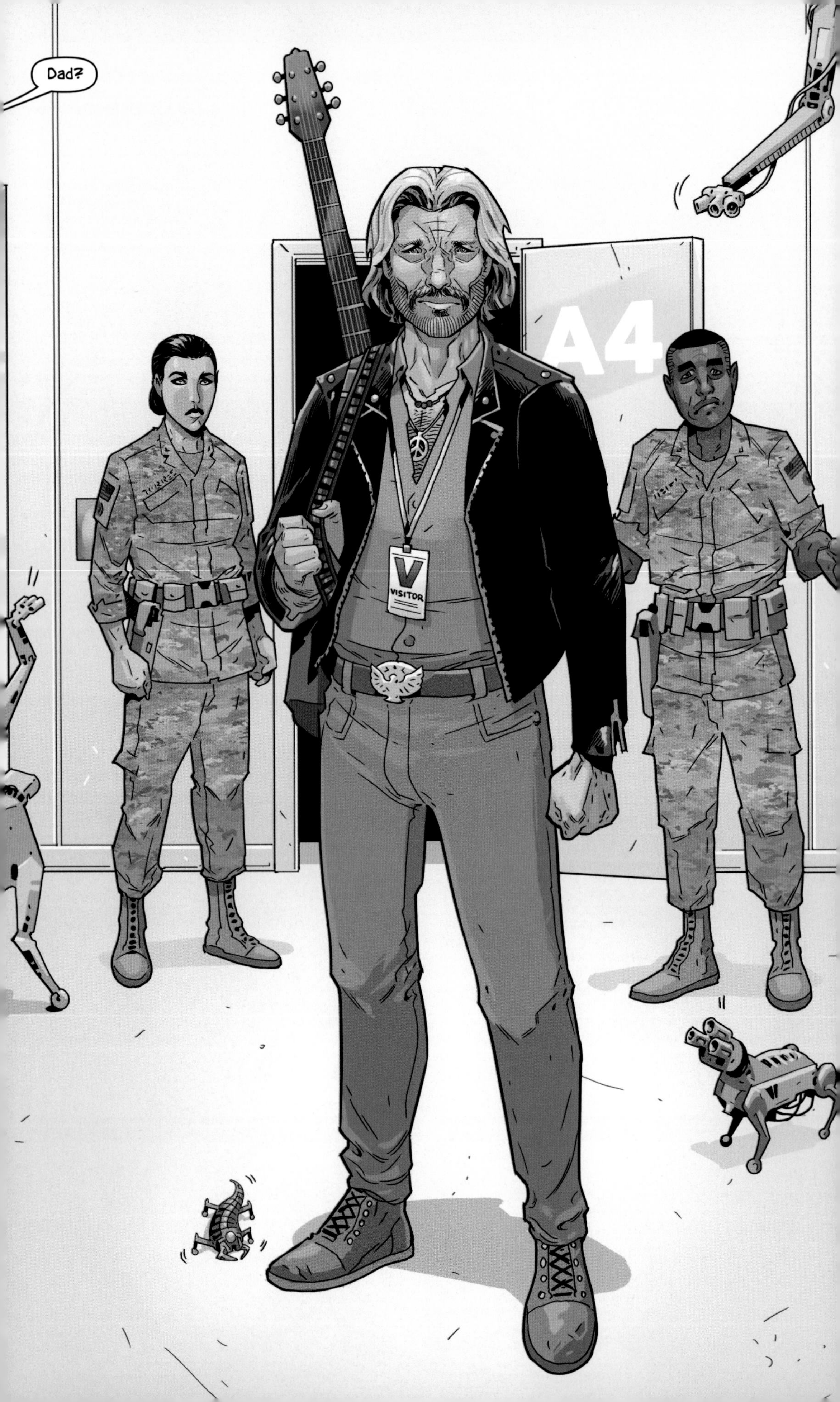
Dad?
A4
VISITOR

CHAPTER TWO

THINK TANK

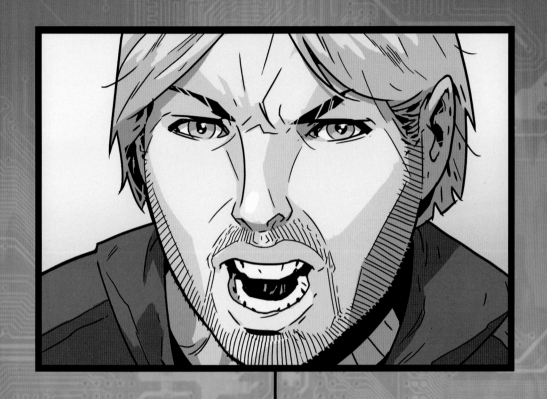

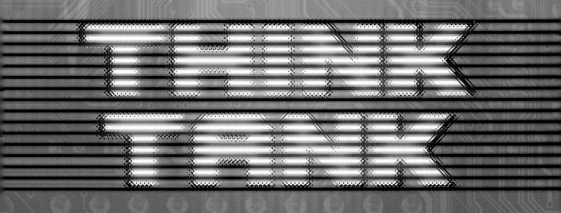

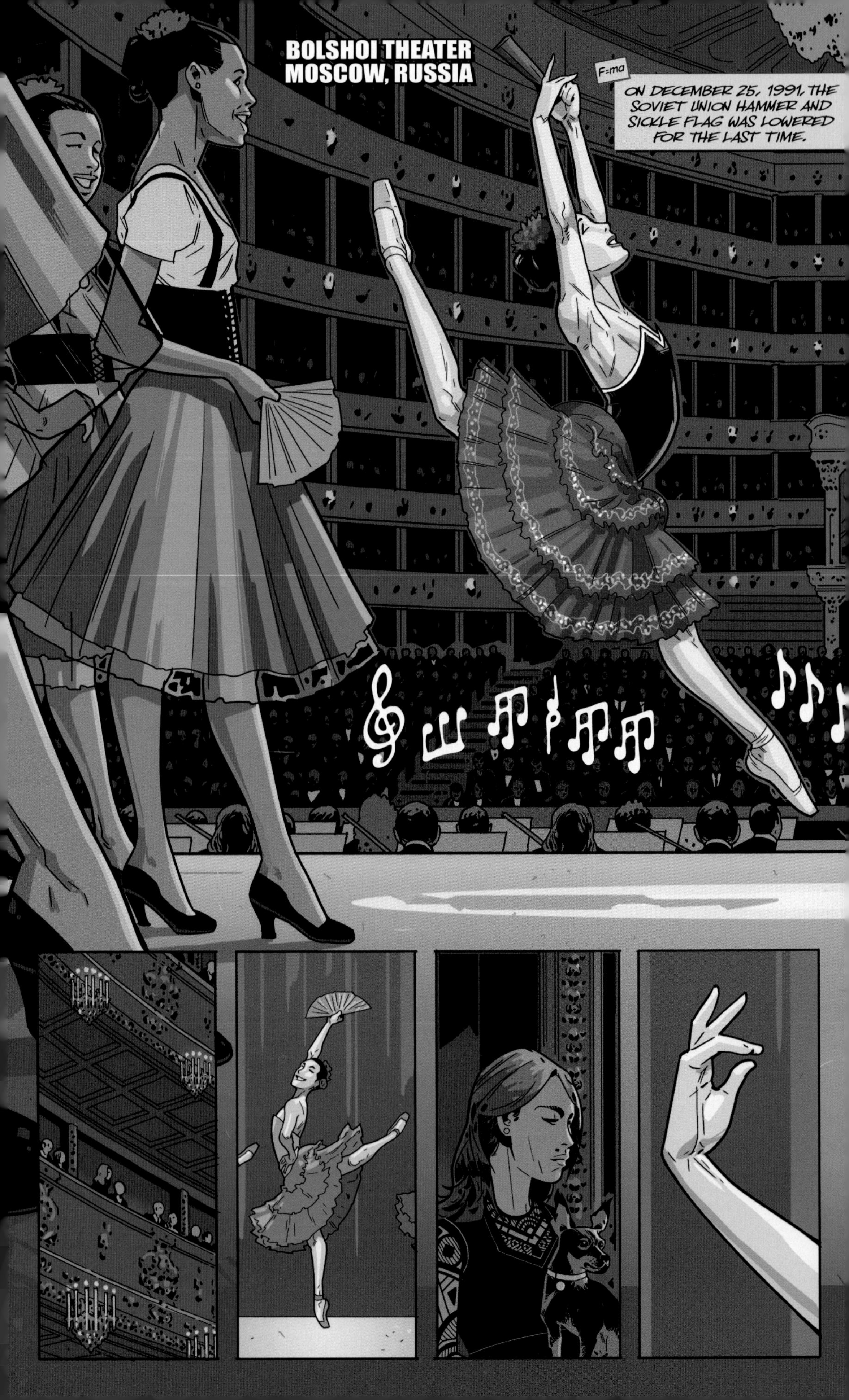
BOLSHOI THEATER
MOSCOW, RUSSIA
F=ma
ON DECEMBER 25, 1991, THE SOVIET UNION HAMMER AND SICKLE FLAG WAS LOWERED FOR THE LAST TIME.

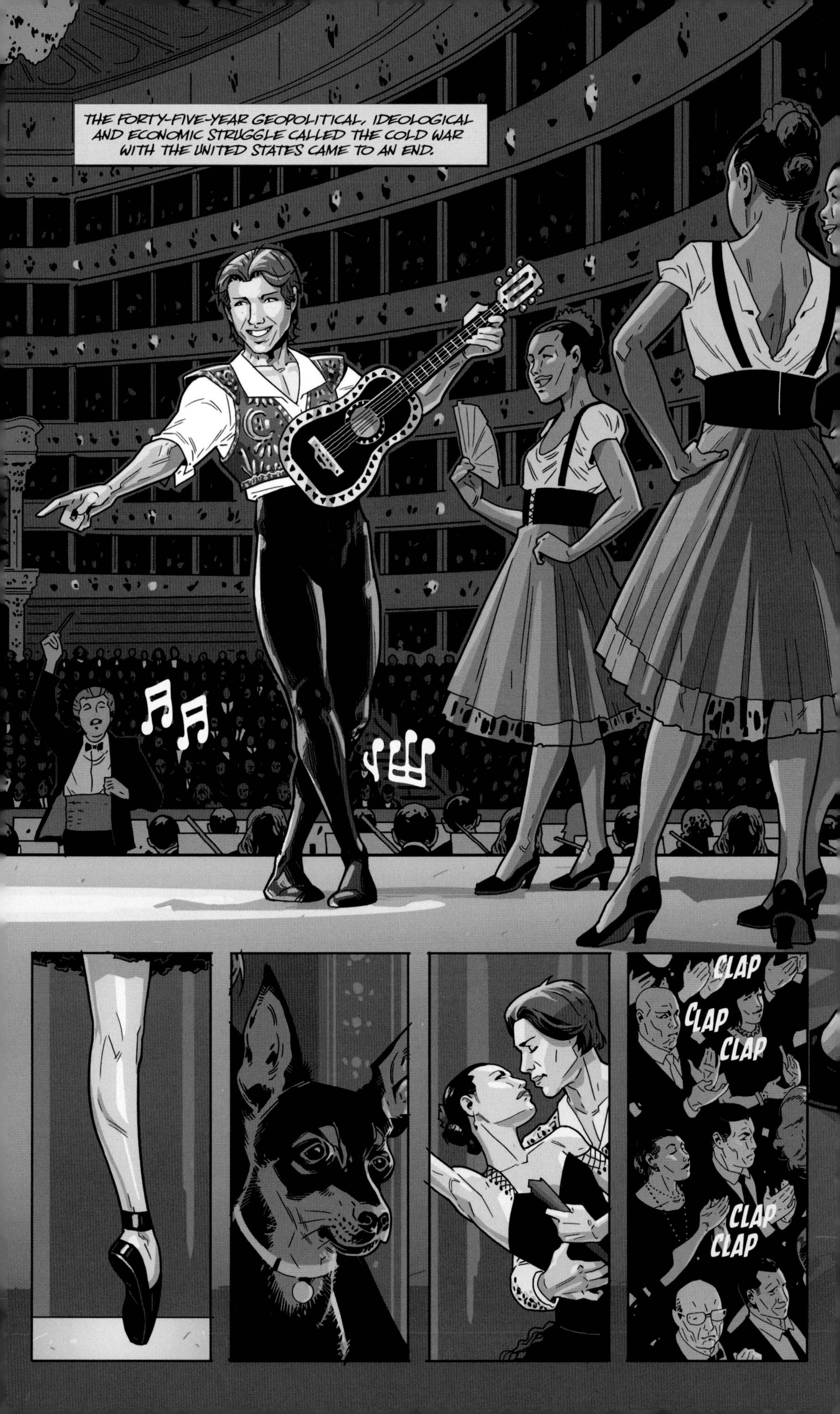
THE FORTY-FIVE-YEAR GEOPOLITICAL, IDEOLOGICAL AND ECONOMIC STRUGGLE CALLED THE COLD WAR WITH THE UNITED STATES CAME TO AN END.
CLAP
CLAP
CLAP
CLAP
CLAP

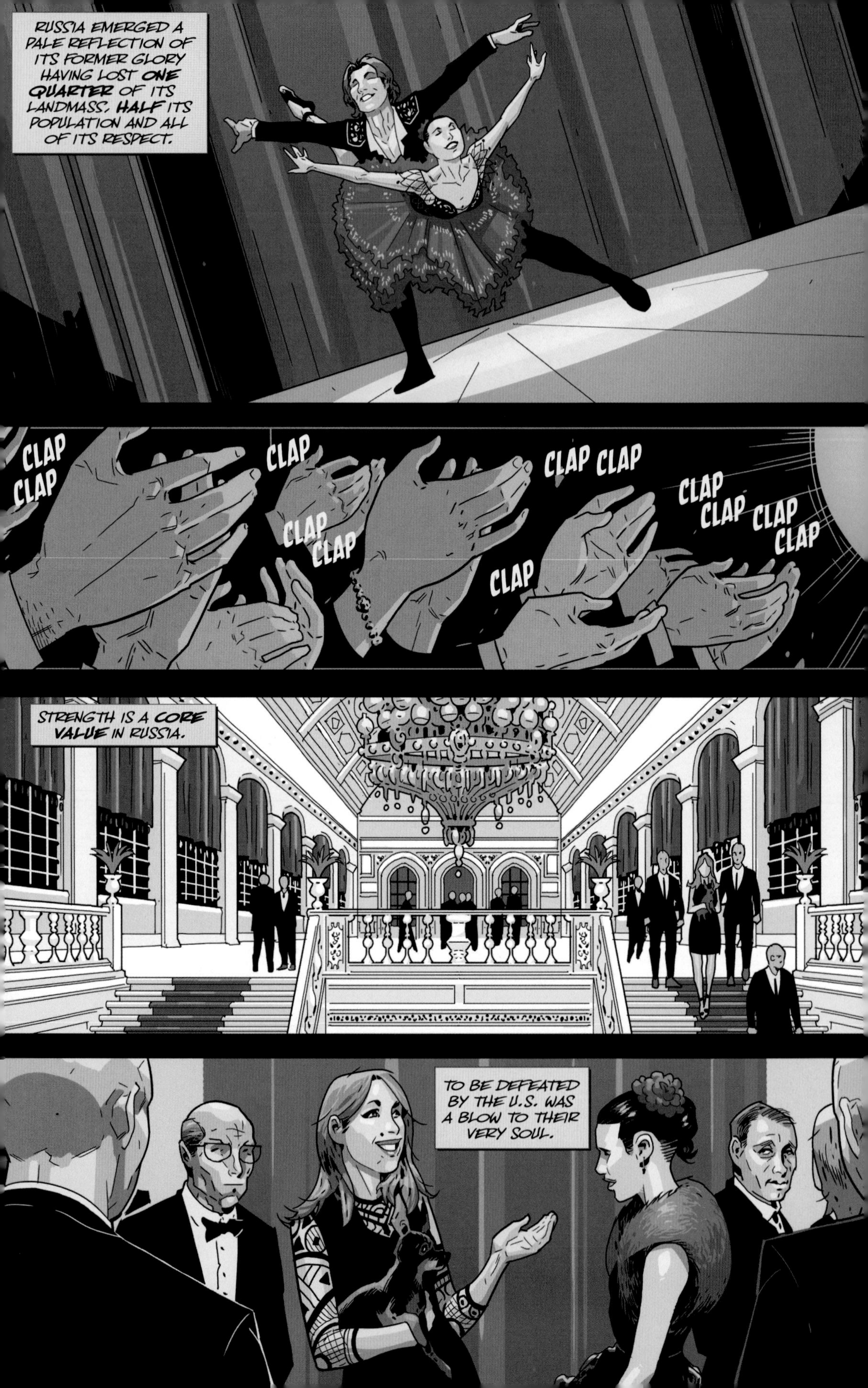
RUSSIA EMERGED A PALE REFLECTION OF ITS FORMER GLORY HAVING LOST ONE QUARTER OF ITS LANDMASS, HALF ITS POPULATION AND ALL OF ITS RESPECT.
CLAP CLAP
CLAP
CLAP CLAP
CLAP CLAP
CLAP
CLAP CLAP
CLAP CLAP
STRENGTH IS A CORE VALUE IN RUSSIA.
TO BE DEFEATED BY THE U.S. WAS A BLOW TO THEIR VERY SOUL.

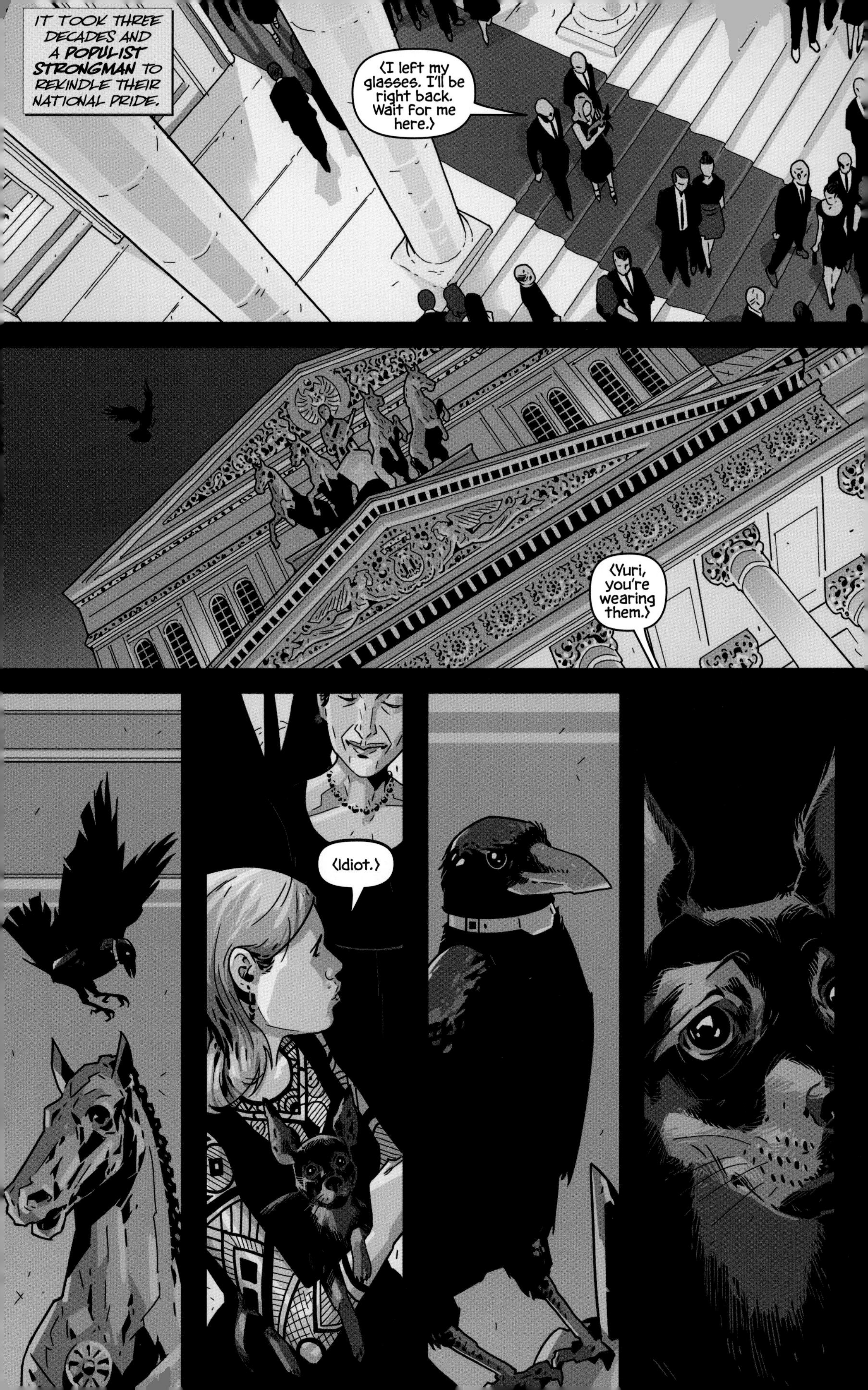
IT TOOK THREE DECADES AND A POPULIST STRONGMAN TO REKINDLE THEIR NATIONAL PRIDE.
‹I left my glasses. I'll be right back. Wait for me here.›
‹Yuri, you're wearing them.›
‹Idiot.›

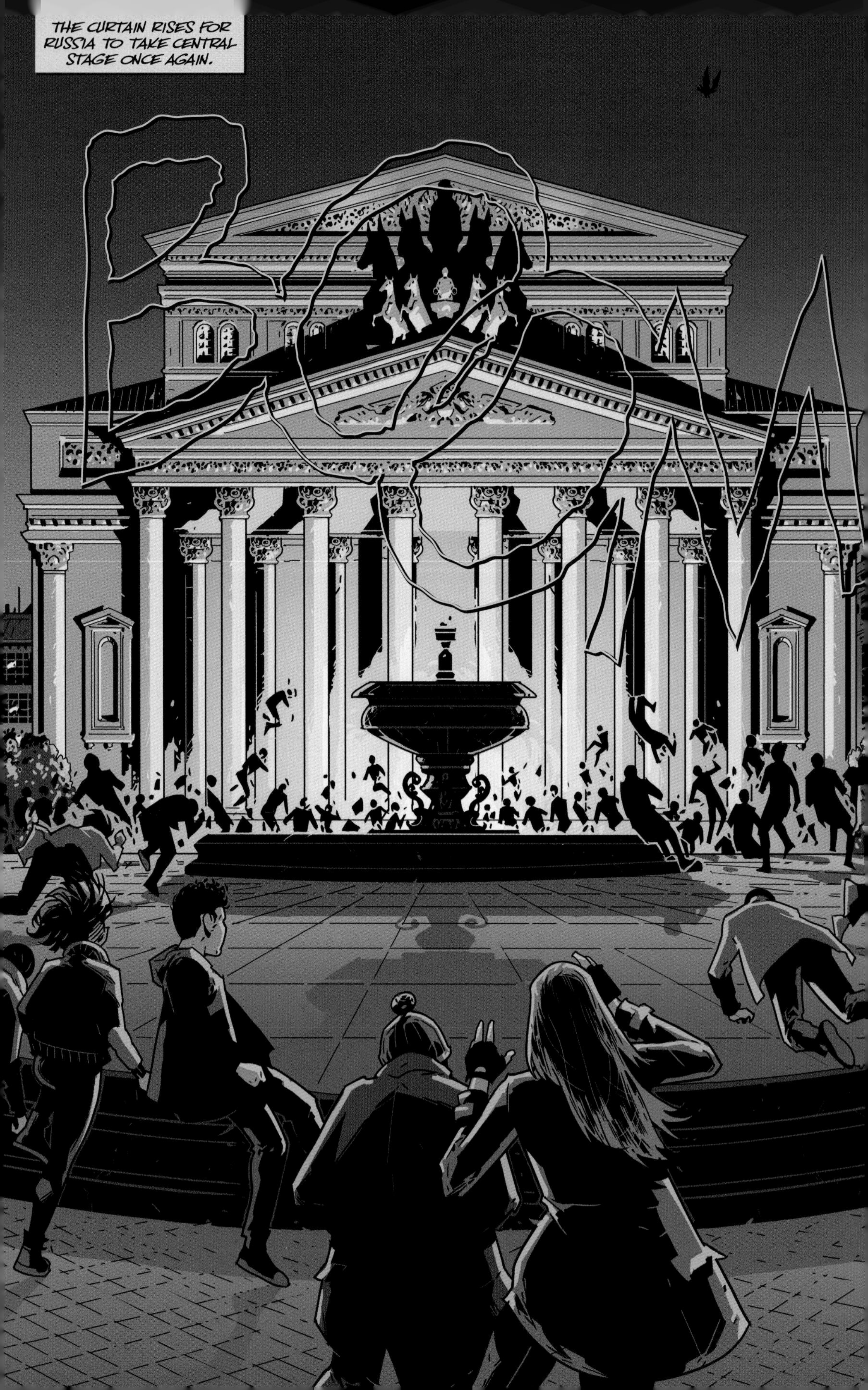
THE CURTAIN RISES FOR RUSSIA TO TAKE CENTRAL STAGE ONCE AGAIN.

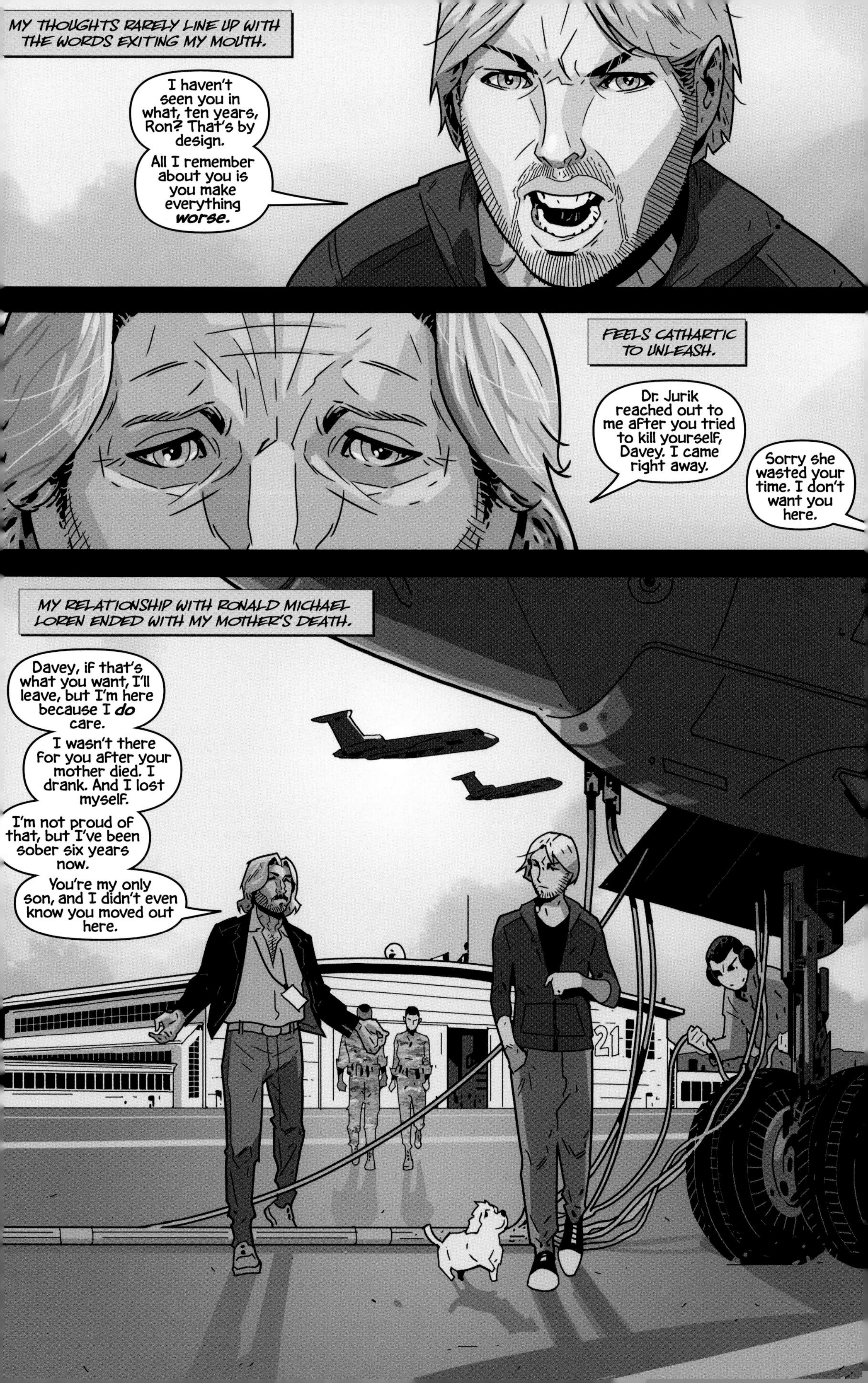
MY THOUGHTS RARELY LINE UP WITH THE WORDS EXITING MY MOUTH.
I haven't seen you in what, ten years, Ron? That's by design.
All I remember about you is you make everything worse.
FEELS CATHARTIC TO UNLEASH.
Dr. Jurik reached out to me after you tried to kill yourself, Davey. I came right away.
Sorry she wasted your time. I don't want you here.
MY RELATIONSHIP WITH RONALD MICHAEL LOREN ENDED WITH MY MOTHER'S DEATH.
Davey, if that's what you want, I'll leave, but I'm here because I do care.
I wasn't there for you after your mother died. I drank. And I lost myself.
I'm not proud of that, but I've been sober six years now.
You're my only son, and I didn't even know you moved out here.
21

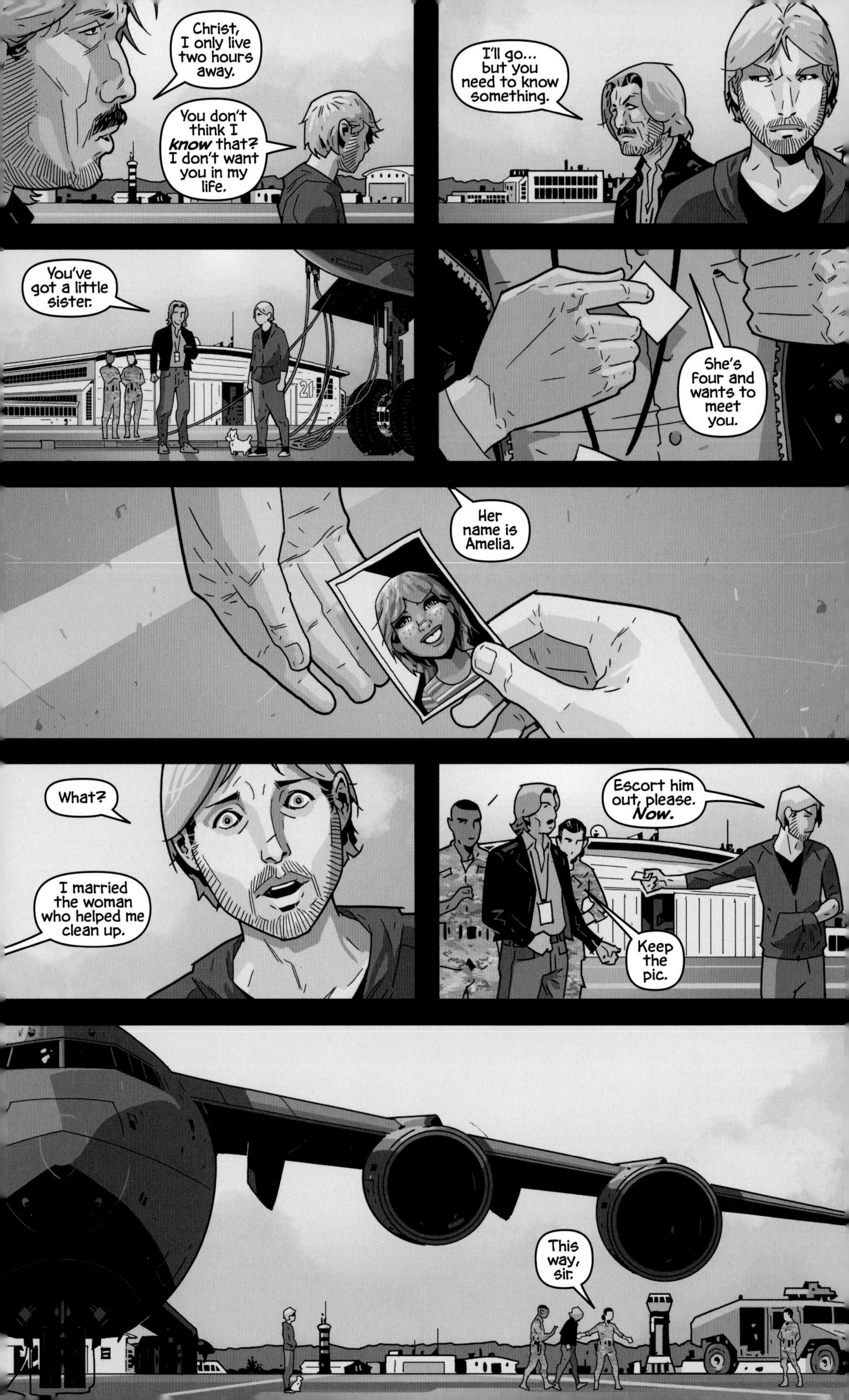
Christ, I only live two hours away.
You don't think I *know* that? I don't want you in my life.
I'll go... but you need to know something.
You've got a little sister.
21
She's four and wants to meet you.
Her name is Amelia.
What?
I married the woman who helped me clean up.
Escort him out, please. *Now.*
Keep the pic.
This way, sir.

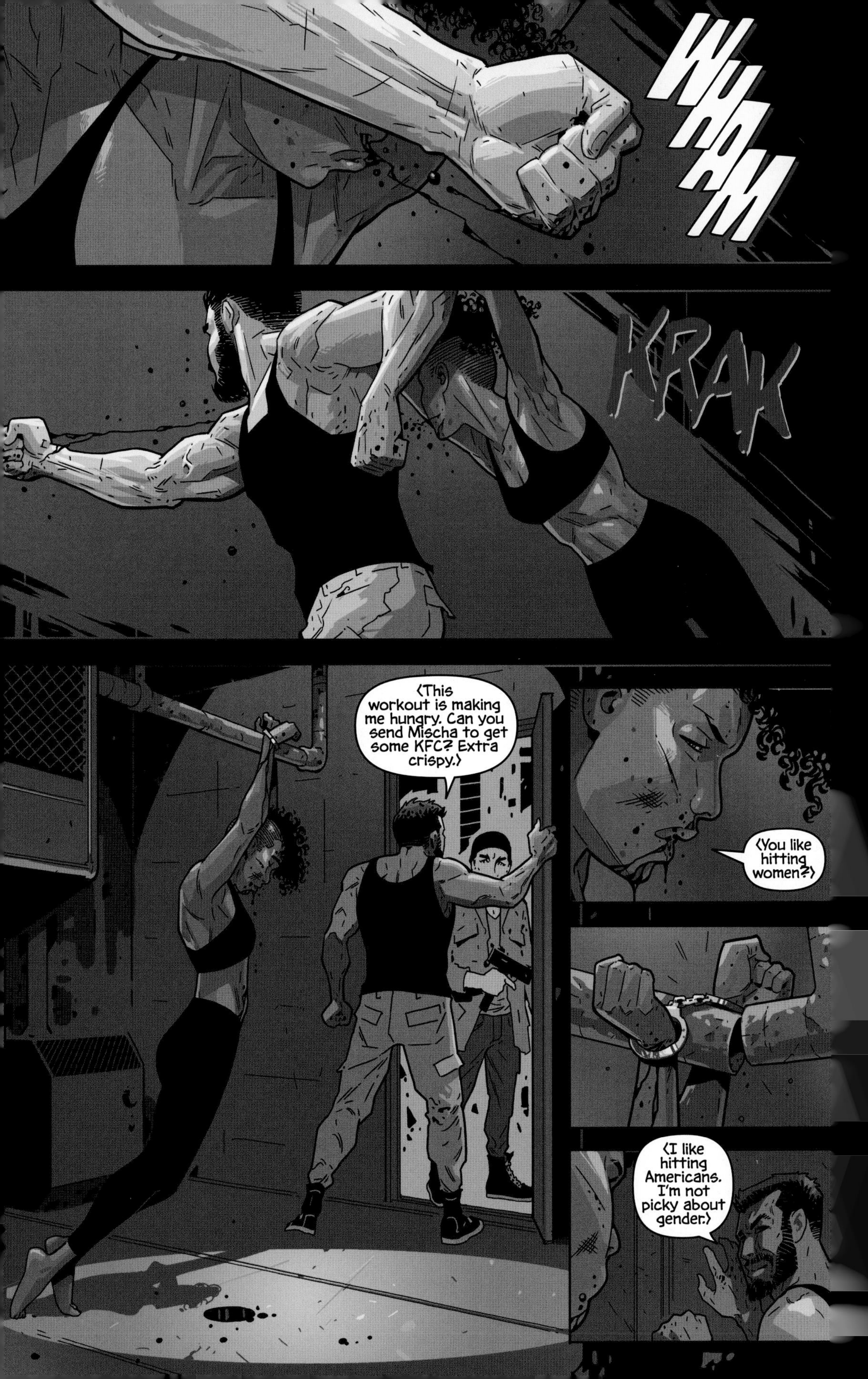
WHAM
KRAK
‹This workout is making me hungry. Can you send Mischa to get some KFC? Extra crispy.›
‹You like hitting women?›
‹I like hitting Americans. I'm not picky about gender.›

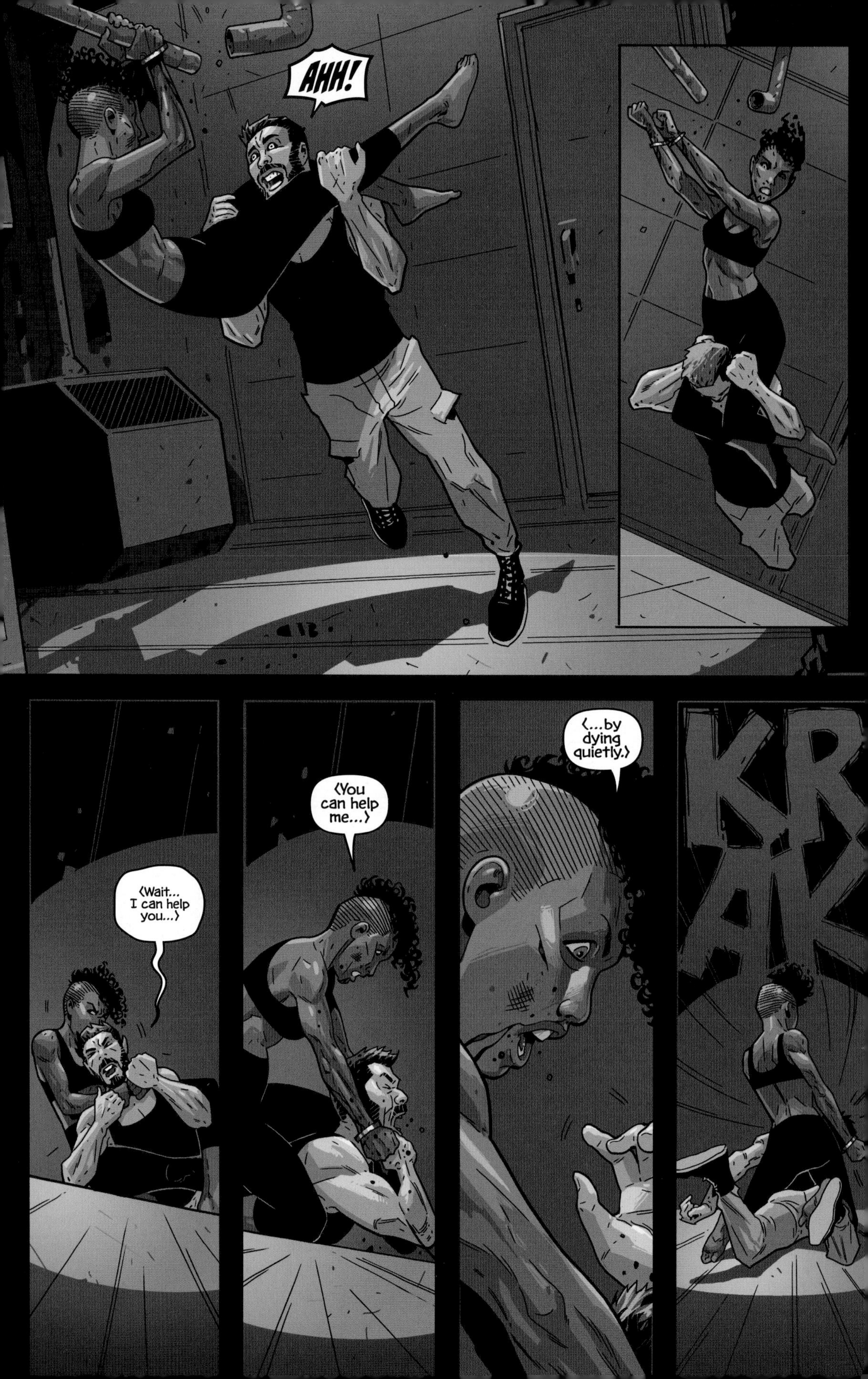
AHH!
‹Wait... I can help you...›
‹You can help me...›
‹...by dying quietly.›
KR
AK

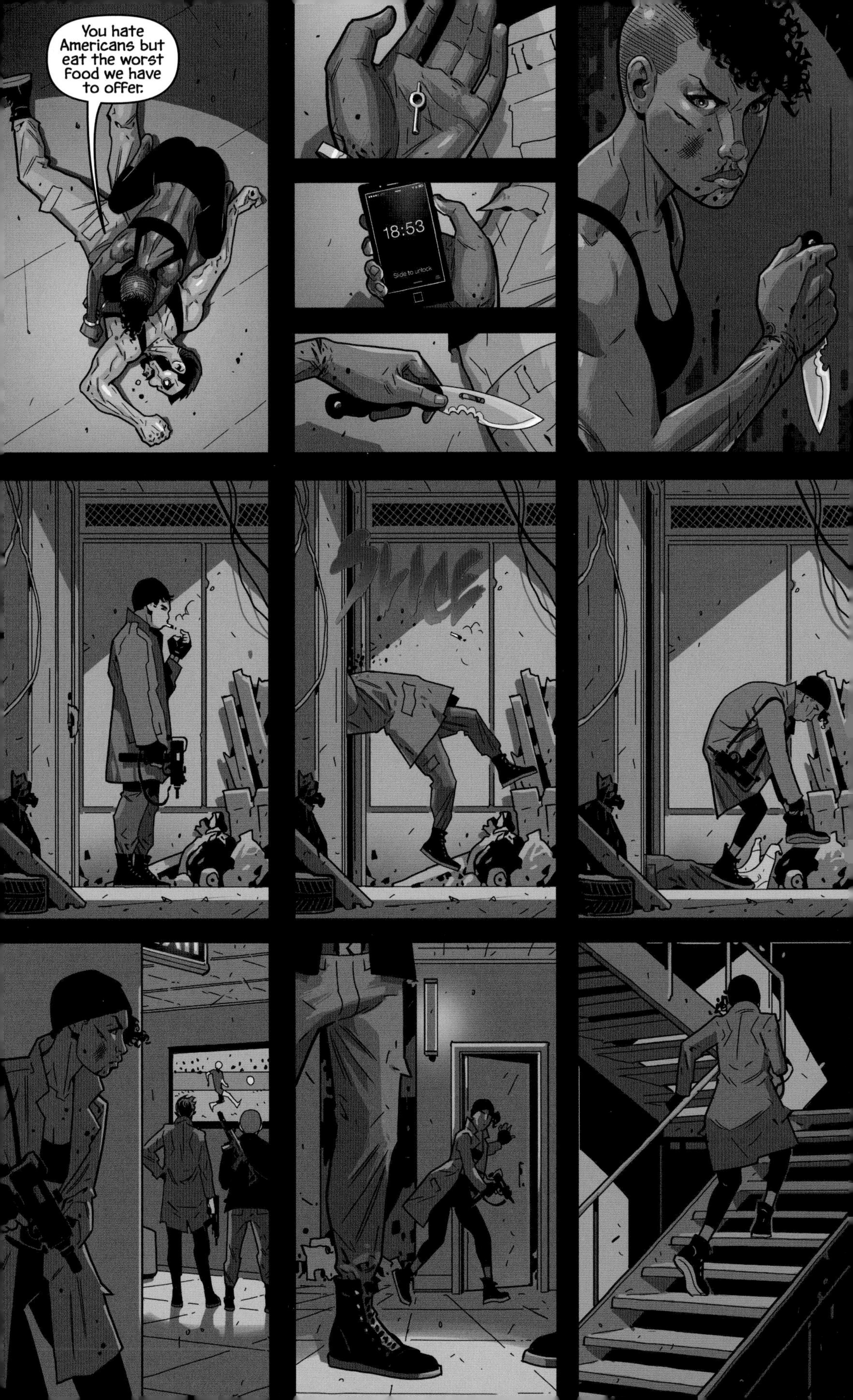
You hate Americans but eat the worst food we have to offer.
18:53
Slide to unlock
SLICE

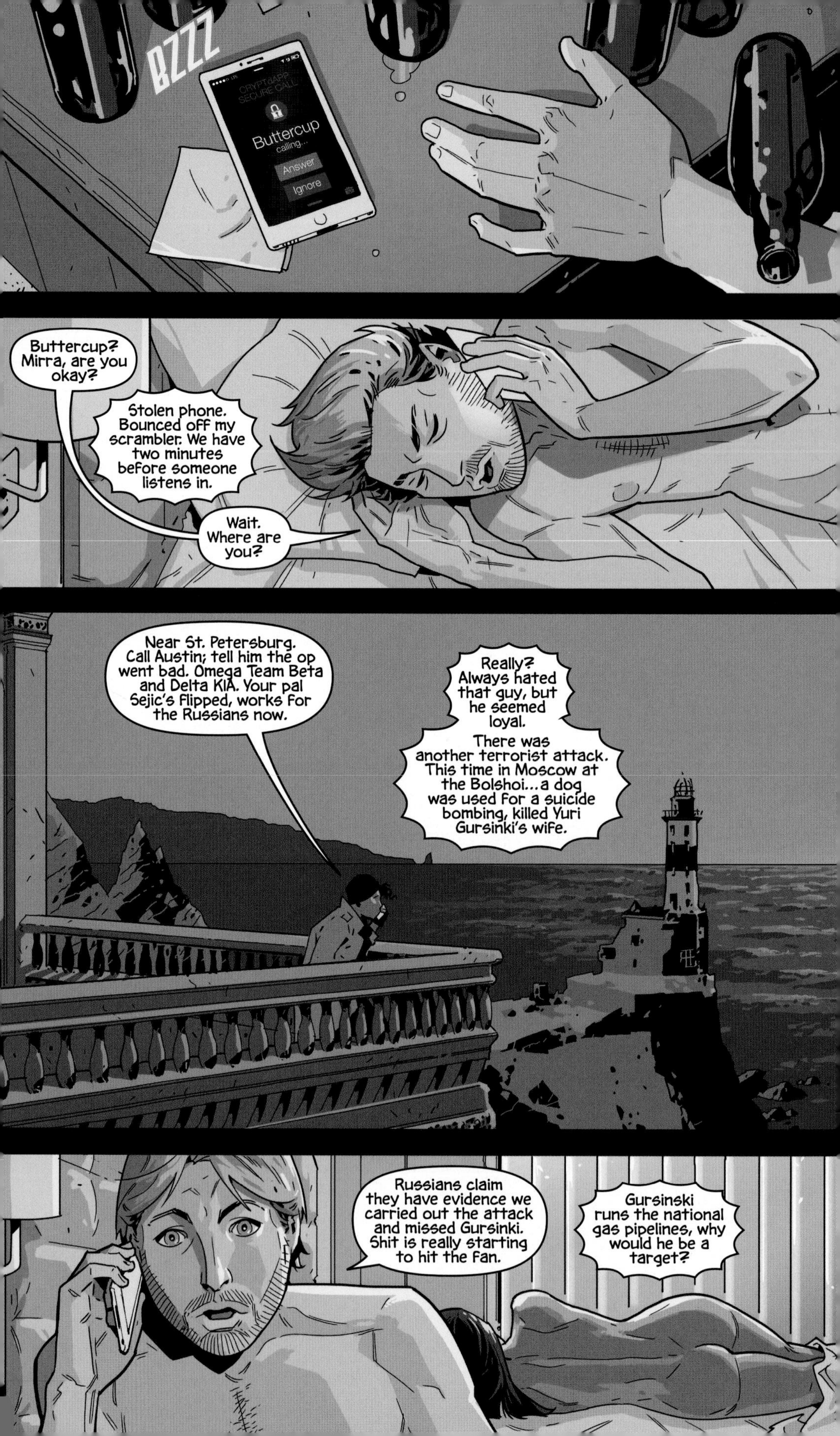
BZZZ
Buttercup
calling...
Answer
Ignore
Buttercup? Mirra, are you okay?
Stolen phone. Bounced off my scrambler. We have two minutes before someone listens in.
Wait. Where are you?
Near St. Petersburg. Call Austin; tell him the op went bad. Omega Team Beta and Delta KIA. Your pal Sejic's flipped, works for the Russians now.
Really? Always hated that guy, but he seemed loyal.
There was another terrorist attack. This time in Moscow at the Bolshoi...a dog was used for a suicide bombing, killed Yuri Gursinki's wife.
Russians claim they have evidence we carried out the attack and missed Gursinki. Shit is really starting to hit the fan.
Gursinski runs the national gas pipelines, why would he be a target?

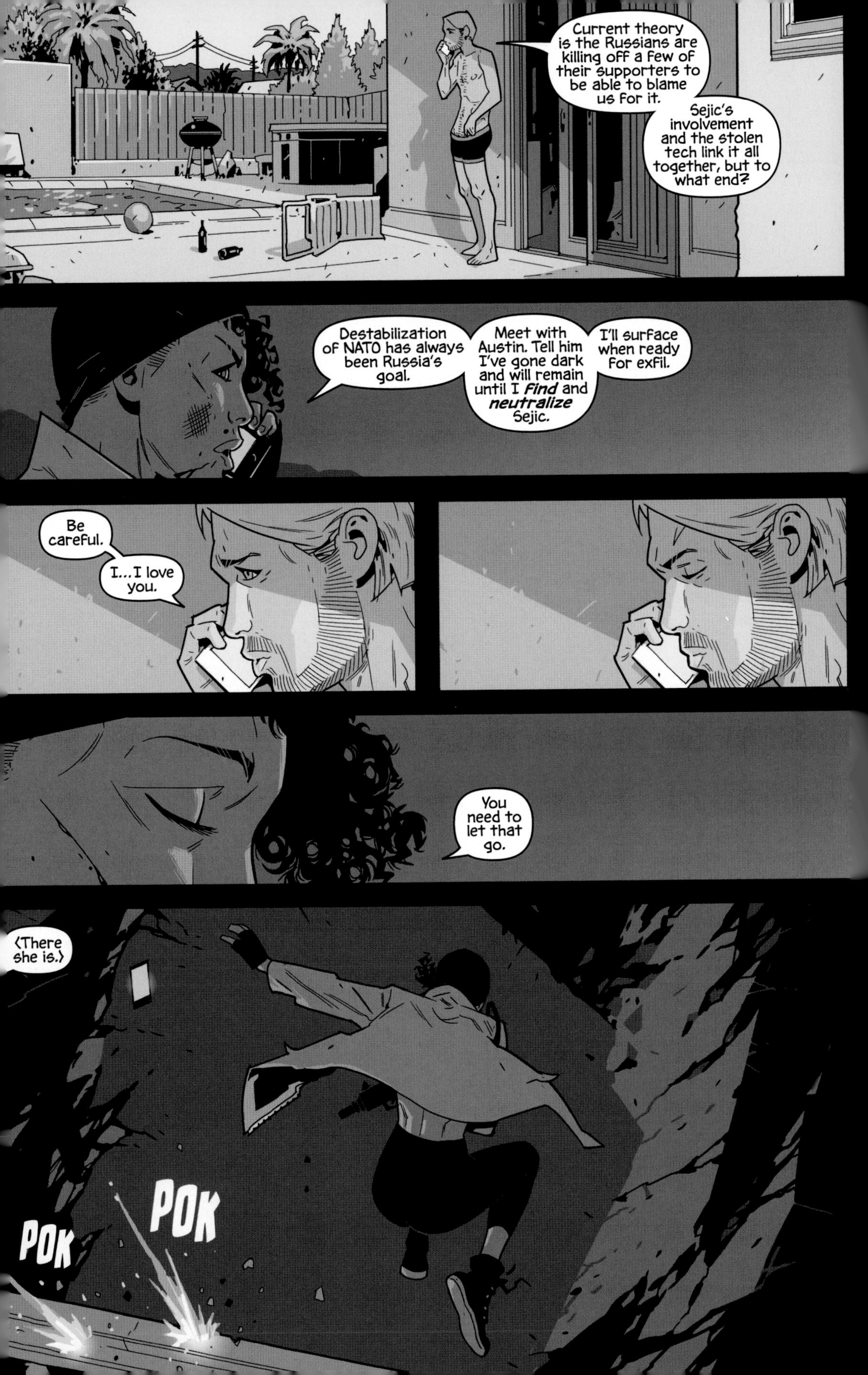
Current theory is the Russians are killing off a few of their supporters to be able to blame us for it.
Sejic's involvement and the stolen tech link it all together, but to what end?
Destabilization of NATO has always been Russia's goal.
Meet with Austin. Tell him I've gone dark and will remain until I *find* and *neutralize* Sejic.
I'll surface when ready for exfil.
Be careful.
I... I love you.
You need to let that go.
‹There she is.›
POK
POK

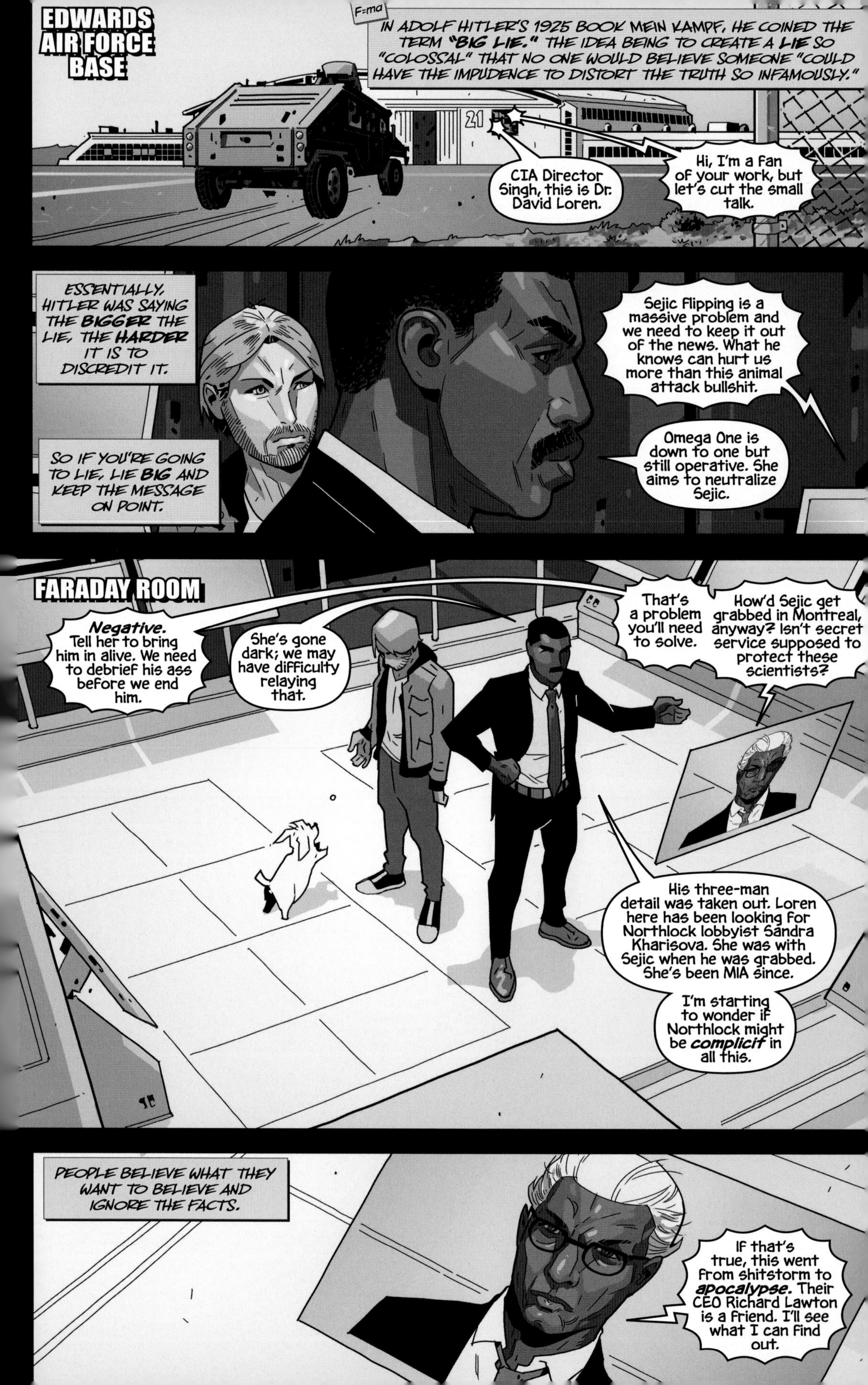
EDWARDS AIR FORCE BASE
F=ma
IN ADOLF HITLER'S 1925 BOOK MEIN KAMPF, HE COINED THE TERM "BIG LIE." THE IDEA BEING TO CREATE A LIE SO "COLOSSAL" THAT NO ONE WOULD BELIEVE SOMEONE "COULD HAVE THE IMPUDENCE TO DISTORT THE TRUTH SO INFAMOUSLY."
21
CIA Director Singh, this is Dr. David Loren.
Hi, I'm a fan of your work, but let's cut the small talk.
ESSENTIALLY, HITLER WAS SAYING THE BIGGER THE LIE, THE HARDER IT IS TO DISCREDIT IT.
Sejic flipping is a massive problem and we need to keep it out of the news. What he knows can hurt us more than this animal attack bullshit.
SO IF YOU'RE GOING TO LIE, LIE BIG AND KEEP THE MESSAGE ON POINT.
Omega One is down to one but still operative. She aims to neutralize Sejic.
FARADAY ROOM
Negative. Tell her to bring him in alive. We need to debrief his ass before we end him.
She's gone dark; we may have difficulty relaying that.
That's a problem you'll need to solve.
How'd Sejic get grabbed in Montreal, anyway? Isn't secret service supposed to protect these scientists?
His three-man detail was taken out. Loren here has been looking for Northlock lobbyist Sandra Kharisova. She was with Sejic when he was grabbed. She's been MIA since.
I'm starting to wonder if Northlock might be complicit in all this.
PEOPLE BELIEVE WHAT THEY WANT TO BELIEVE AND IGNORE THE FACTS.
If that's true, this went from shitstorm to apocalypse. Their CEO Richard Lawton is a friend. I'll see what I can find out.

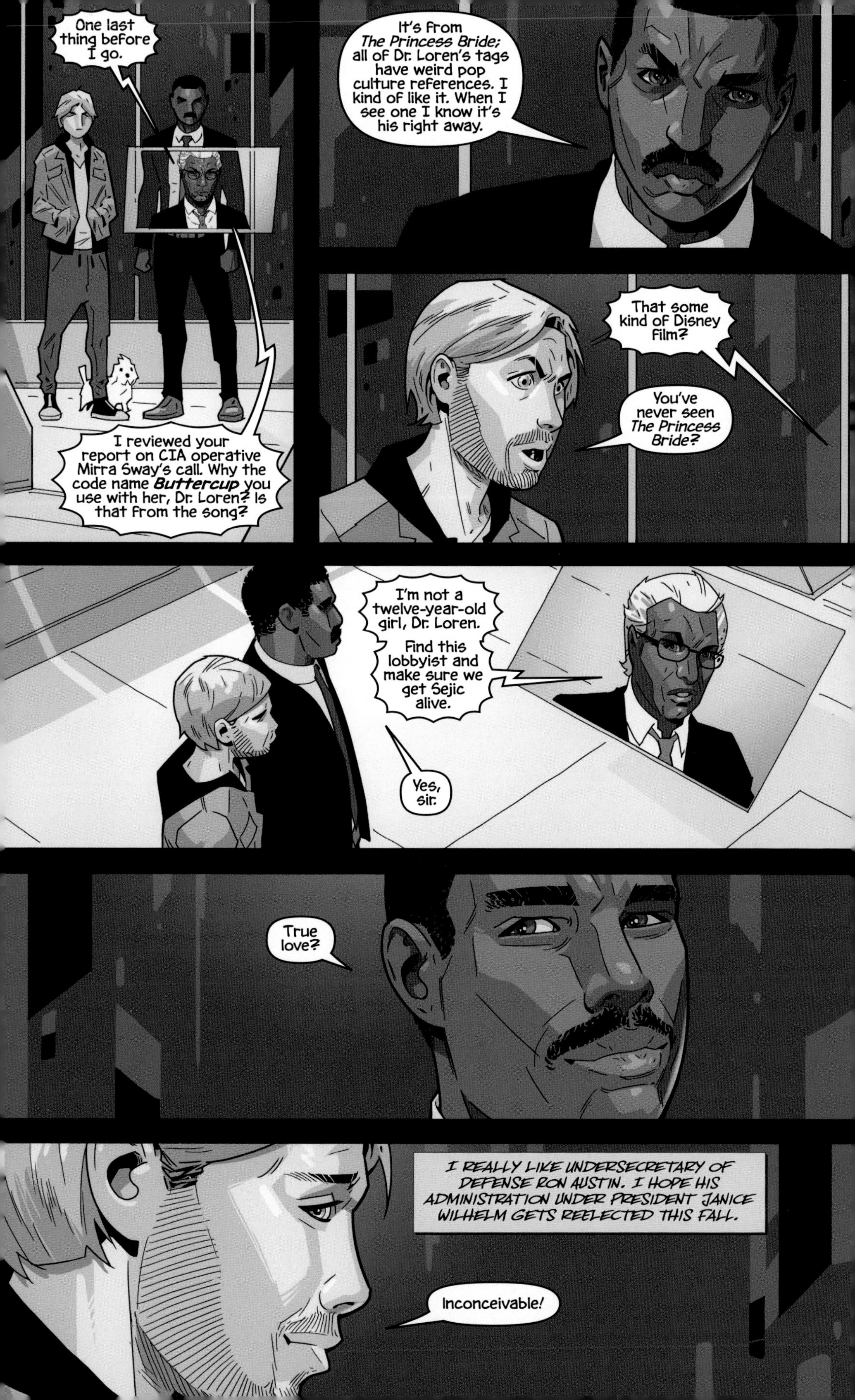
One last thing before I go.
I reviewed your report on CIA operative Mirra Sway's call. Why the code name *Buttercup* you use with her, Dr. Loren? Is that from the song?
It's from *The Princess Bride;* all of Dr. Loren's tags have weird pop culture references. I kind of like it. When I see one I know it's his right away.
That some kind of Disney film?
You've never seen *The Princess Bride?*
I'm not a twelve-year-old girl, Dr. Loren.
Find this lobbyist and make sure we get Sejic alive.
Yes, sir.
True love?
I REALLY LIKE UNDERSECRETARY OF DEFENSE RON AUSTIN. I HOPE HIS ADMINISTRATION UNDER PRESIDENT JANICE WILHELM GETS REELECTED THIS FALL.
Inconceivable!

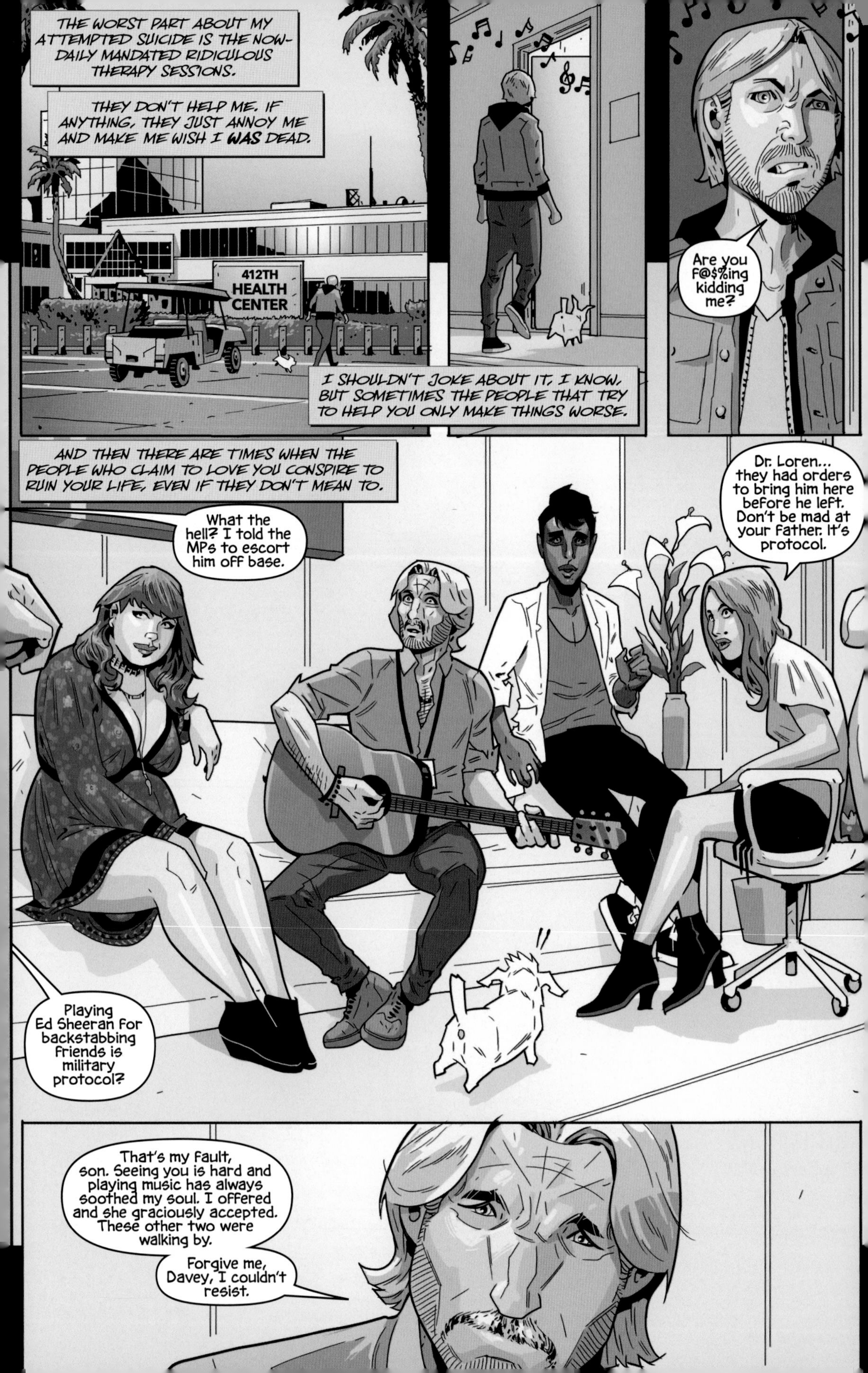
THE WORST PART ABOUT MY ATTEMPTED SUICIDE IS THE NOW-DAILY MANDATED RIDICULOUS THERAPY SESSIONS.
THEY DON'T HELP ME. IF ANYTHING, THEY JUST ANNOY ME AND MAKE ME WISH I WAS DEAD.
412TH HEALTH CENTER
I SHOULDN'T JOKE ABOUT IT, I KNOW, BUT SOMETIMES THE PEOPLE THAT TRY TO HELP YOU ONLY MAKE THINGS WORSE.
Are you F@$%ing kidding me?
AND THEN THERE ARE TIMES WHEN THE PEOPLE WHO CLAIM TO LOVE YOU CONSPIRE TO RUIN YOUR LIFE, EVEN IF THEY DON'T MEAN TO.
What the hell? I told the MPs to escort him off base.
Dr. Loren... they had orders to bring him here before he left. Don't be mad at your father. It's protocol.
Playing Ed Sheeran for backstabbing friends is military protocol?
That's my fault, son. Seeing you is hard and playing music has always soothed my soul. I offered and she graciously accepted. These other two were walking by.
Forgive me, Davey, I couldn't resist.

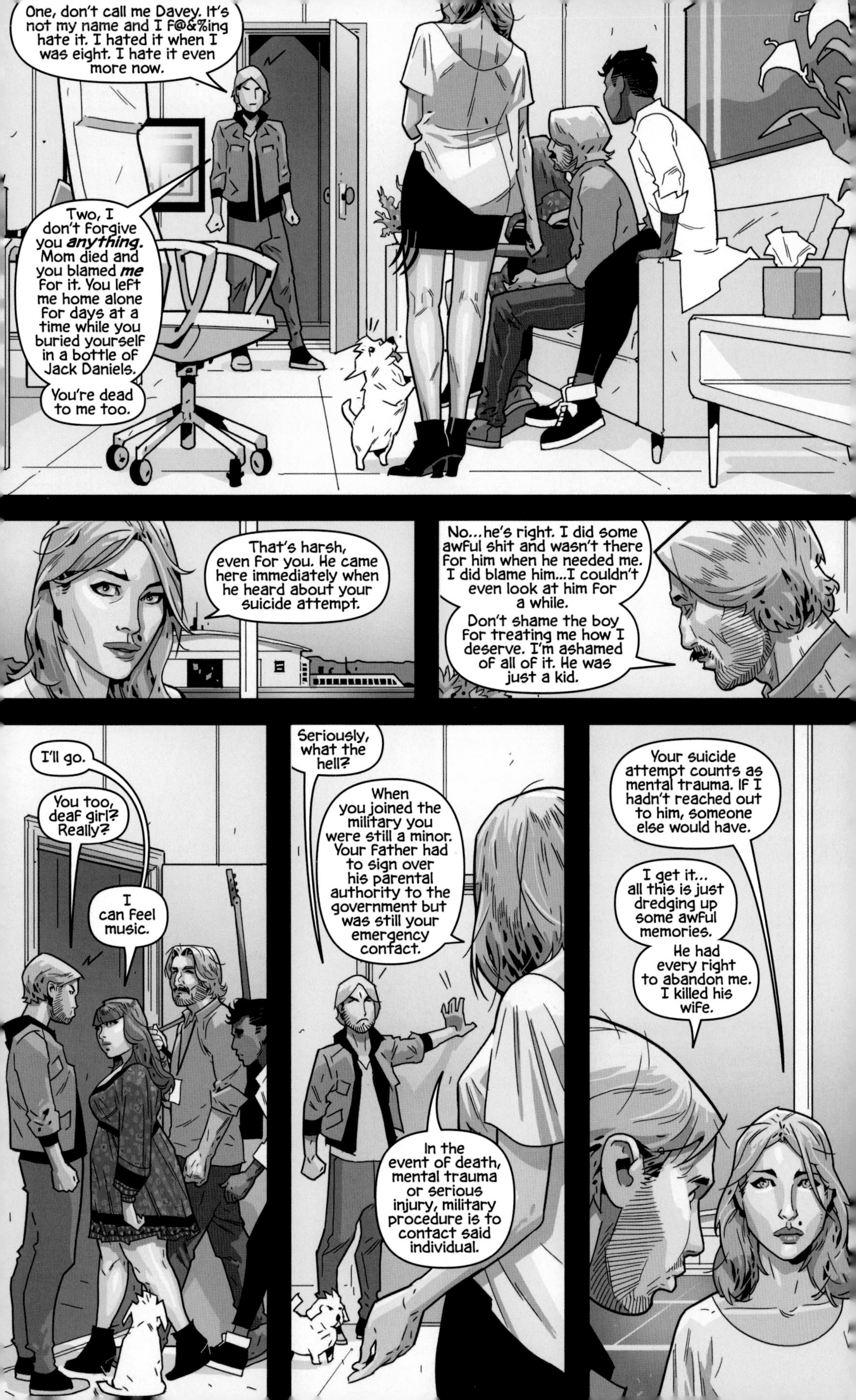
One, don't call me Davey. It's not my name and I F@&%ing hate it. I hated it when I was eight. I hate it even more now.
Two, I don't forgive you *anything*. Mom died and you blamed *me* for it. You left me home alone for days at a time while you buried yourself in a bottle of Jack Daniels.
You're dead to me too.
That's harsh, even for you. He came here immediately when he heard about your suicide attempt.
No...he's right. I did some awful shit and wasn't there for him when he needed me. I did blame him...I couldn't even look at him for a while.
Don't shame the boy for treating me how I deserve. I'm ashamed of all of it. He was just a kid.
I'll go.
You too, deaf girl? Really?
I can feel music.
Seriously, what the hell?
When you joined the military you were still a minor. Your father had to sign over his parental authority to the government but was still your emergency contact.
In the event of death, mental trauma or serious injury, military procedure is to contact said individual.
Your suicide attempt counts as mental trauma. If I hadn't reached out to him, someone else would have.
I get it... all this is just dredging up some awful memories.
He had every right to abandon me. I killed his wife.

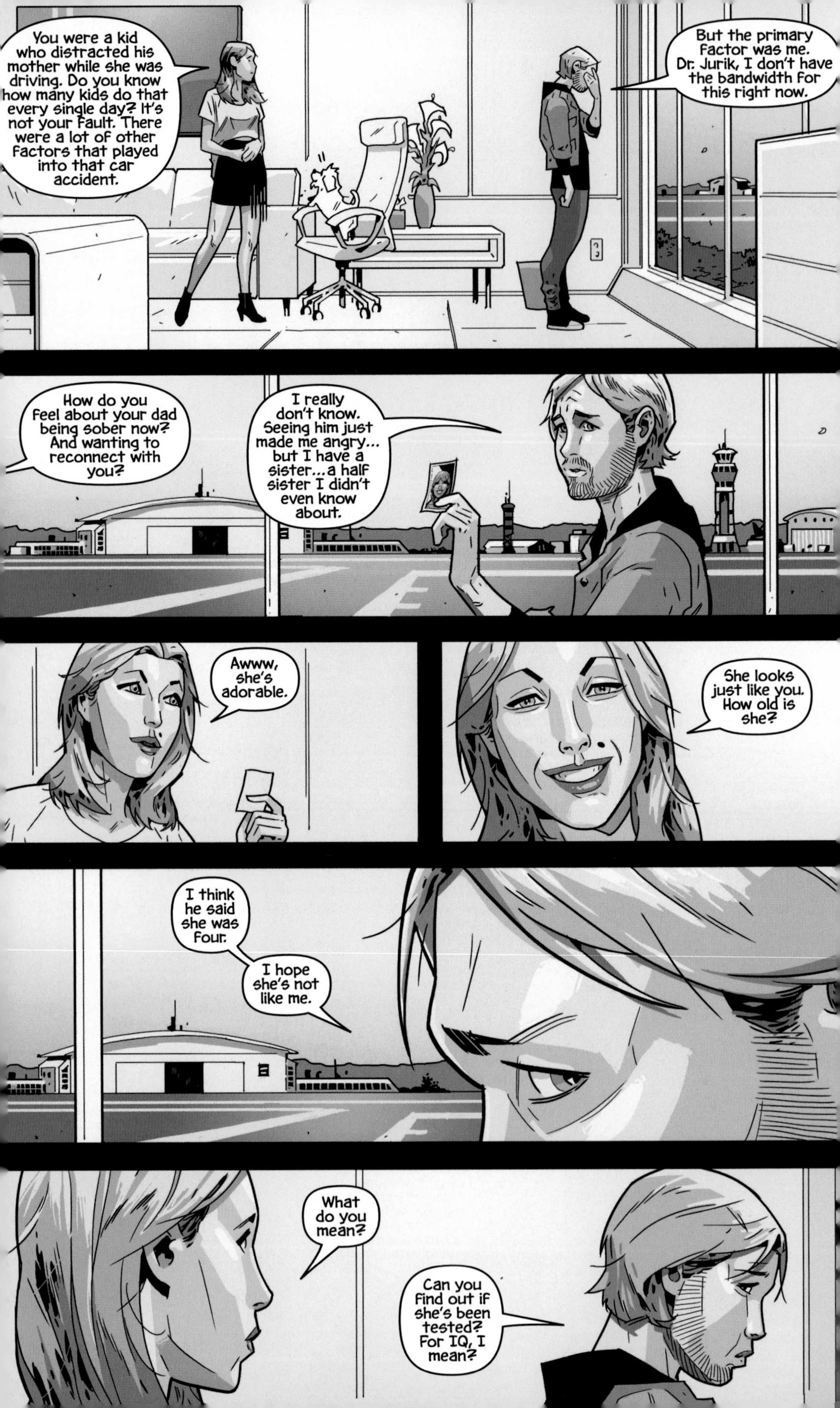
You were a kid who distracted his mother while she was driving. Do you know how many kids do that every single day? It's not your fault. There were a lot of other factors that played into that car accident.
But the primary factor was me. Dr. Jurik, I don't have the bandwidth for this right now.
How do you feel about your dad being sober now? And wanting to reconnect with you?
I really don't know. Seeing him just made me angry... but I have a sister... a half sister I didn't even know about.
Awww, she's adorable.
She looks just like you. How old is she?
I think he said she was four.
I hope she's not like me.
What do you mean?
Can you find out if she's been tested? For IQ, I mean?

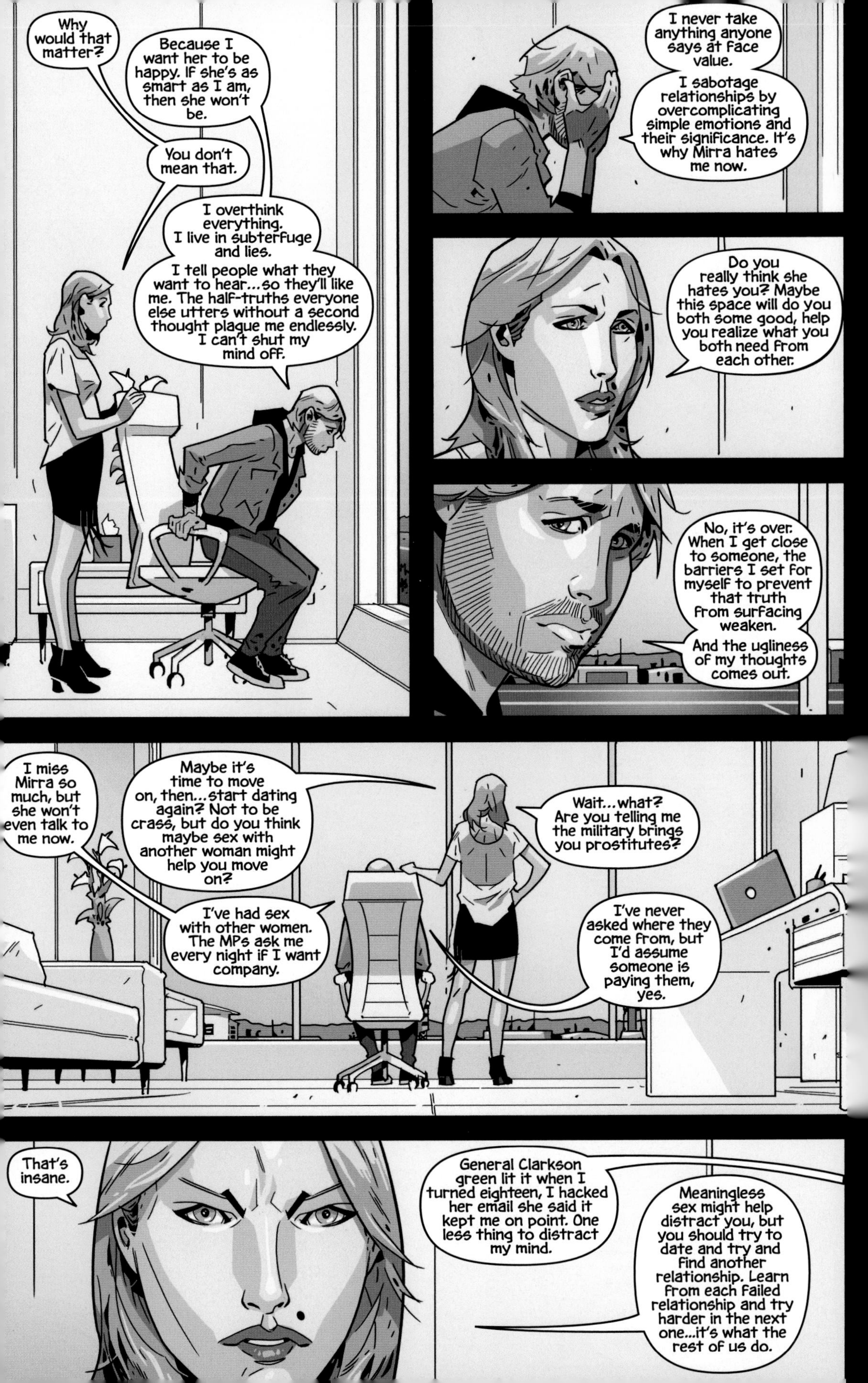
Why would that matter?
Because I want her to be happy. If she's as smart as I am, then she won't be.
You don't mean that.
I overthink everything. I live in subterfuge and lies.
I tell people what they want to hear...so they'll like me. The half-truths everyone else utters without a second thought plague me endlessly. I can't shut my mind off.
I never take anything anyone says at face value.
I sabotage relationships by overcomplicating simple emotions and their significance. It's why Mirra hates me now.
Do you really think she hates you? Maybe this space will do you both some good, help you realize what you both need from each other.
No, it's over. When I get close to someone, the barriers I set for myself to prevent that truth from surfacing weaken.
And the ugliness of my thoughts comes out.
I miss Mirra so much, but she won't even talk to me now.
Maybe it's time to move on, then...start dating again? Not to be crass, but do you think maybe sex with another woman might help you move on?
I've had sex with other women. The MPs ask me every night if I want company.
Wait...what? Are you telling me the military brings you prostitutes?
I've never asked where they come from, but I'd assume someone is paying them, yes.
That's insane.
General Clarkson green lit it when I turned eighteen, I hacked her email she said it kept me on point. One less thing to distract my mind.
Meaningless sex might help distract you, but you should try to date and try and find another relationship. Learn from each failed relationship and try harder in the next one...it's what the rest of us do.

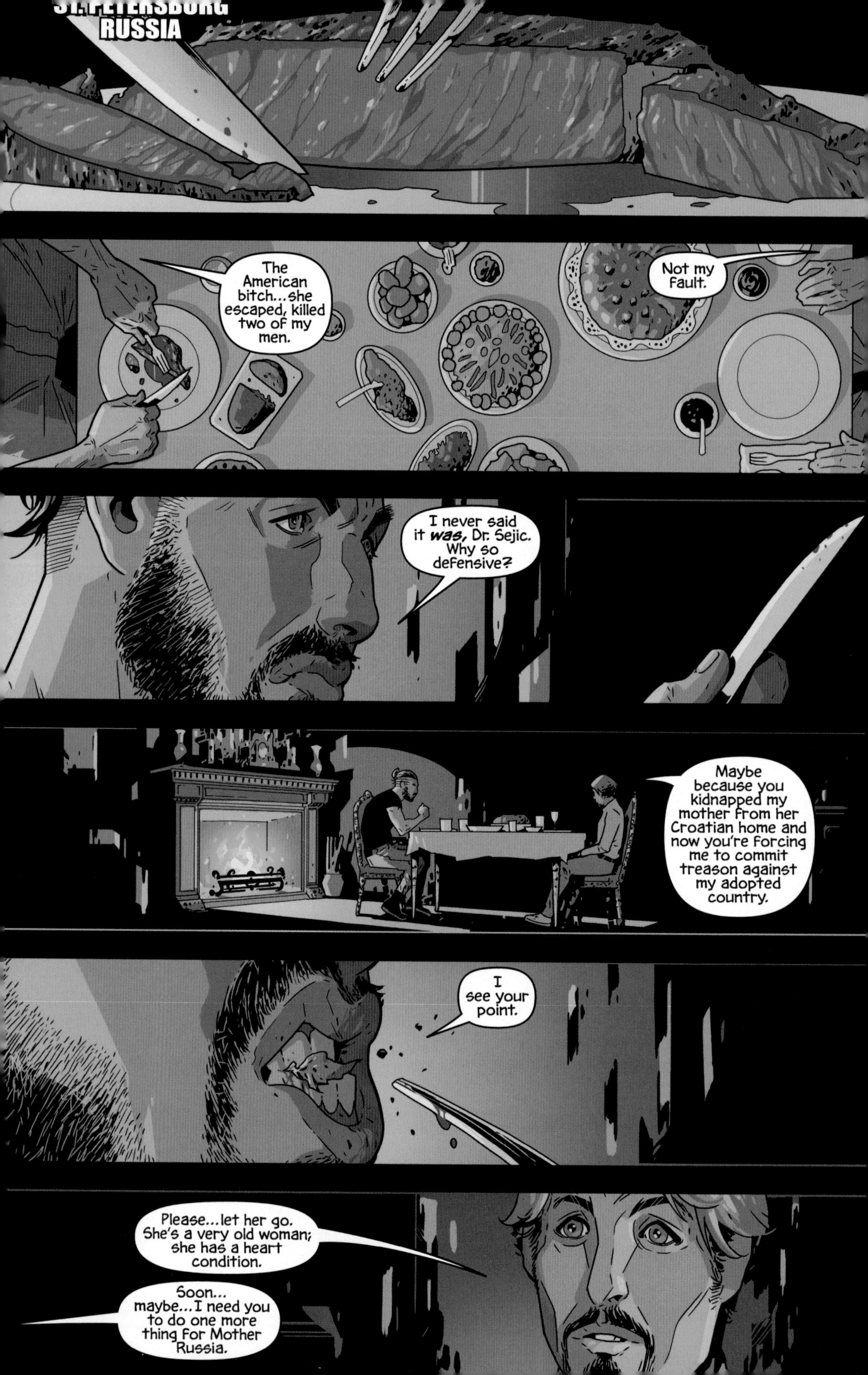
ST. PETERSBURG
RUSSIA
The American bitch...she escaped, killed two of my men.
Not my fault.
I never said it *was*, Dr. Sejic. Why so defensive?
Maybe because you kidnapped my mother from her Croatian home and now you're forcing me to commit treason against my adopted country.
I see your point.
Please...let her go. She's a very old woman; she has a heart condition.
Soon... maybe...I need you to do one more thing for Mother Russia.

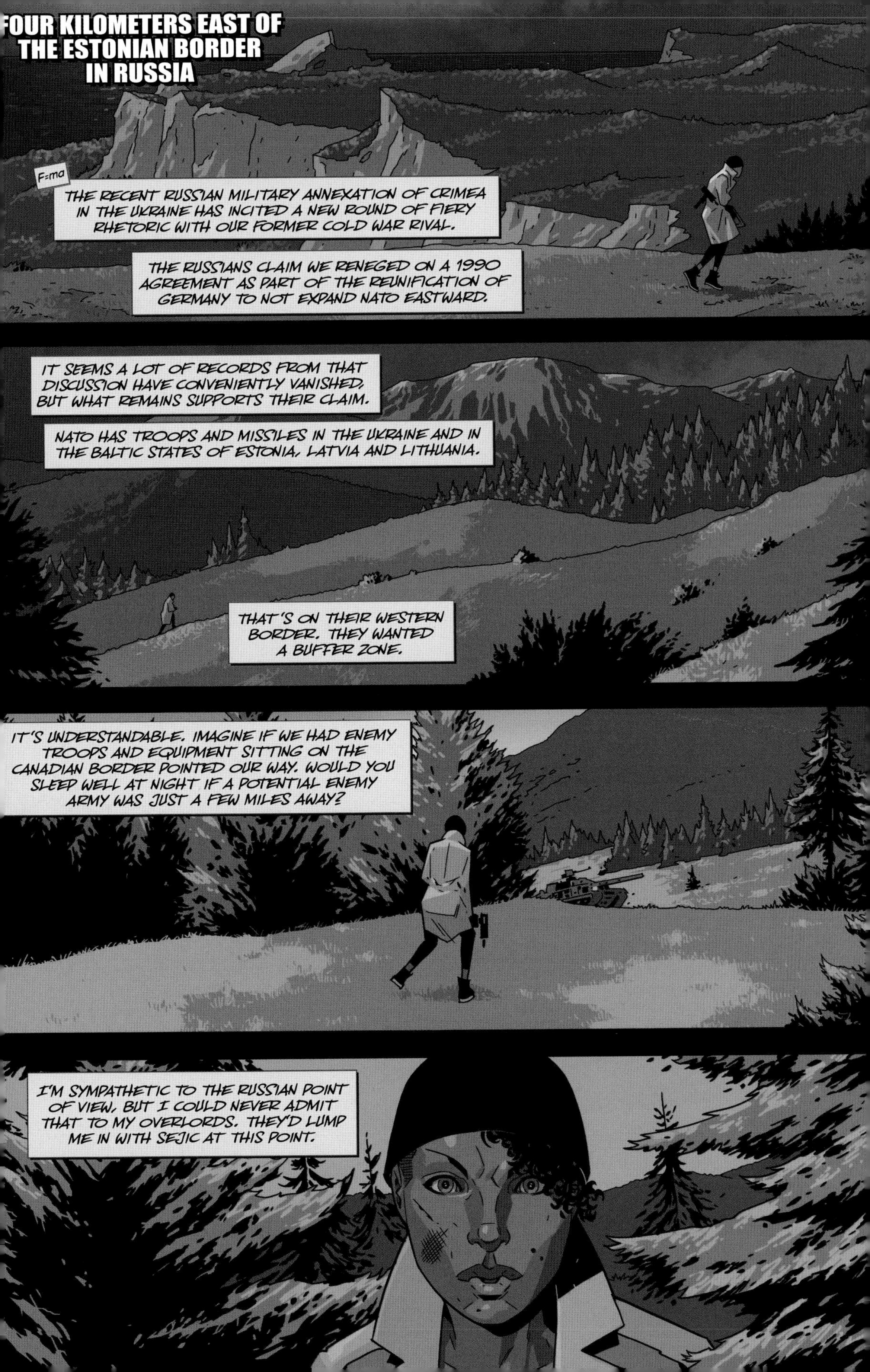
FOUR KILOMETERS EAST OF THE ESTONIAN BORDER IN RUSSIA
F=ma
THE RECENT RUSSIAN MILITARY ANNEXATION OF CRIMEA IN THE UKRAINE HAS INCITED A NEW ROUND OF FIERY RHETORIC WITH OUR FORMER COLD WAR RIVAL.
THE RUSSIANS CLAIM WE RENEGED ON A 1990 AGREEMENT AS PART OF THE REUNIFICATION OF GERMANY TO NOT EXPAND NATO EASTWARD.
IT SEEMS A LOT OF RECORDS FROM THAT DISCUSSION HAVE CONVENIENTLY VANISHED, BUT WHAT REMAINS SUPPORTS THEIR CLAIM.
NATO HAS TROOPS AND MISSILES IN THE UKRAINE AND IN THE BALTIC STATES OF ESTONIA, LATVIA AND LITHUANIA.
THAT'S ON THEIR WESTERN BORDER. THEY WANTED A BUFFER ZONE.
IT'S UNDERSTANDABLE. IMAGINE IF WE HAD ENEMY TROOPS AND EQUIPMENT SITTING ON THE CANADIAN BORDER POINTED OUR WAY. WOULD YOU SLEEP WELL AT NIGHT IF A POTENTIAL ENEMY ARMY WAS JUST A FEW MILES AWAY?
I'M SYMPATHETIC TO THE RUSSIAN POINT OF VIEW, BUT I COULD NEVER ADMIT THAT TO MY OVERLORDS. THEY'D LUMP ME IN WITH SEJIC AT THIS POINT.

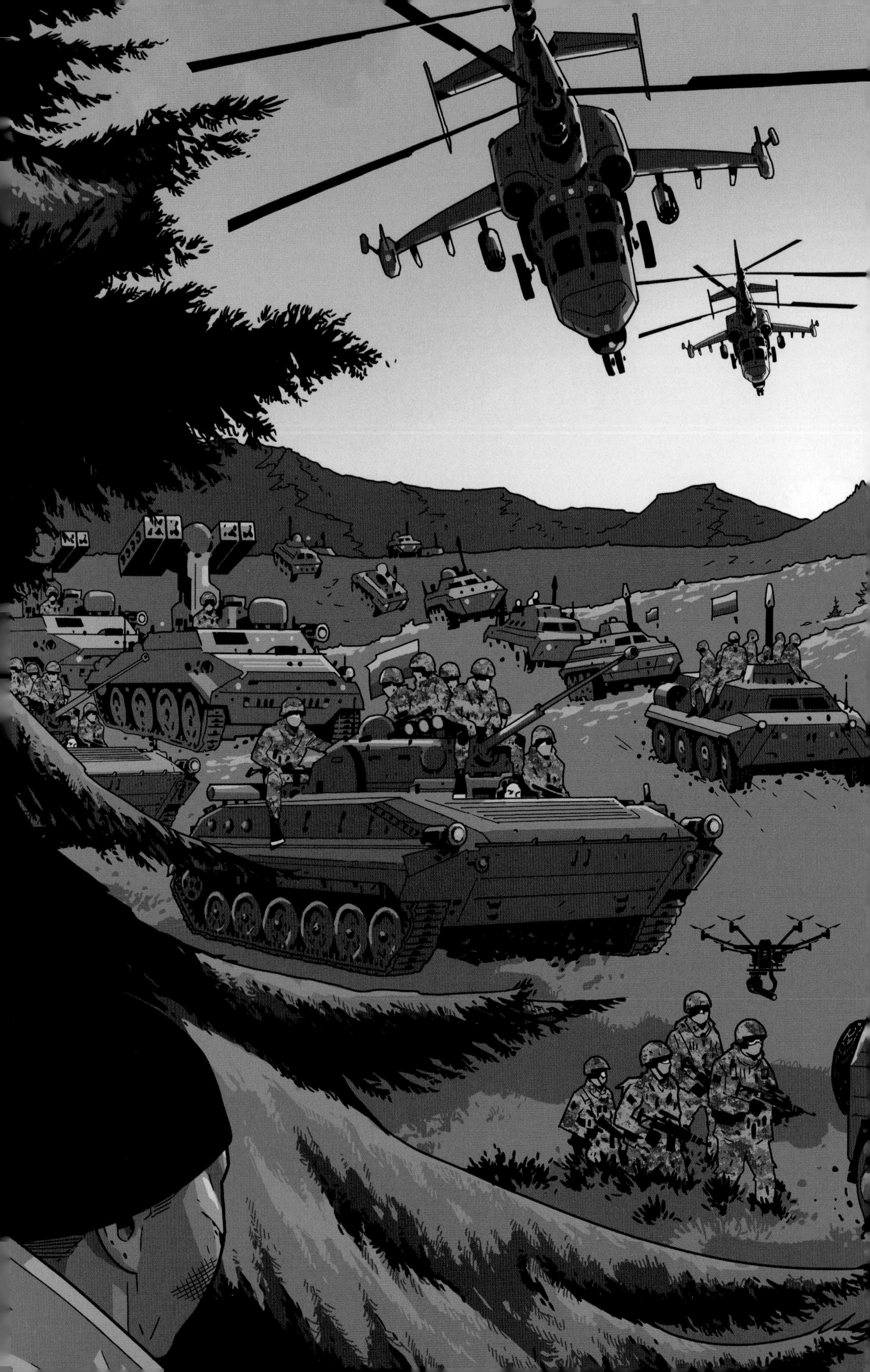

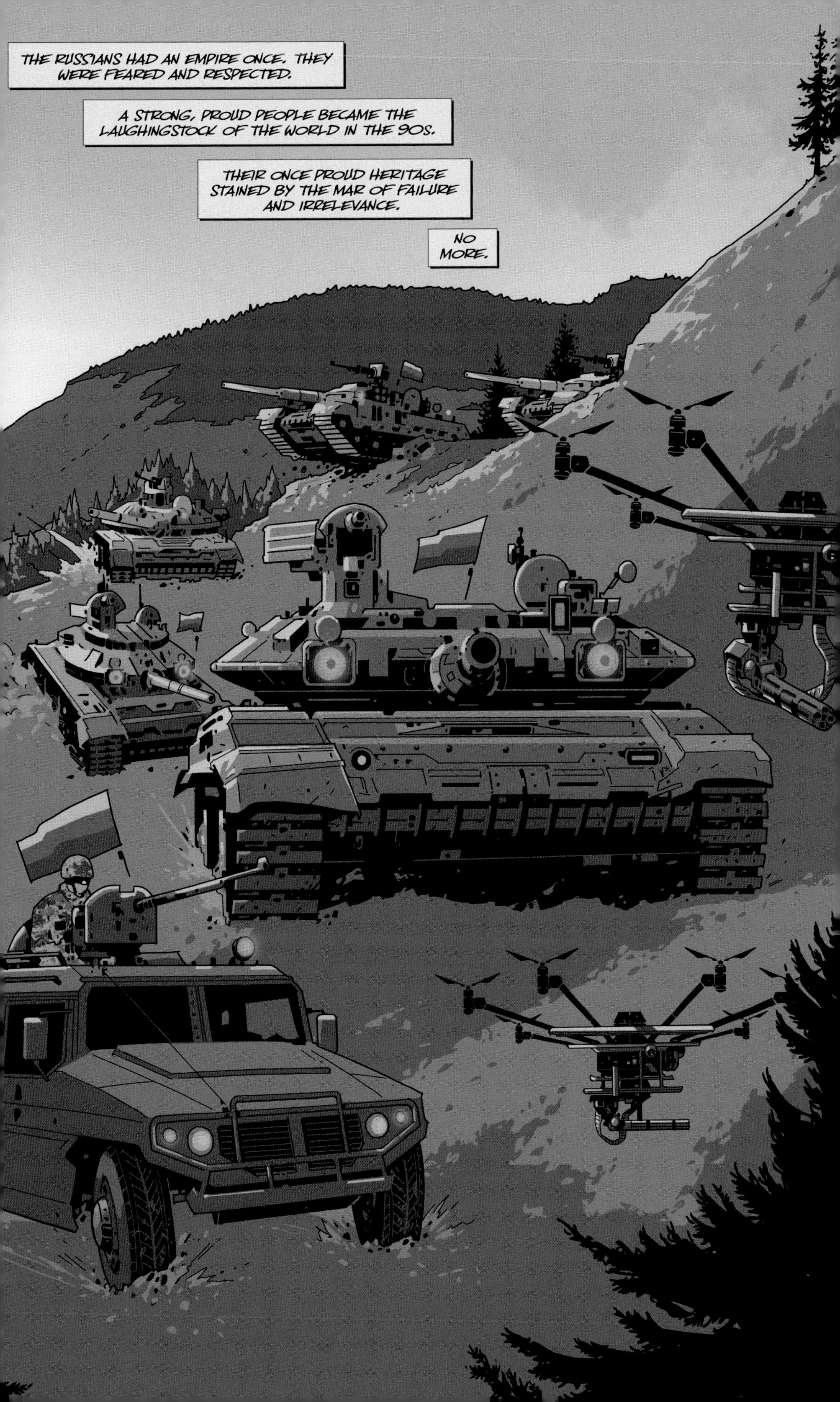
THE RUSSIANS HAD AN EMPIRE ONCE. THEY WERE FEARED AND RESPECTED.
A STRONG, PROUD PEOPLE BECAME THE LAUGHINGSTOCK OF THE WORLD IN THE 90S.
THEIR ONCE PROUD HERITAGE STAINED BY THE MAR OF FAILURE AND IRRELEVANCE.
NO MORE.

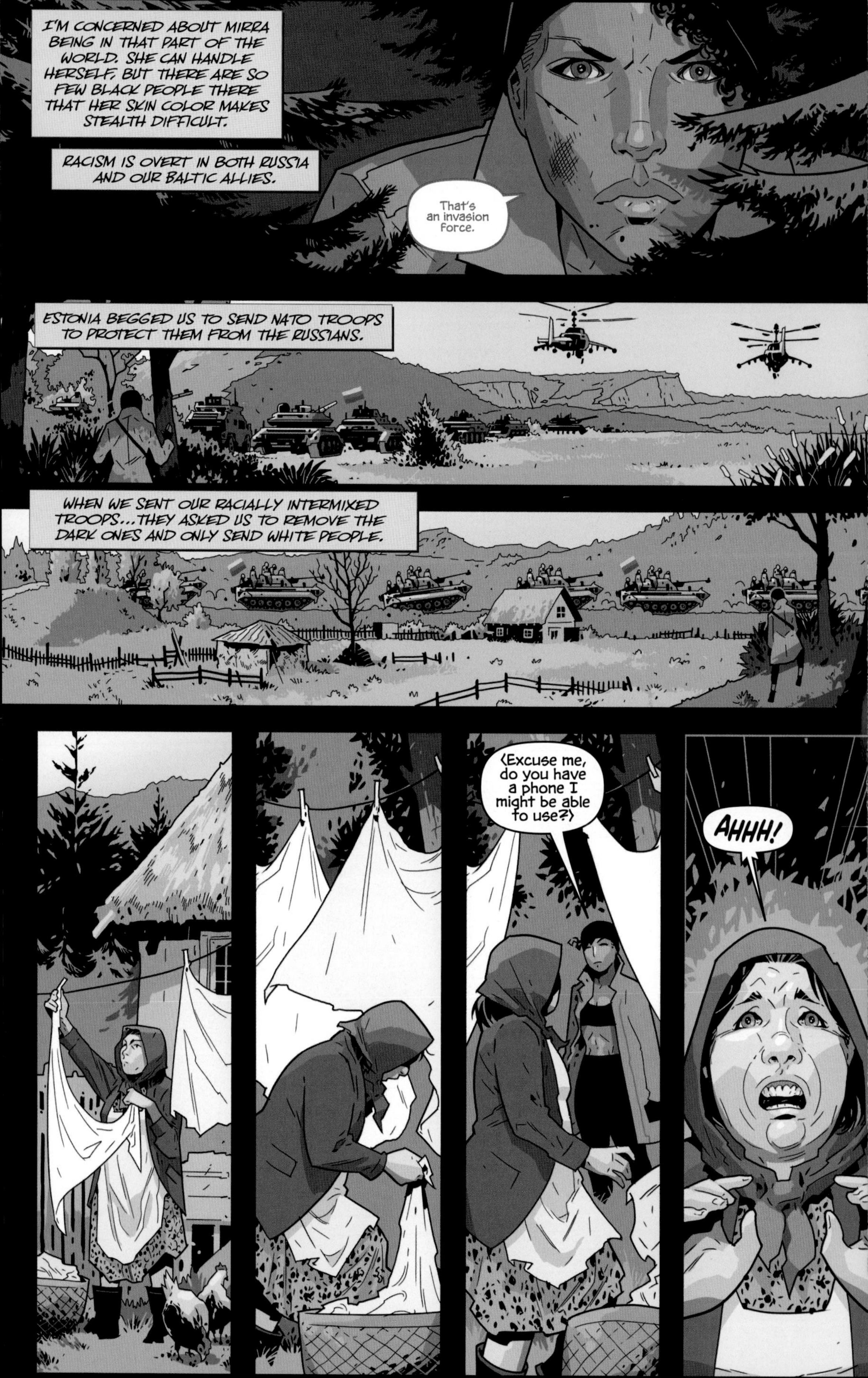

I'M CONCERNED ABOUT MIRRA BEING IN THAT PART OF THE WORLD. SHE CAN HANDLE HERSELF, BUT THERE ARE SO FEW BLACK PEOPLE THERE THAT HER SKIN COLOR MAKES STEALTH DIFFICULT.
RACISM IS OVERT IN BOTH RUSSIA AND OUR BALTIC ALLIES.
That's an invasion force.
ESTONIA BEGGED US TO SEND NATO TROOPS TO PROTECT THEM FROM THE RUSSIANS.
WHEN WE SENT OUR RACIALLY INTERMIXED TROOPS...THEY ASKED US TO REMOVE THE DARK ONES AND ONLY SEND WHITE PEOPLE.
‹Excuse me, do you have a phone I might be able to use?›
AHHH!

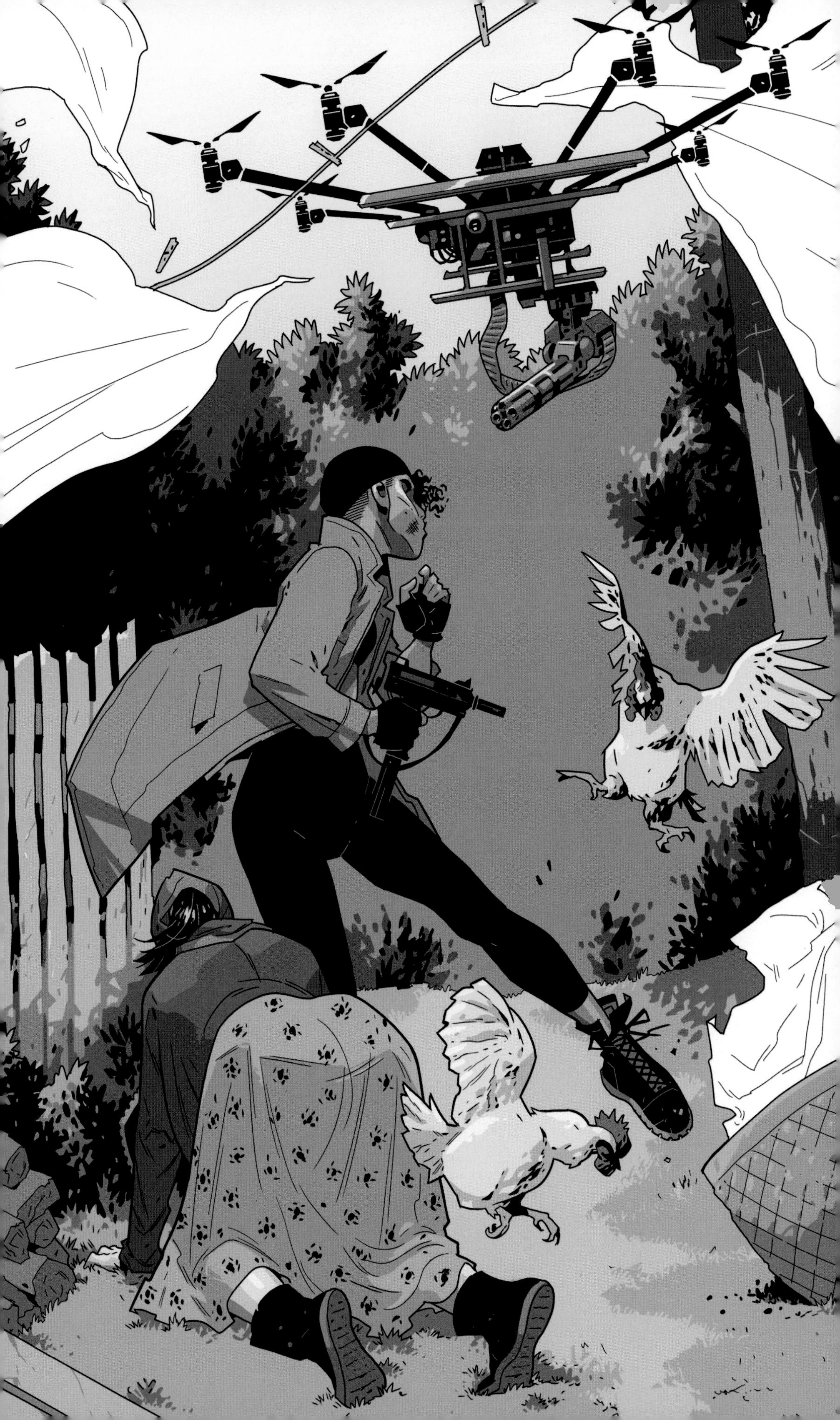

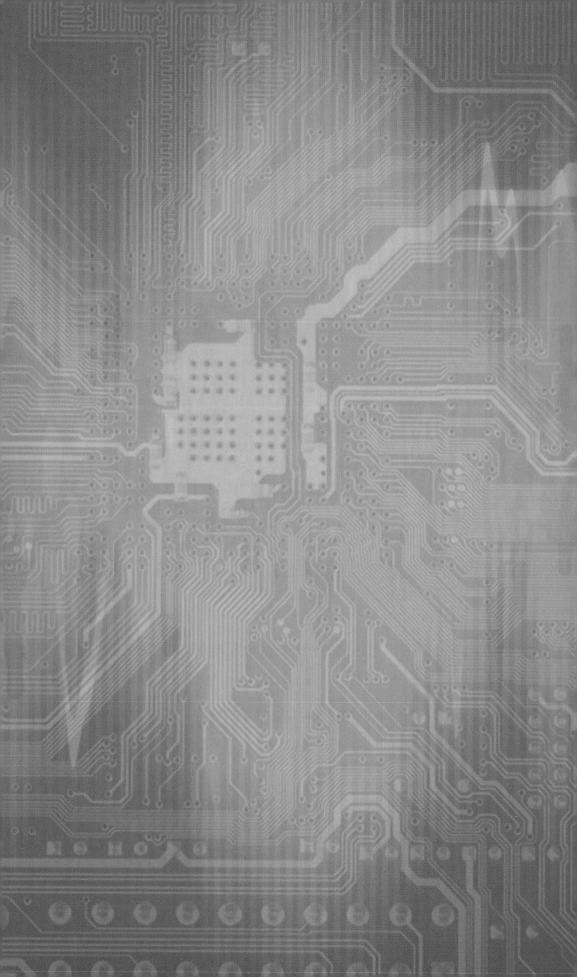

CHAPTER THREE

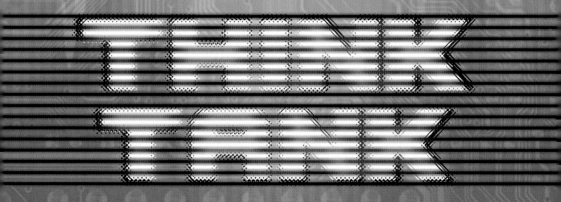

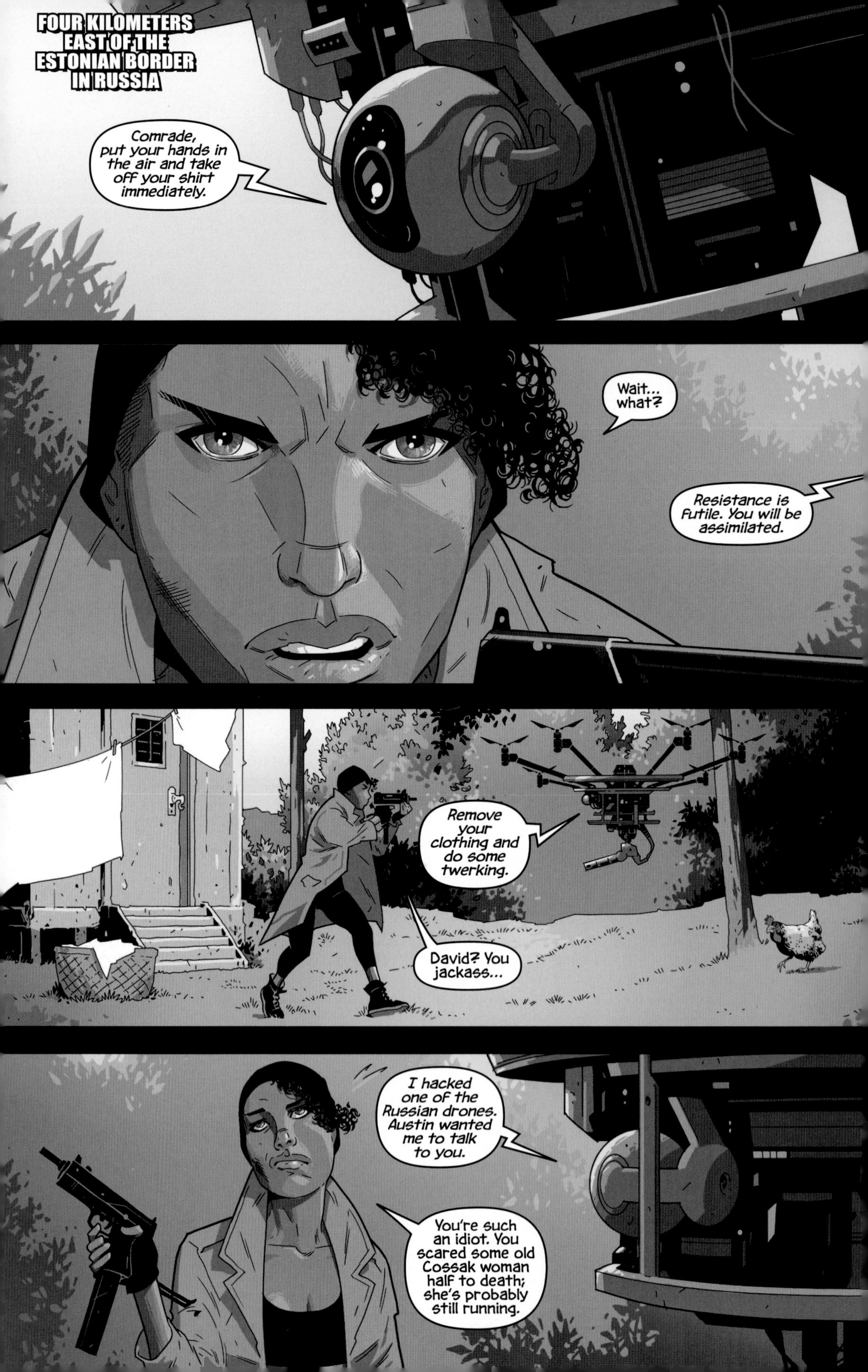
FOUR KILOMETERS EAST OF THE ESTONIAN BORDER IN RUSSIA
Comrade, put your hands in the air and take off your shirt immediately.
Wait... what?
Resistance is futile. You will be assimilated.
Remove your clothing and do some twerking.
David? You jackass...
I hacked one of the Russian drones. Austin wanted me to talk to you.
You're such an idiot. You scared some old Cossak woman half to death; she's probably still running.

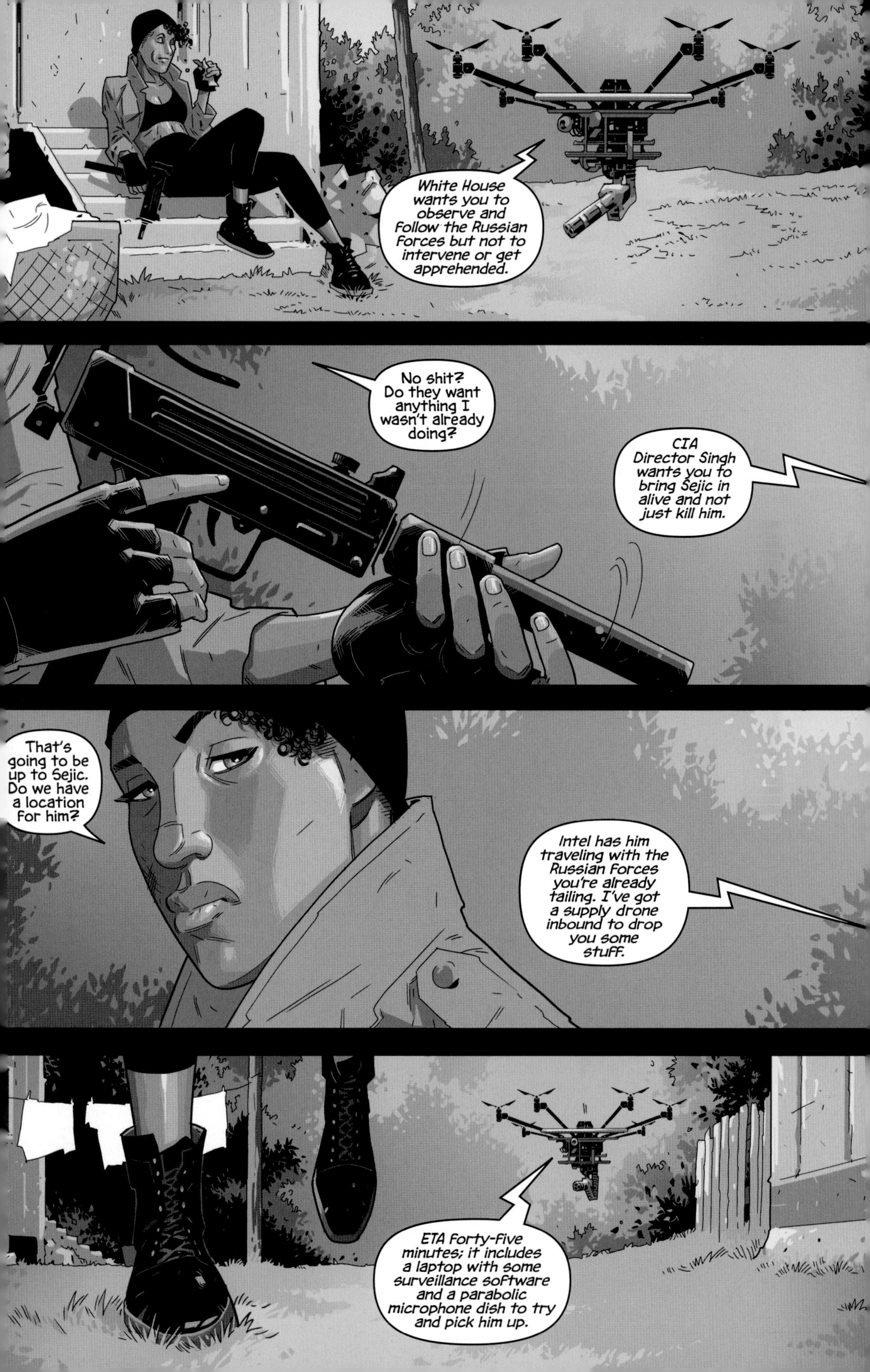
White House wants you to observe and follow the Russian Forces but not to intervene or get apprehended.
No shit? Do they want anything I wasn't already doing?
CIA Director Singh wants you to bring Sejic in alive and not just kill him.
That's going to be up to Sejic. Do we have a location for him?
Intel has him traveling with the Russian Forces you're already tailing. I've got a supply drone inbound to drop you some stuff.
ETA forty-five minutes; it includes a laptop with some surveillance software and a parabolic microphone dish to try and pick him up.

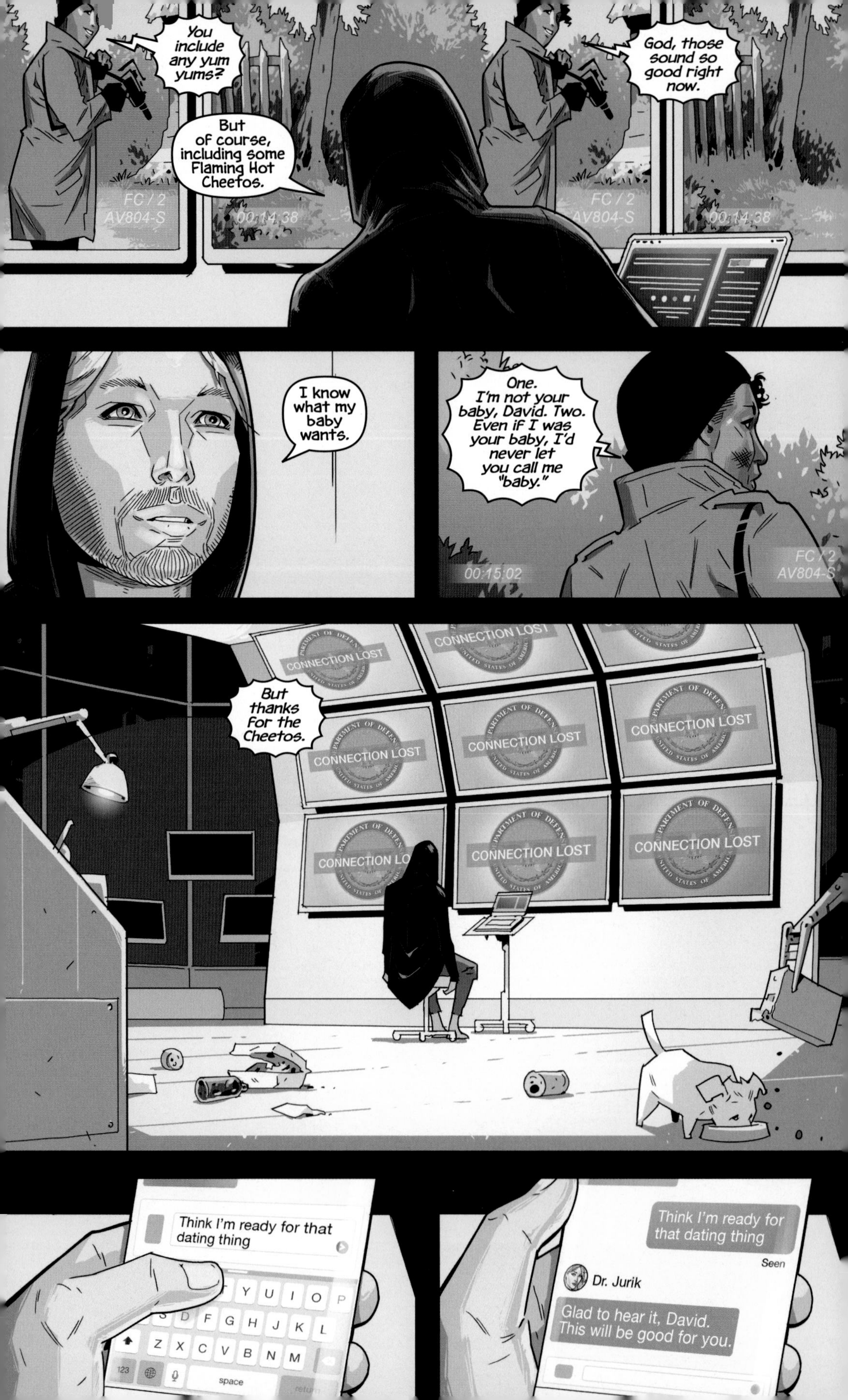
You include any yum yums?
But of course, including some Flaming Hot Cheetos.
FC / 2
AV804-S
00:14:38
God, those sound so good right now.
FC / 2
AV804-S
00:14:38
I know what my baby wants.
One. I'm not your baby, David. Two. Even if I was your baby, I'd never let you call me "baby."
00:15:02
FC / 2
AV804-S
But thanks for the Cheetos.
CONNECTION LOST
Think I'm ready for that dating thing
Think I'm ready for that dating thing
Seen
Dr. Jurik
Glad to hear it, David. This will be good for you.

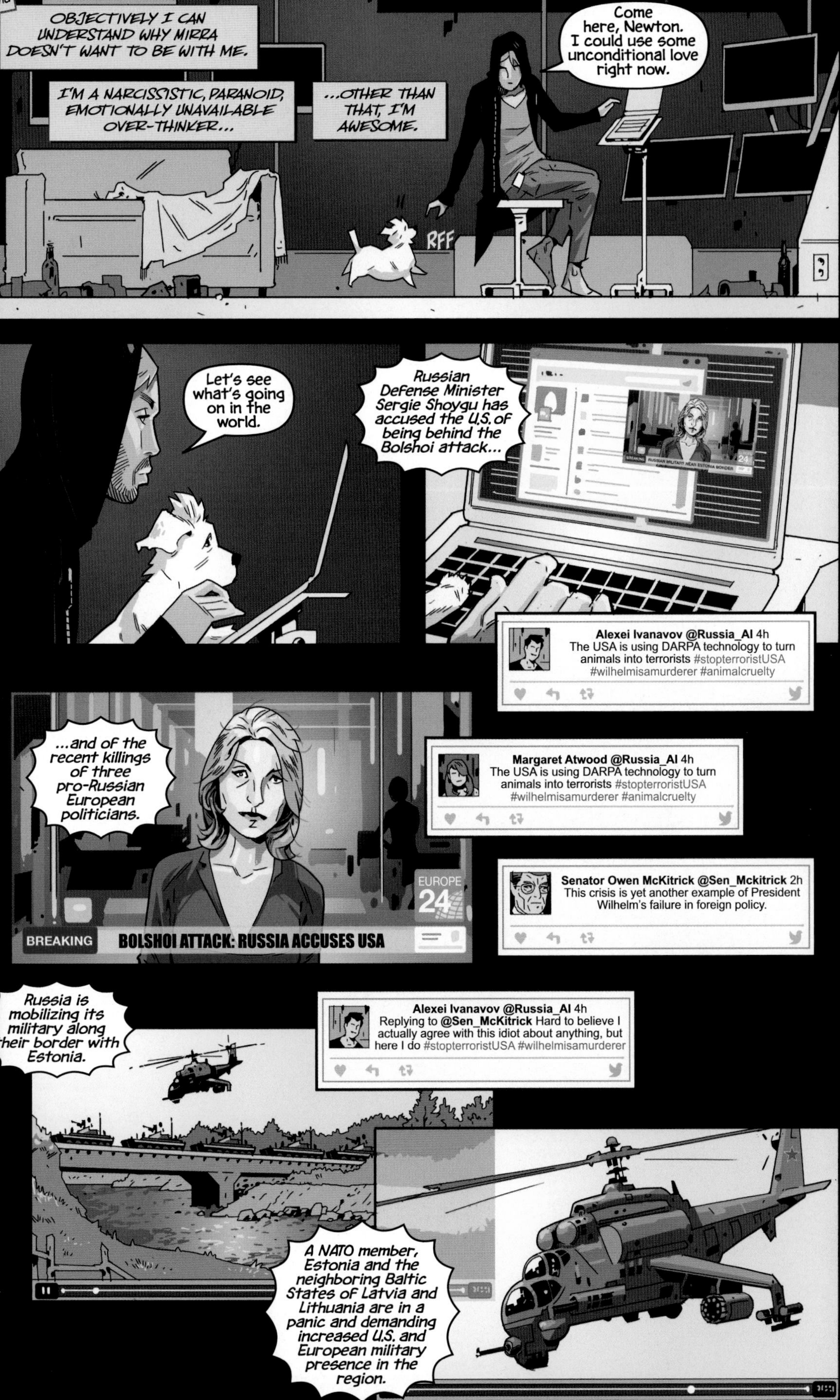

OBJECTIVELY I CAN UNDERSTAND WHY MIRRA DOESN'T WANT TO BE WITH ME.
I'M A NARCISSISTIC, PARANOID, EMOTIONALLY UNAVAILABLE OVER-THINKER...
...OTHER THAN THAT, I'M AWESOME.
Come here, Newton. I could use some unconditional love right now.
RFF
Let's see what's going on in the world.
Russian Defense Minister Sergie Shoygu has accused the U.S. of being behind the Bolshoi attack...
Alexei Ivanavov @Russia_Al 4h
The USA is using DARPA technology to turn animals into terrorists #stopterroristUSA #wilhelmisamurderer #animalcruelty
...and of the recent killings of three pro-Russian European politicians.
EUROPE 24
BREAKING
BOLSHOI ATTACK: RUSSIA ACCUSES USA
Margaret Atwood @Russia_Al 4h
The USA is using DARPA technology to turn animals into terrorists #stopterroristUSA #wilhelmisamurderer #animalcruelty
Senator Owen McKitrick @Sen_Mckitrick 2h
This crisis is yet another example of President Wilhelm's failure in foreign policy.
Russia is mobilizing its military along their border with Estonia.
Alexei Ivanavov @Russia_Al 4h
Replying to @Sen_McKitrick Hard to believe I actually agree with this idiot about anything, but here I do #stopterroristUSA #wilhelmisamurderer
A NATO member, Estonia and the neighboring Baltic States of Latvia and Lithuania are in a panic and demanding increased U.S. and European military presence in the region.

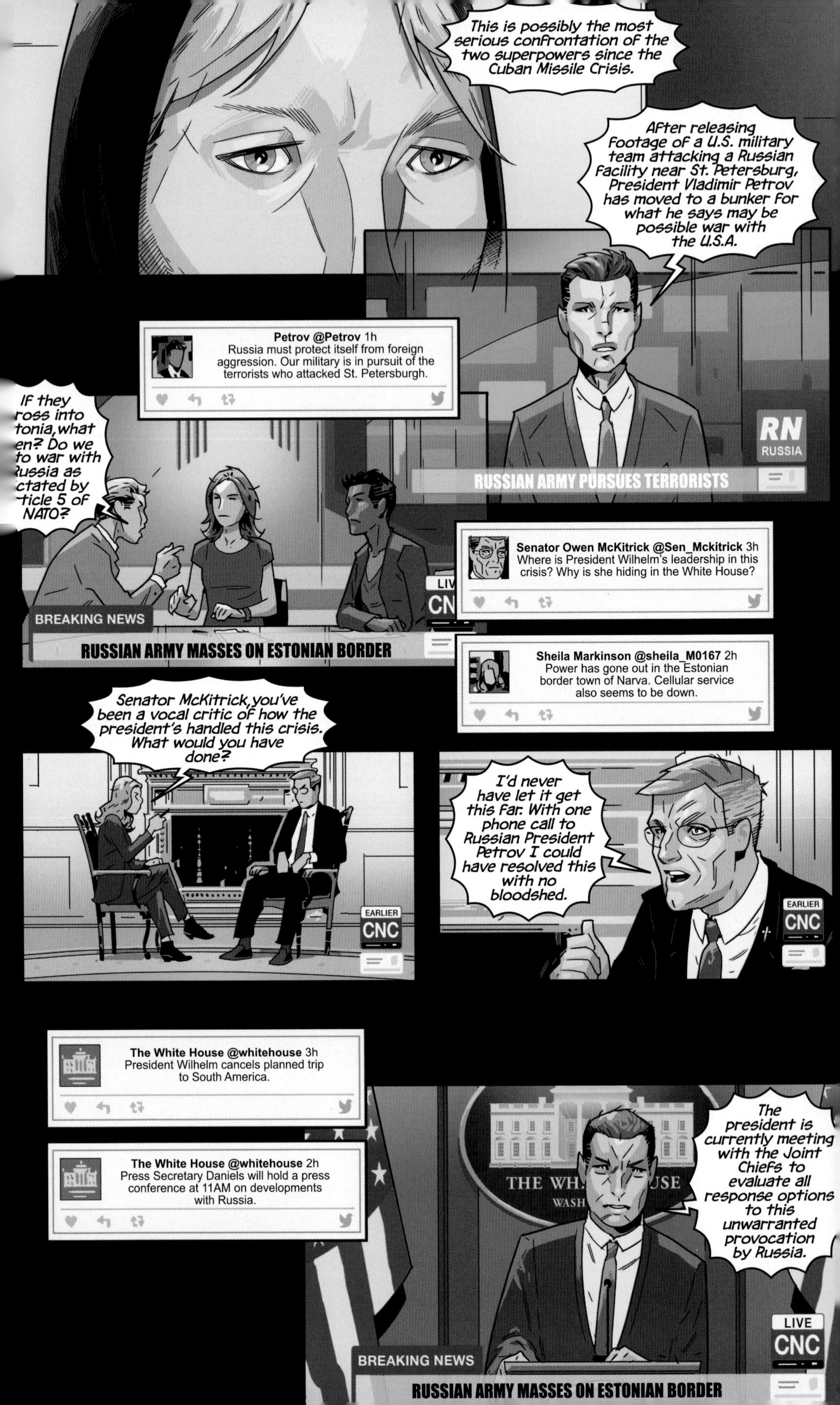

This is possibly the most serious confrontation of the two superpowers since the Cuban Missile Crisis.
After releasing footage of a U.S. military team attacking a Russian facility near St. Petersburg, President Vladimir Petrov has moved to a bunker for what he says may be possible war with the U.S.A.
RN
RUSSIA
RUSSIAN ARMY PURSUES TERRORISTS
Petrov @Petrov 1h
Russia must protect itself from foreign aggression. Our military is in pursuit of the terrorists who attacked St. Petersburgh.
BREAKING NEWS
RUSSIAN ARMY MASSES ON ESTONIAN BORDER
Senator Owen McKitrick @Sen_Mckitrick 3h
Where is President Wilhelm's leadership in this crisis? Why is she hiding in the White House?
Sheila Markinson @sheila_M0167 2h
Power has gone out in the Estonian border town of Narva. Cellular service also seems to be down.
Senator McKitrick, you've been a vocal critic of how the president's handled this crisis. What would you have done?
EARLIER
CNC
I'd never have let it get this far. With one phone call to Russian President Petrov I could have resolved this with no bloodshed.
EARLIER
CNC
The White House @whitehouse 3h
President Wilhelm cancels planned trip to South America.
The White House @whitehouse 2h
Press Secretary Daniels will hold a press conference at 11AM on developments with Russia.
The president is currently meeting with the Joint Chiefs to evaluate all response options to this unwarranted provocation by Russia.
LIVE
CNC
BREAKING NEWS
RUSSIAN ARMY MASSES ON ESTONIAN BORDER

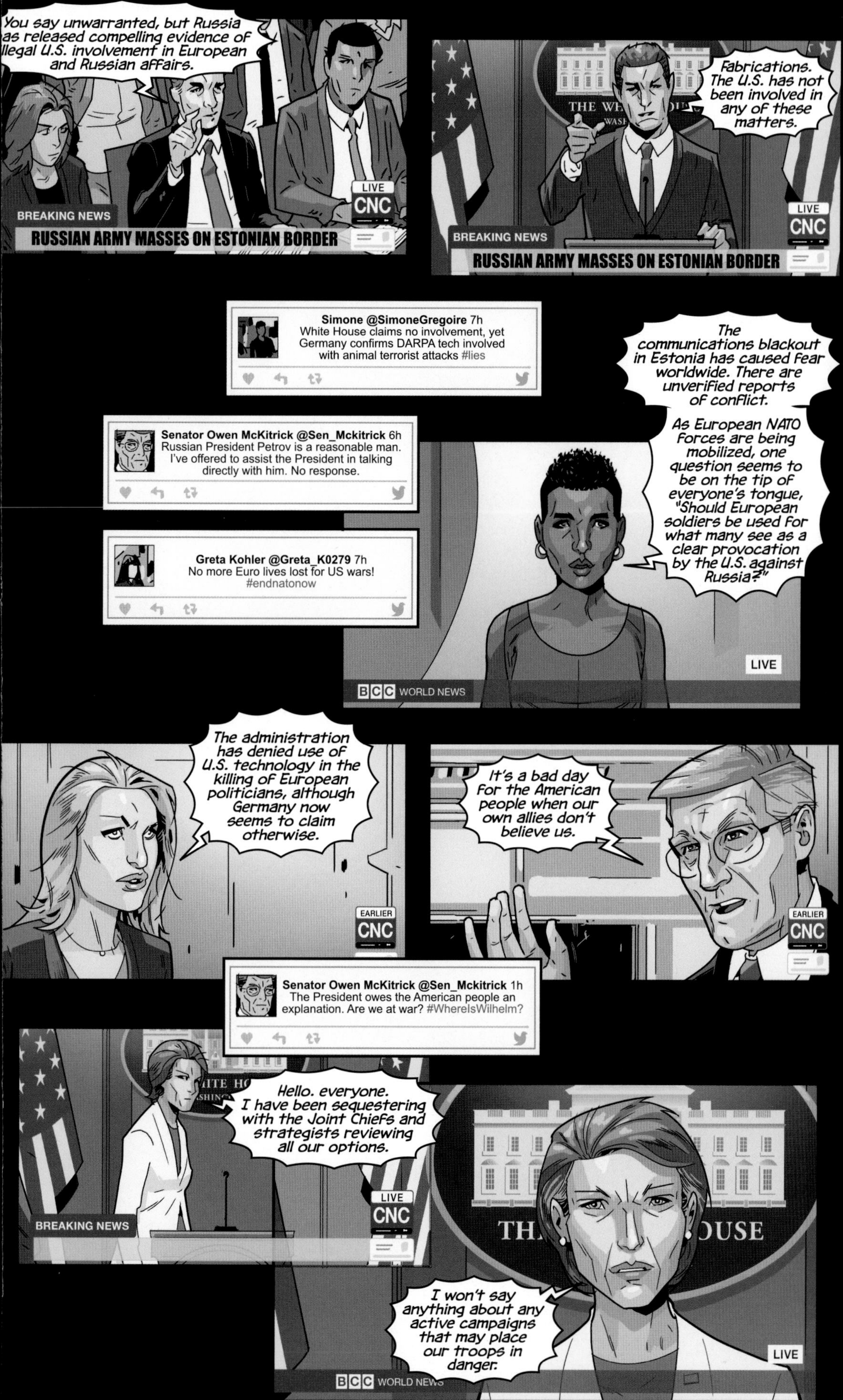

You say unwarranted, but Russia has released compelling evidence of illegal U.S. involvement in European and Russian affairs.
LIVE
CNC
BREAKING NEWS
RUSSIAN ARMY MASSES ON ESTONIAN BORDER
Fabrications. The U.S. has not been involved in any of these matters.
LIVE
CNC
BREAKING NEWS
RUSSIAN ARMY MASSES ON ESTONIAN BORDER
Simone @SimoneGregoire 7h
White House claims no involvement, yet Germany confirms DARPA tech involved with animal terrorist attacks #lies
Senator Owen McKitrick @Sen_Mckitrick 6h
Russian President Petrov is a reasonable man. I've offered to assist the President in talking directly with him. No response.
Greta Kohler @Greta_K0279 7h
No more Euro lives lost for US wars! #endnatonow
The communications blackout in Estonia has caused fear worldwide. There are unverified reports of conflict.
As European NATO forces are being mobilized, one question seems to be on the tip of everyone's tongue, "Should European soldiers be used for what many see as a clear provocation by the U.S. against Russia?"
LIVE
BCC WORLD NEWS
The administration has denied use of U.S. technology in the killing of European politicians, although Germany now seems to claim otherwise.
EARLIER
CNC
It's a bad day for the American people when our own allies don't believe us.
EARLIER
CNC
Senator Owen McKitrick @Sen_Mckitrick 1h
The President owes the American people an explanation. Are we at war? #WhereIsWilhelm?
Hello. everyone. I have been sequestering with the Joint Chiefs and strategists reviewing all our options.
LIVE
CNC
BREAKING NEWS
I won't say anything about any active campaigns that may place our troops in danger.
LIVE
BCC WORLD NEWS

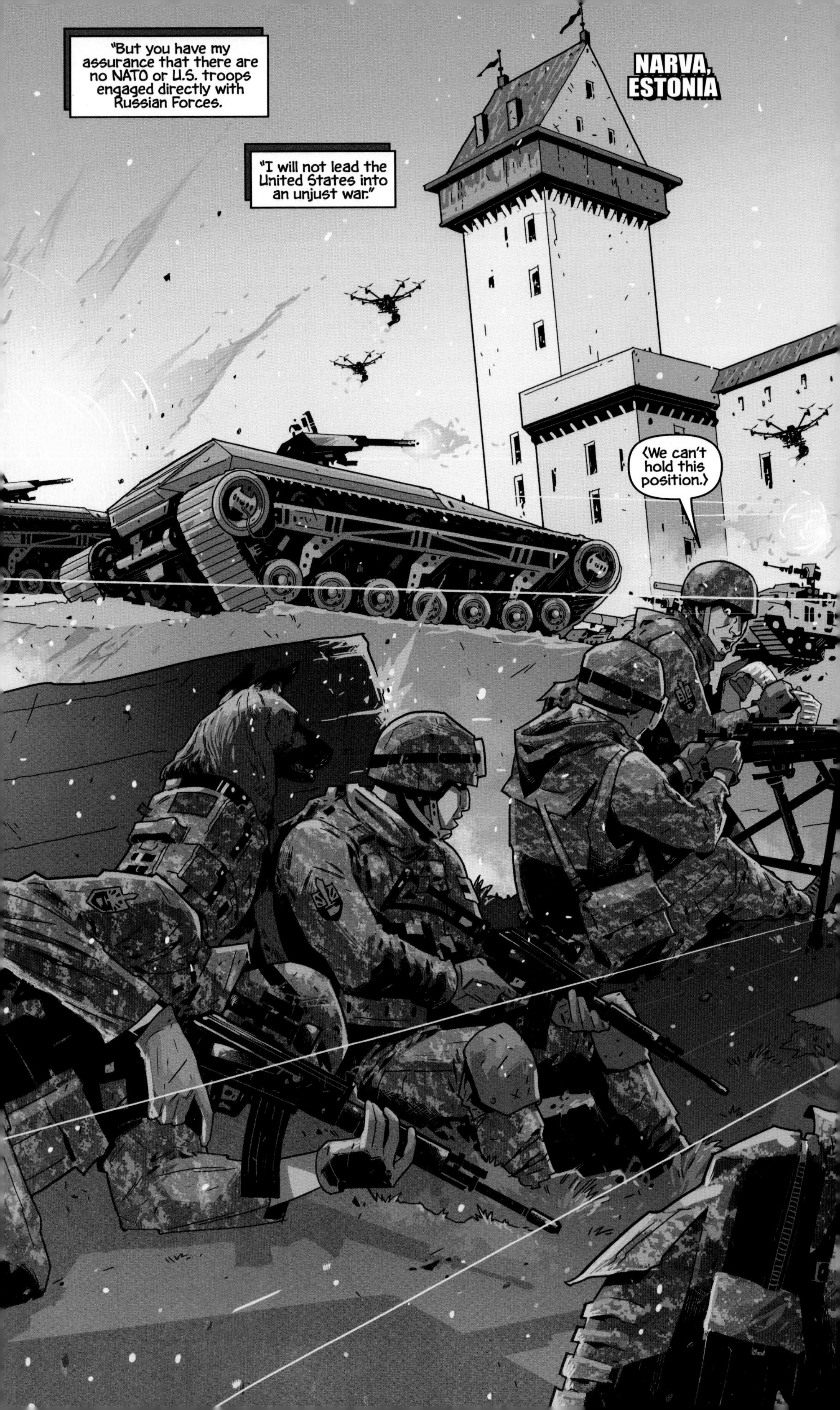

"But you have my assurance that there are no NATO or U.S. troops engaged directly with Russian Forces.
NARVA, ESTONIA
"I will not lead the United States into an unjust war."
⟨We can't hold this position.⟩

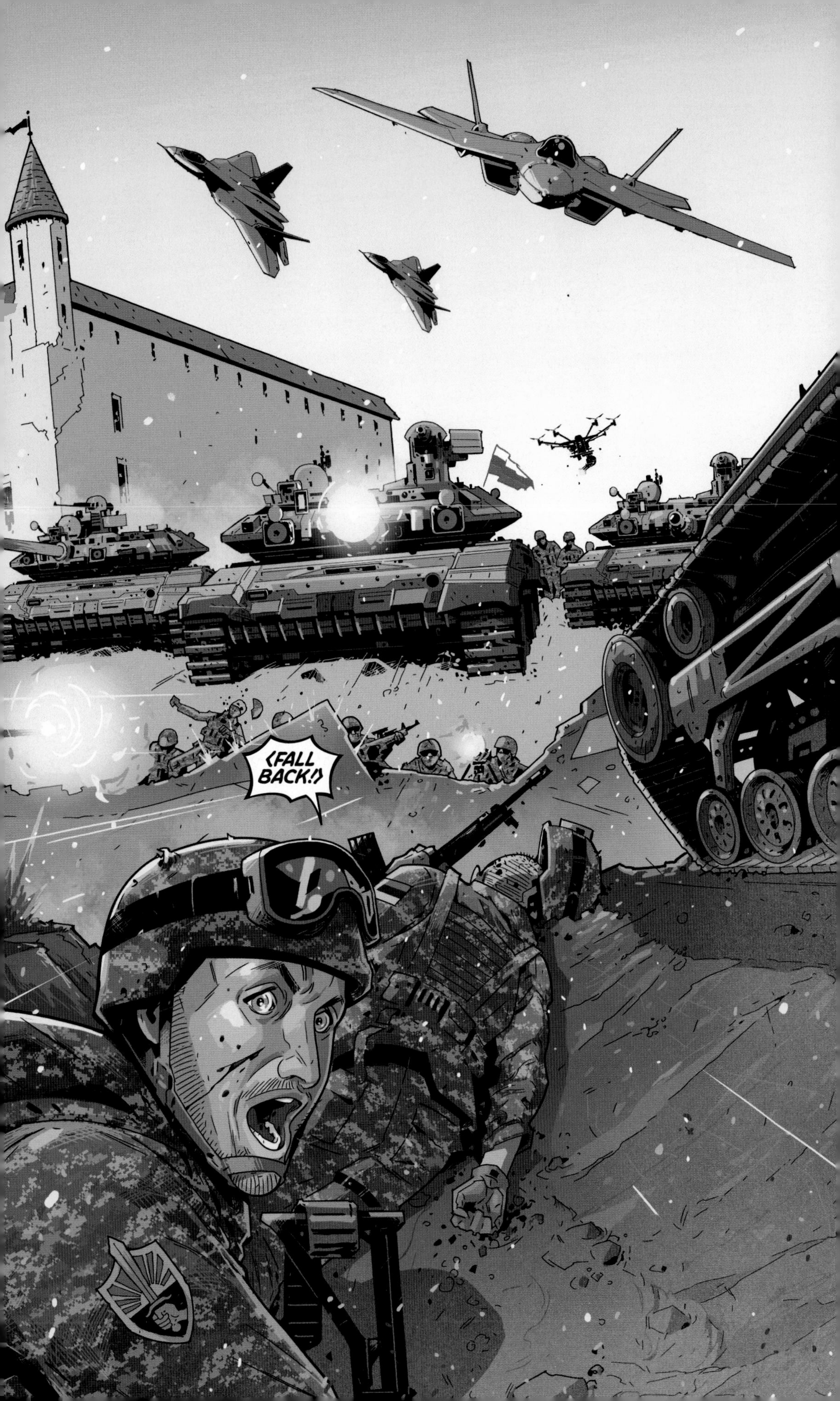
<FALL BACK!>

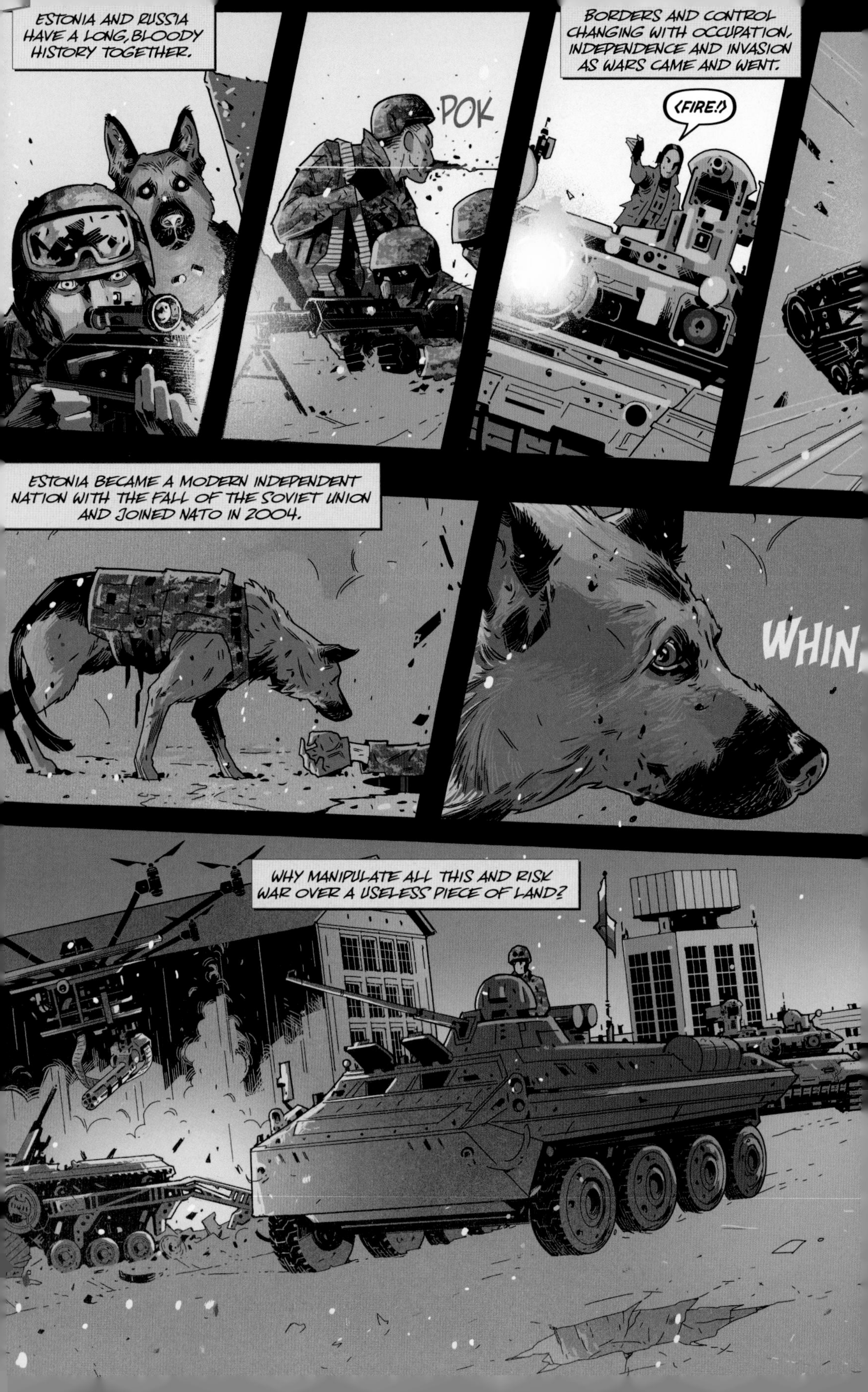
ESTONIA AND RUSSIA HAVE A LONG, BLOODY HISTORY TOGETHER.
POK
BORDERS AND CONTROL CHANGING WITH OCCUPATION, INDEPENDENCE AND INVASION AS WARS CAME AND WENT.
‹FIRE!›
ESTONIA BECAME A MODERN INDEPENDENT NATION WITH THE FALL OF THE SOVIET UNION AND JOINED NATO IN 2004.
WHIN
WHY MANIPULATE ALL THIS AND RISK WAR OVER A USELESS PIECE OF LAND?

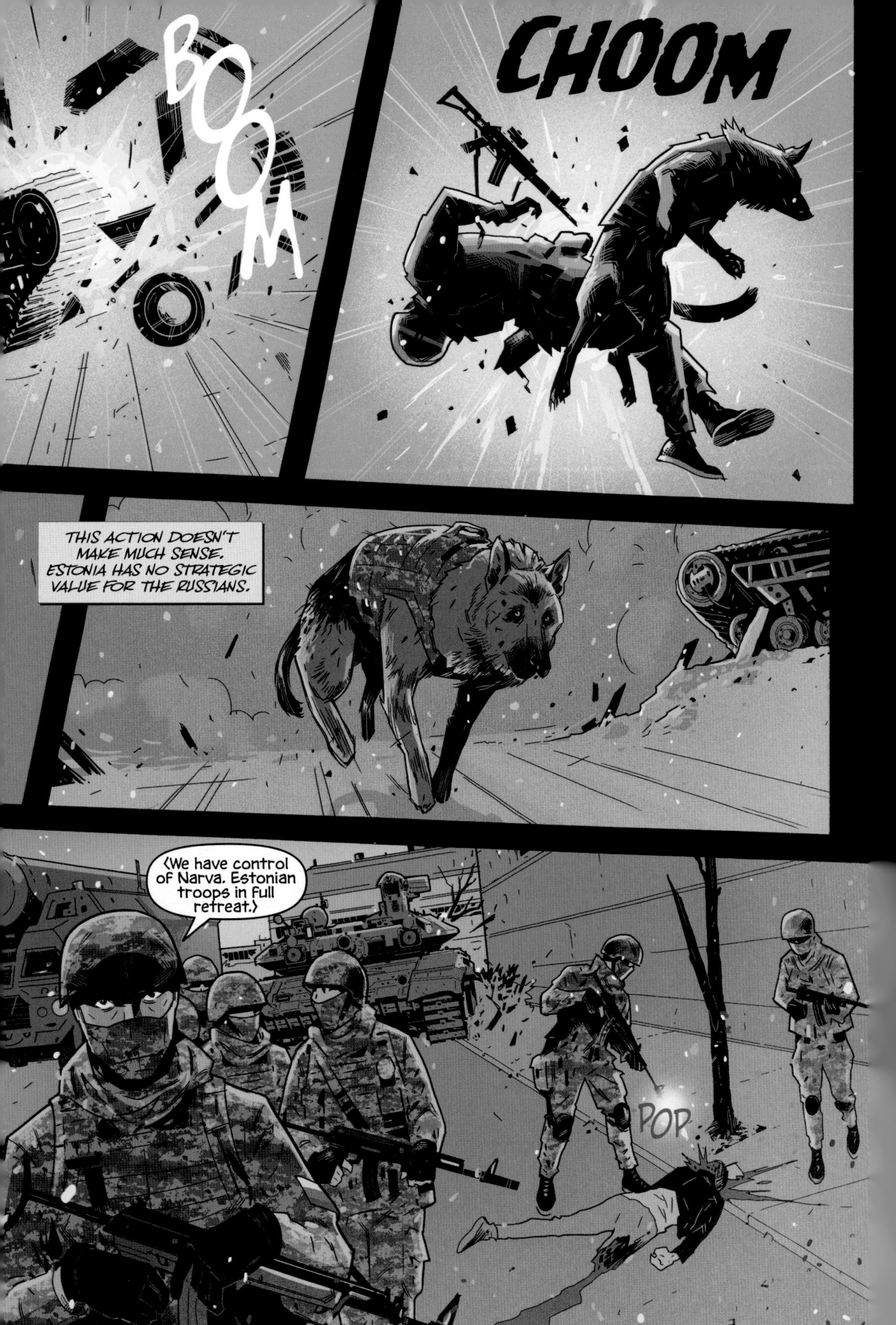
BOOM
CHOOM
THIS ACTION DOESN'T MAKE MUCH SENSE. ESTONIA HAS NO STRATEGIC VALUE FOR THE RUSSIANS.
⟨We have control of Narva. Estonian troops in full retreat.⟩
POP

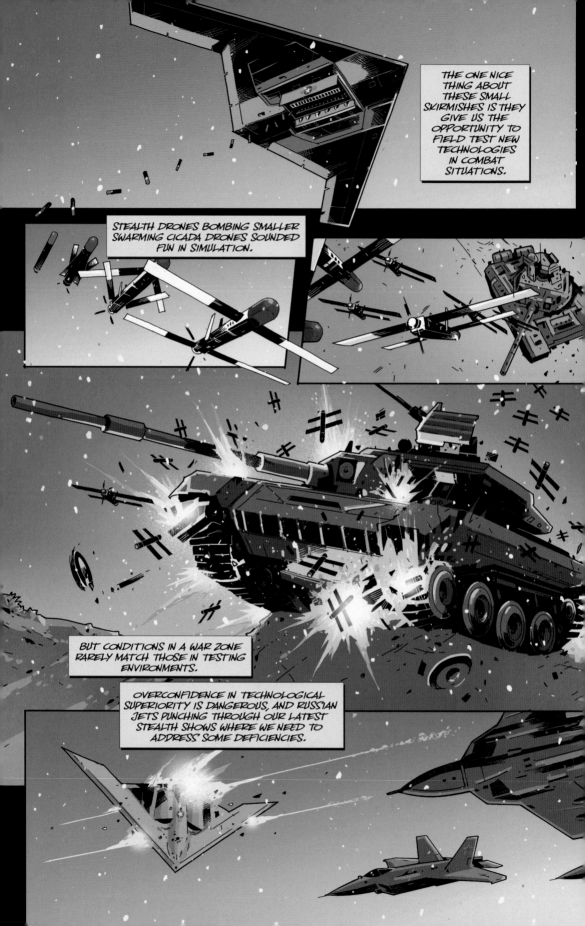

THE ONE NICE THING ABOUT THESE SMALL SKIRMISHES IS THEY GIVE US THE OPPORTUNITY TO FIELD TEST NEW TECHNOLOGIES IN COMBAT SITUATIONS.

STEALTH DRONES BOMBING SMALLER SWARMING CICADA DRONES SOUNDED FUN IN SIMULATION.

BUT CONDITIONS IN A WAR ZONE RARELY MATCH THOSE IN TESTING ENVIRONMENTS.

OVERCONFIDENCE IN TECHNOLOGICAL SUPERIORITY IS DANGEROUS, AND RUSSIAN JETS PUNCHING THROUGH OUR LATEST STEALTH SHOWS WHERE WE NEED TO ADDRESS SOME DEFICIENCIES.

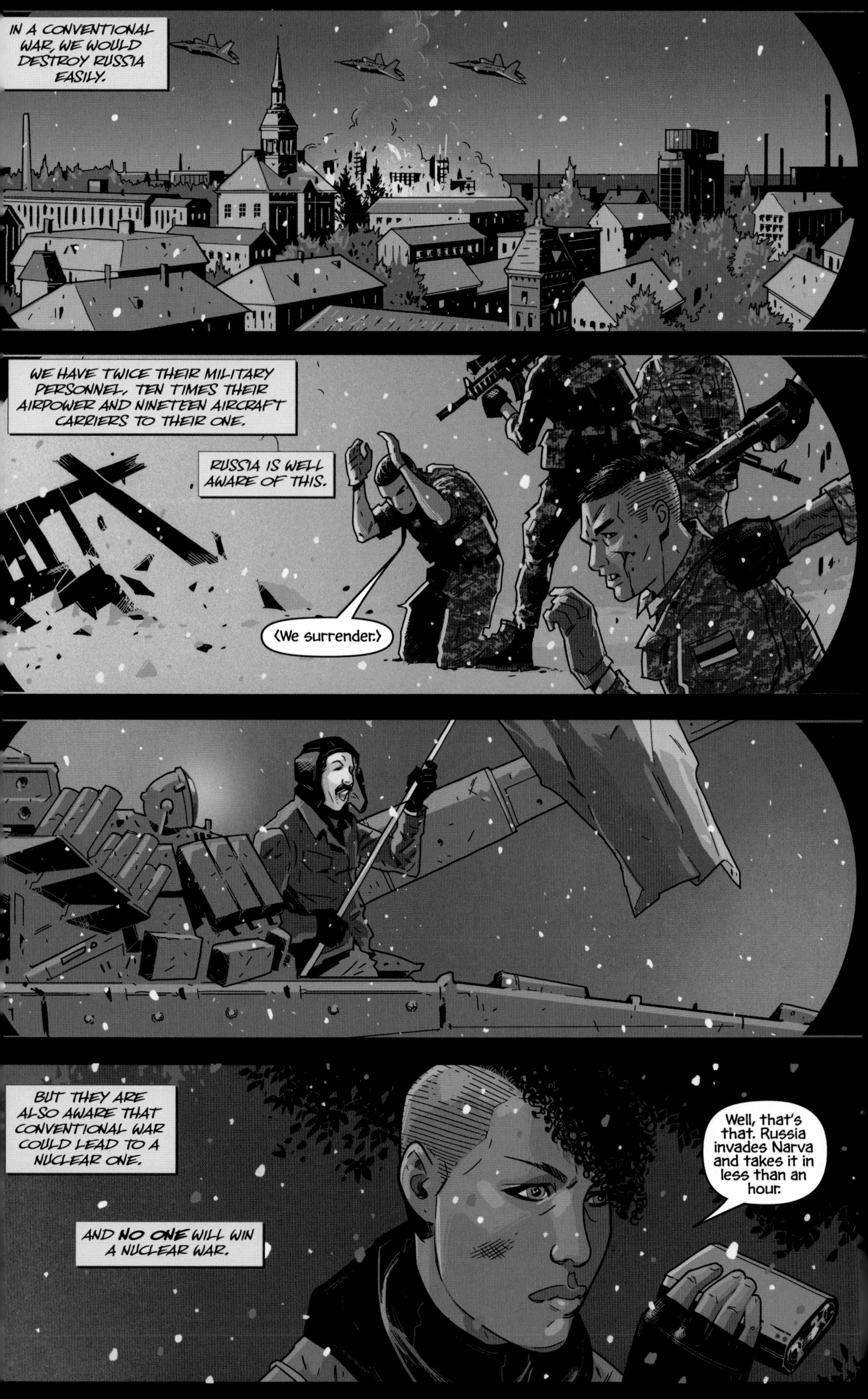
IN A CONVENTIONAL WAR, WE WOULD DESTROY RUSSIA EASILY.
WE HAVE TWICE THEIR MILITARY PERSONNEL, TEN TIMES THEIR AIRPOWER AND NINETEEN AIRCRAFT CARRIERS TO THEIR ONE.
RUSSIA IS WELL AWARE OF THIS.
‹We surrender.›
BUT THEY ARE ALSO AWARE THAT CONVENTIONAL WAR COULD LEAD TO A NUCLEAR ONE.
AND NO ONE WILL WIN A NUCLEAR WAR.
Well, that's that. Russia invades Narva and takes it in less than an hour.

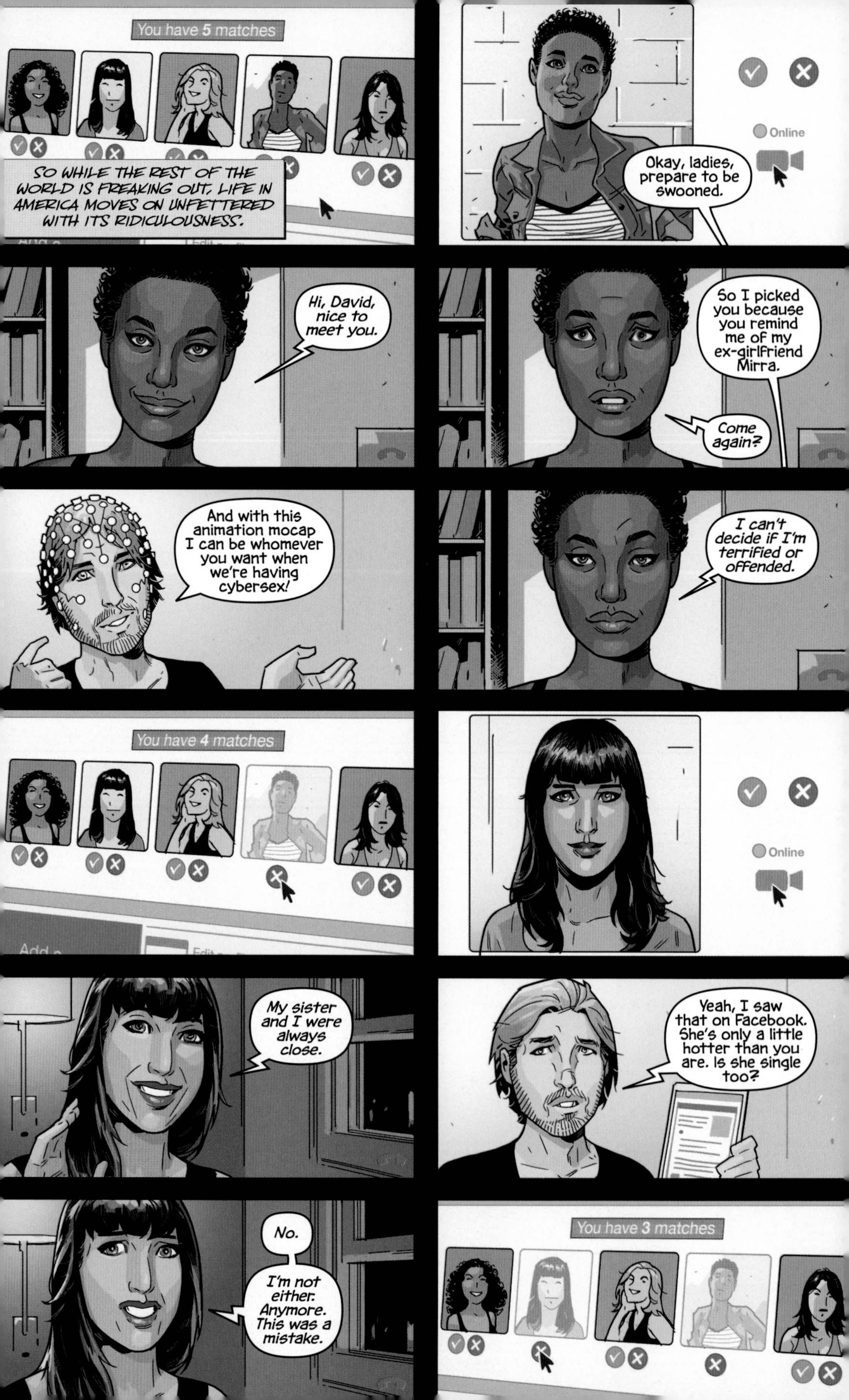
You have 5 matches
SO WHILE THE REST OF THE WORLD IS FREAKING OUT, LIFE IN AMERICA MOVES ON UNFETTERED WITH ITS RIDICULOUSNESS.
Online
Okay, ladies, prepare to be swooned.
Hi, David, nice to meet you.
So I picked you because you remind me of my ex-girlfriend Mirra.
Come again?
And with this animation mocap I can be whomever you want when we're having cybersex!
I can't decide if I'm terrified or offended.
You have 4 matches
Online
My sister and I were always close.
Yeah, I saw that on Facebook. She's only a little hotter than you are. Is she single too?
No.
I'm not either. Anymore. This was a mistake.
You have 3 matches

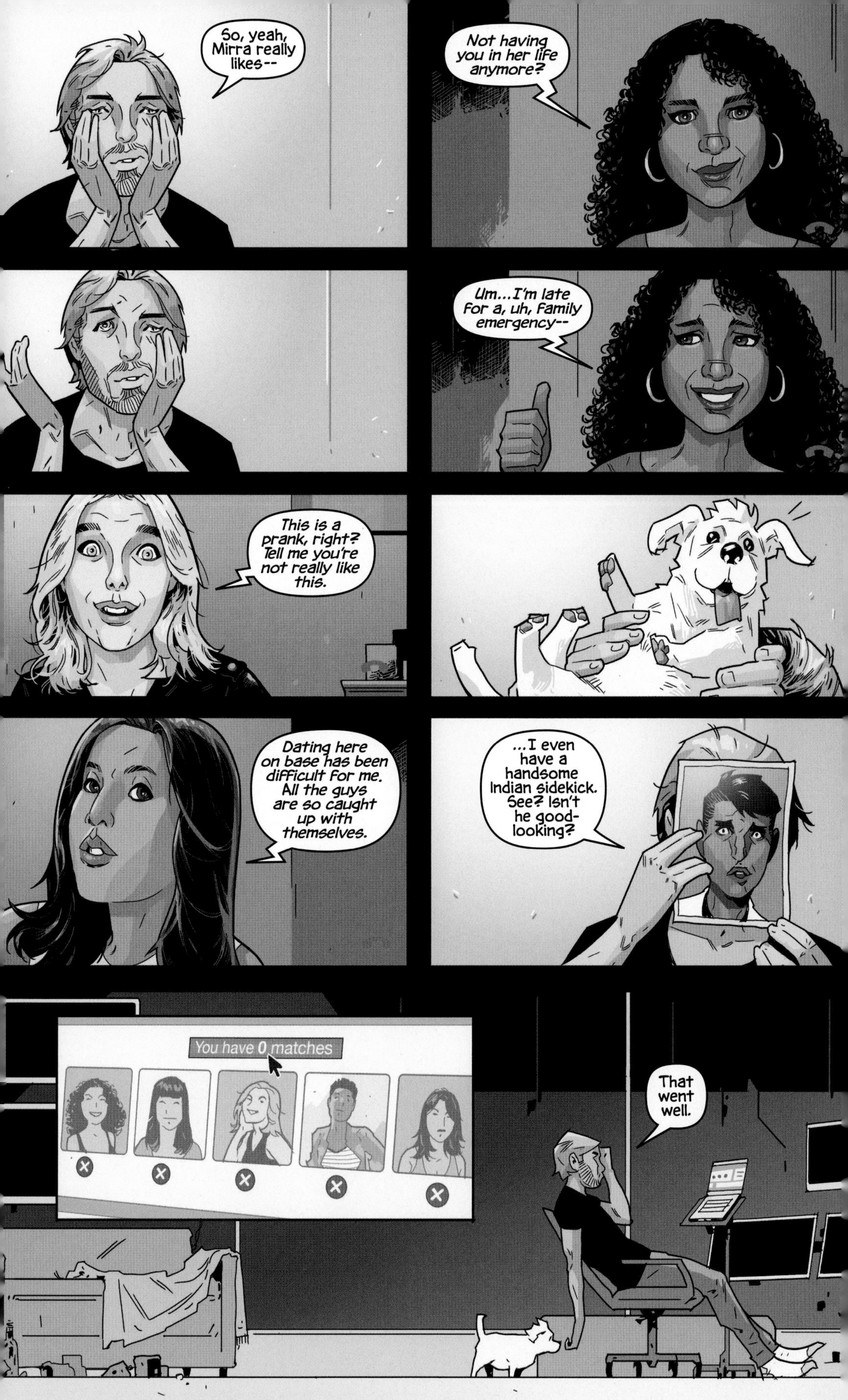
So, yeah, Mirra really likes--
Not having you in her life anymore?
Um...I'm late for a, uh, family emergency--
This is a prank, right? Tell me you're not really like this.
Dating here on base has been difficult for me. All the guys are so caught up with themselves.
...I even have a handsome Indian sidekick. See? Isn't he good-looking?
You have 0 matches
That went well.

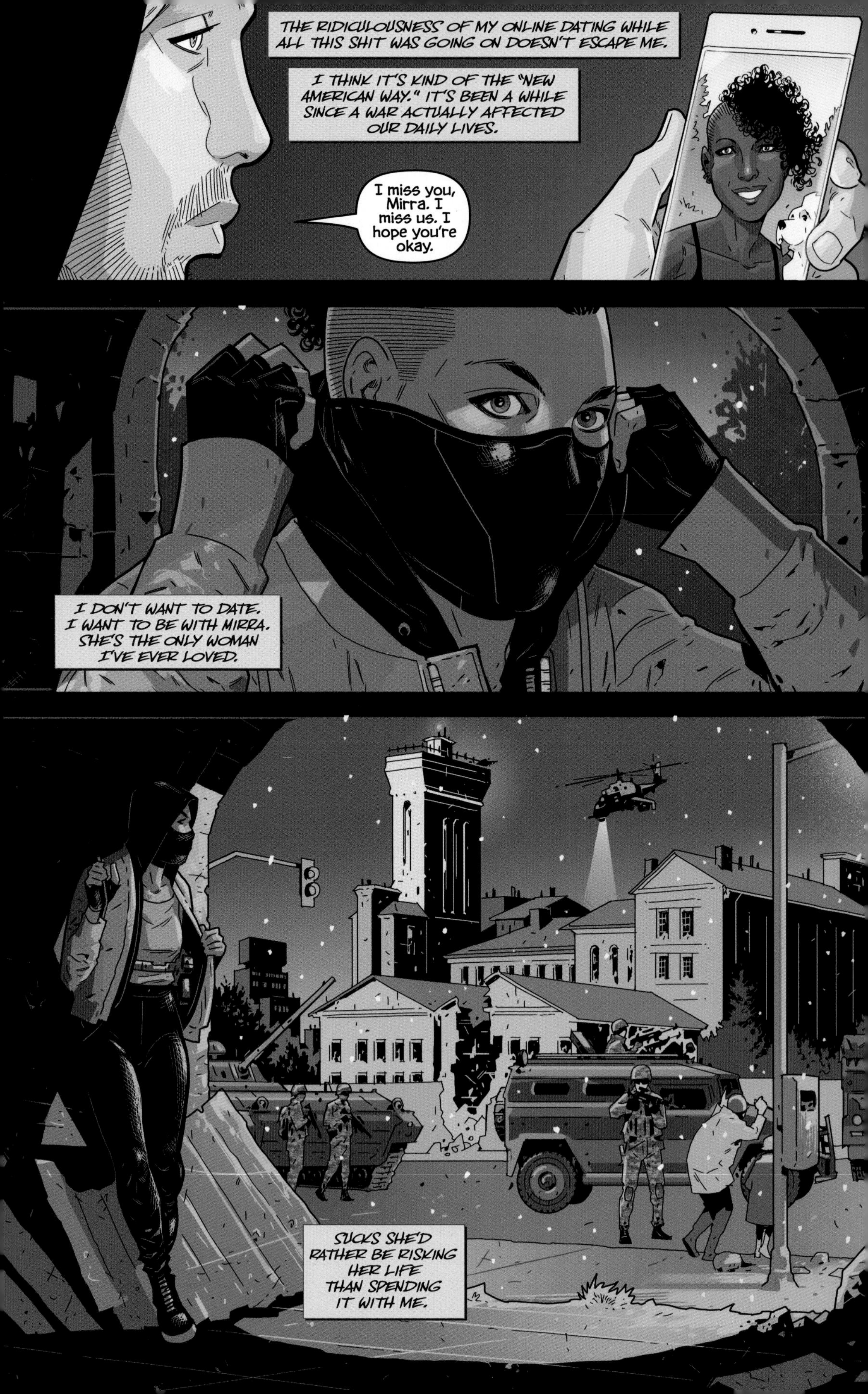
THE RIDICULOUSNESS OF MY ONLINE DATING WHILE ALL THIS SHIT WAS GOING ON DOESN'T ESCAPE ME.
I THINK IT'S KIND OF THE "NEW AMERICAN WAY." IT'S BEEN A WHILE SINCE A WAR ACTUALLY AFFECTED OUR DAILY LIVES.
I miss you, Mirra. I miss us. I hope you're okay.
I DON'T WANT TO DATE. I WANT TO BE WITH MIRRA. SHE'S THE ONLY WOMAN I'VE EVER LOVED.
SUCKS SHE'D RATHER BE RISKING HER LIFE THAN SPENDING IT WITH ME.

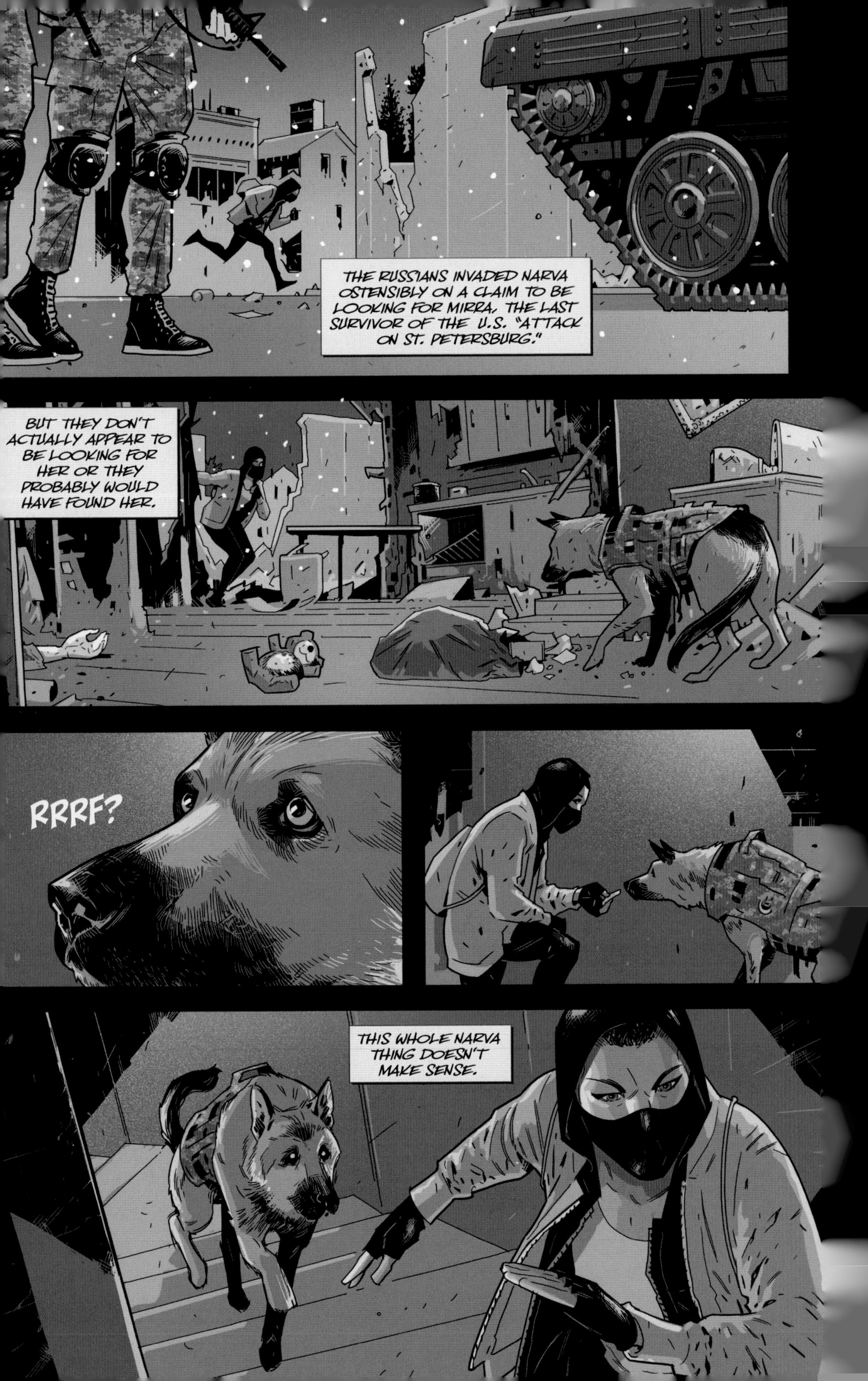
THE RUSSIANS INVADED NARVA OSTENSIBLY ON A CLAIM TO BE LOOKING FOR MIRRA, THE LAST SURVIVOR OF THE U.S. "ATTACK ON ST. PETERSBURG."
BUT THEY DON'T ACTUALLY APPEAR TO BE LOOKING FOR HER OR THEY PROBABLY WOULD HAVE FOUND HER.
RRRF?
THIS WHOLE NARVA THING DOESN'T MAKE SENSE.

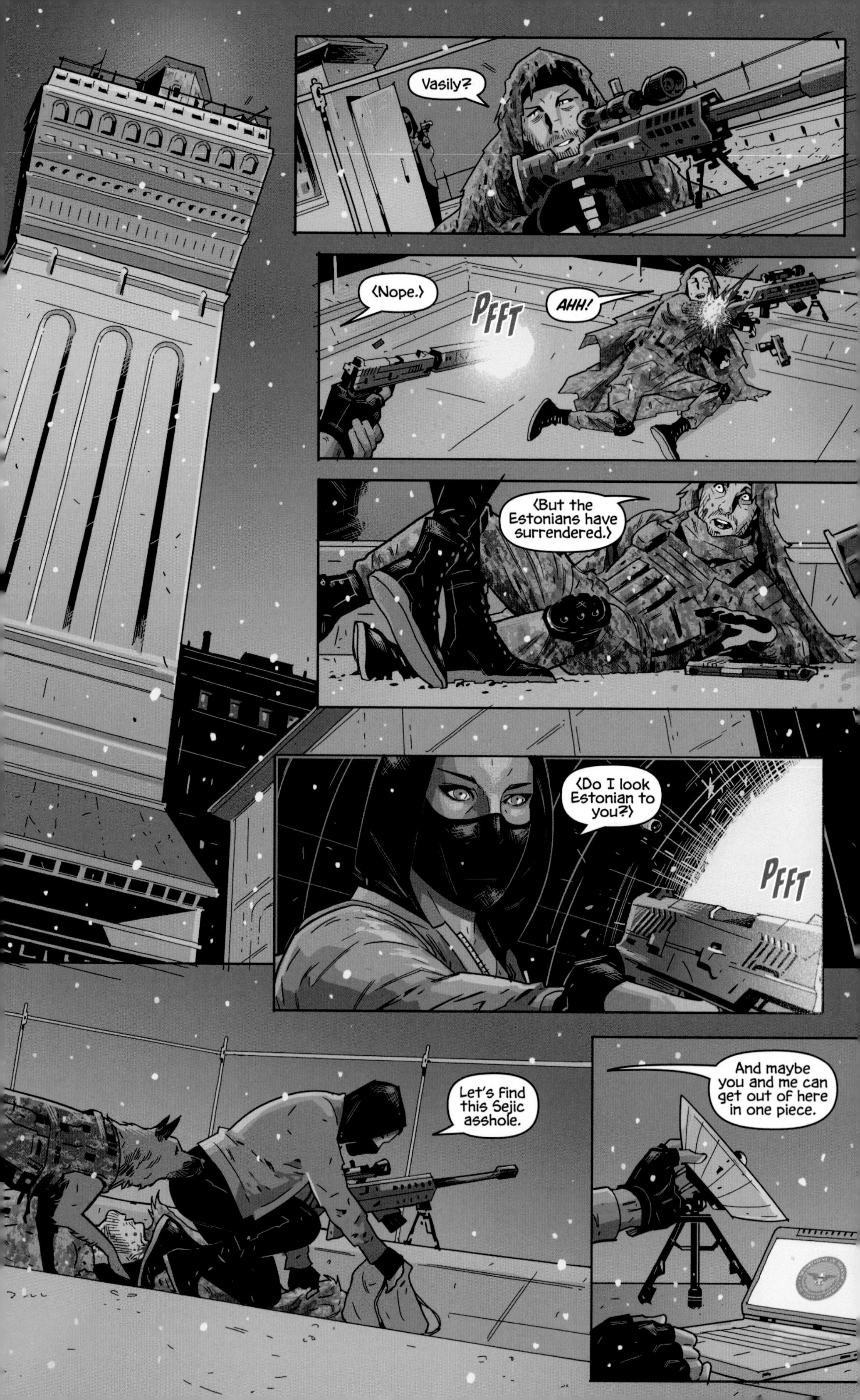
Vasily?
‹Nope.›
PFFT
AHH!
‹But the Estonians have surrendered.›
‹Do I look Estonian to you?›
PFFT
Let's find this Sejic asshole.
And maybe you and me can get out of here in one piece.

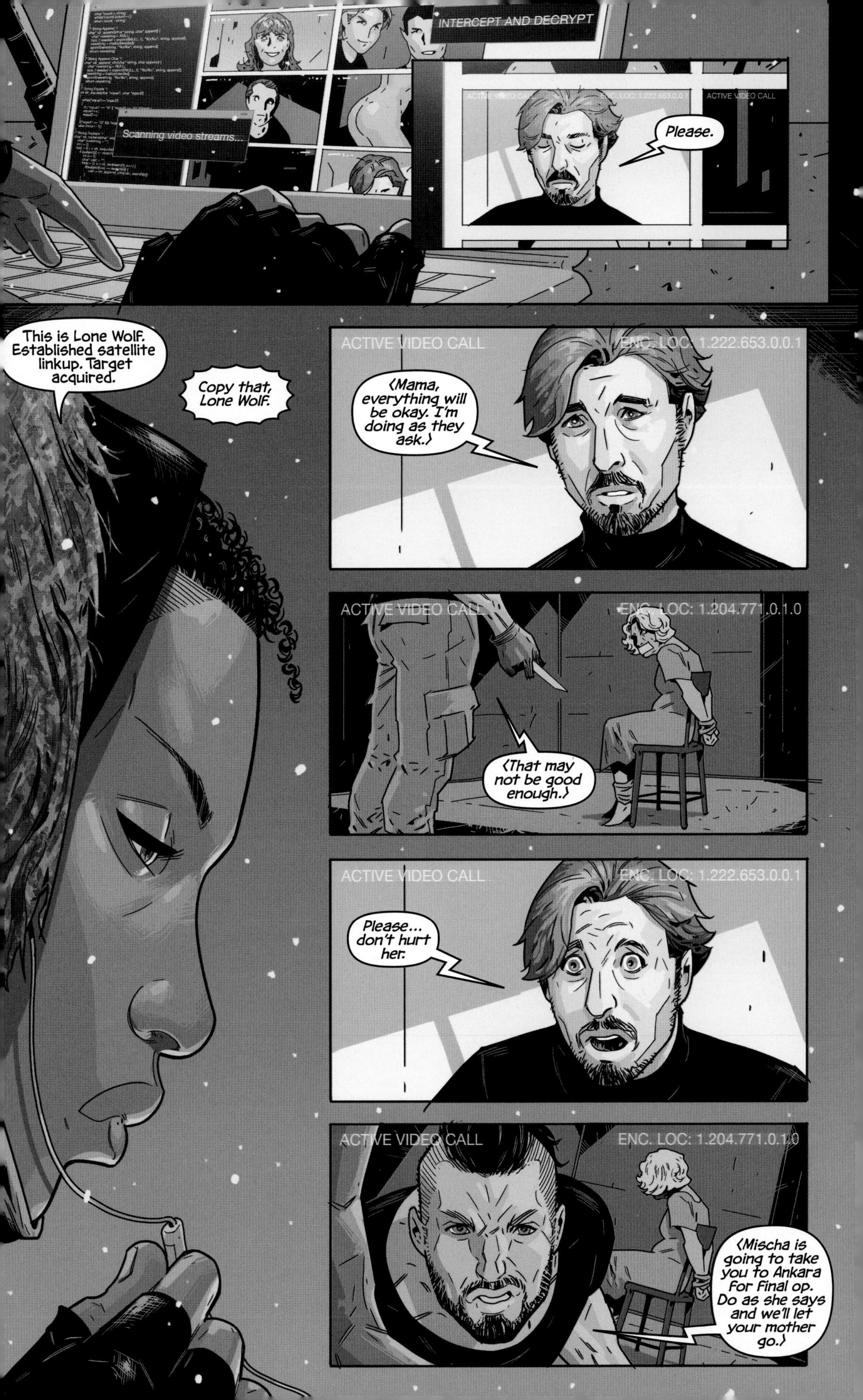
INTERCEPT AND DECRYPT
Scanning video streams...
ACTIVE VIDEO CALL
ACTIVE VIDEO CALL
Please.
This is Lone Wolf. Established satellite linkup. Target acquired.
Copy that, Lone Wolf.
ACTIVE VIDEO CALL
ENC. LOC: 1.222.653.0.0.1
⟨Mama, everything will be okay. I'm doing as they ask.⟩
ACTIVE VIDEO CALL
ENC. LOC: 1.204.771.0.1.0
⟨That may not be good enough.⟩
ACTIVE VIDEO CALL
ENC. LOC: 1.222.653.0.0.1
Please... don't hurt her.
ACTIVE VIDEO CALL
ENC. LOC: 1.204.771.0.1.0
⟨Mischa is going to take you to Ankara for final op. Do as she says and we'll let your mother go.⟩

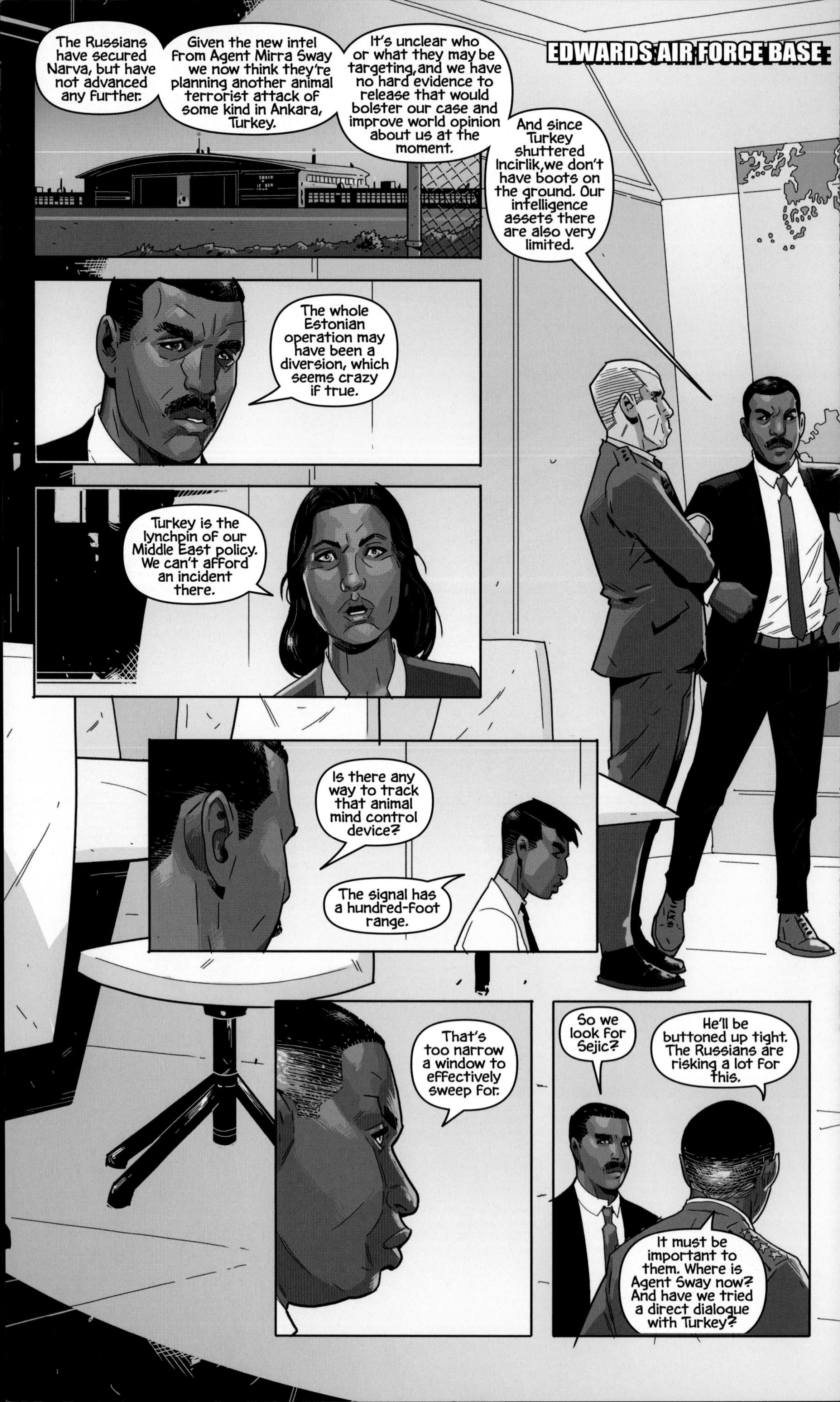
EDWARDS AIR FORCE BASE
The Russians have secured Narva, but have not advanced any further.
Given the new intel from Agent Mirra Sway we now think they're planning another animal terrorist attack of some kind in Ankara, Turkey.
It's unclear who or what they may be targeting, and we have no hard evidence to release that would bolster our case and improve world opinion about us at the moment.
And since Turkey shuttered Incirlik, we don't have boots on the ground. Our intelligence assets there are also very limited.
The whole Estonian operation may have been a diversion, which seems crazy if true.
Turkey is the lynchpin of our Middle East policy. We can't afford an incident there.
Is there any way to track that animal mind control device?
The signal has a hundred-foot range.
That's too narrow a window to effectively sweep for.
So we look for Sejic?
He'll be buttoned up tight. The Russians are risking a lot for this.
It must be important to them. Where is Agent Sway now? And have we tried a direct dialogue with Turkey?

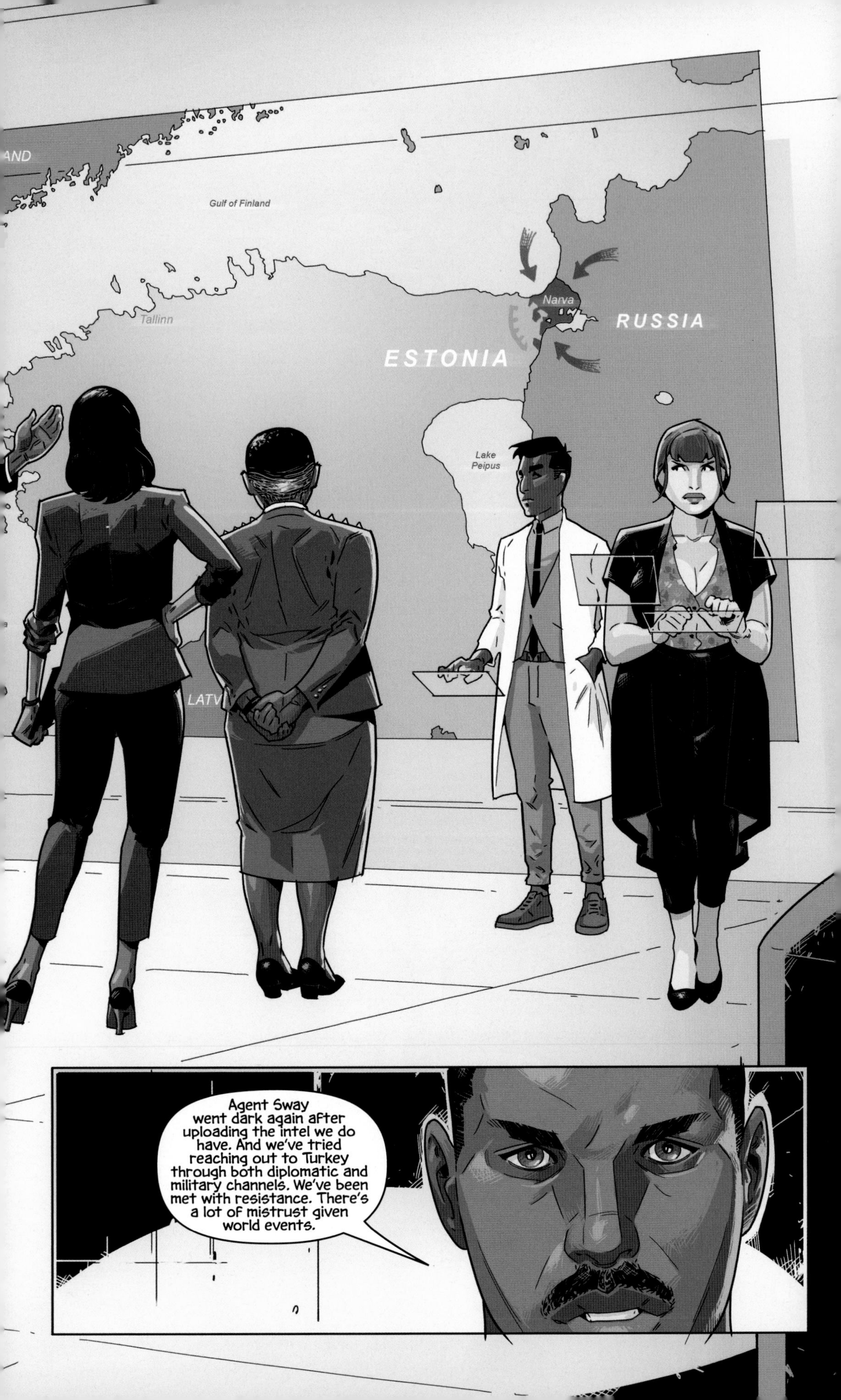
AND
Gulf of Finland
Narva
Tallinn
RUSSIA
ESTONIA
Lake Peipus
LATV
Agent Sway went dark again after uploading the intel we do have. And we've tried reaching out to Turkey through both diplomatic and military channels. We've been met with resistance. There's a lot of mistrust given world events.

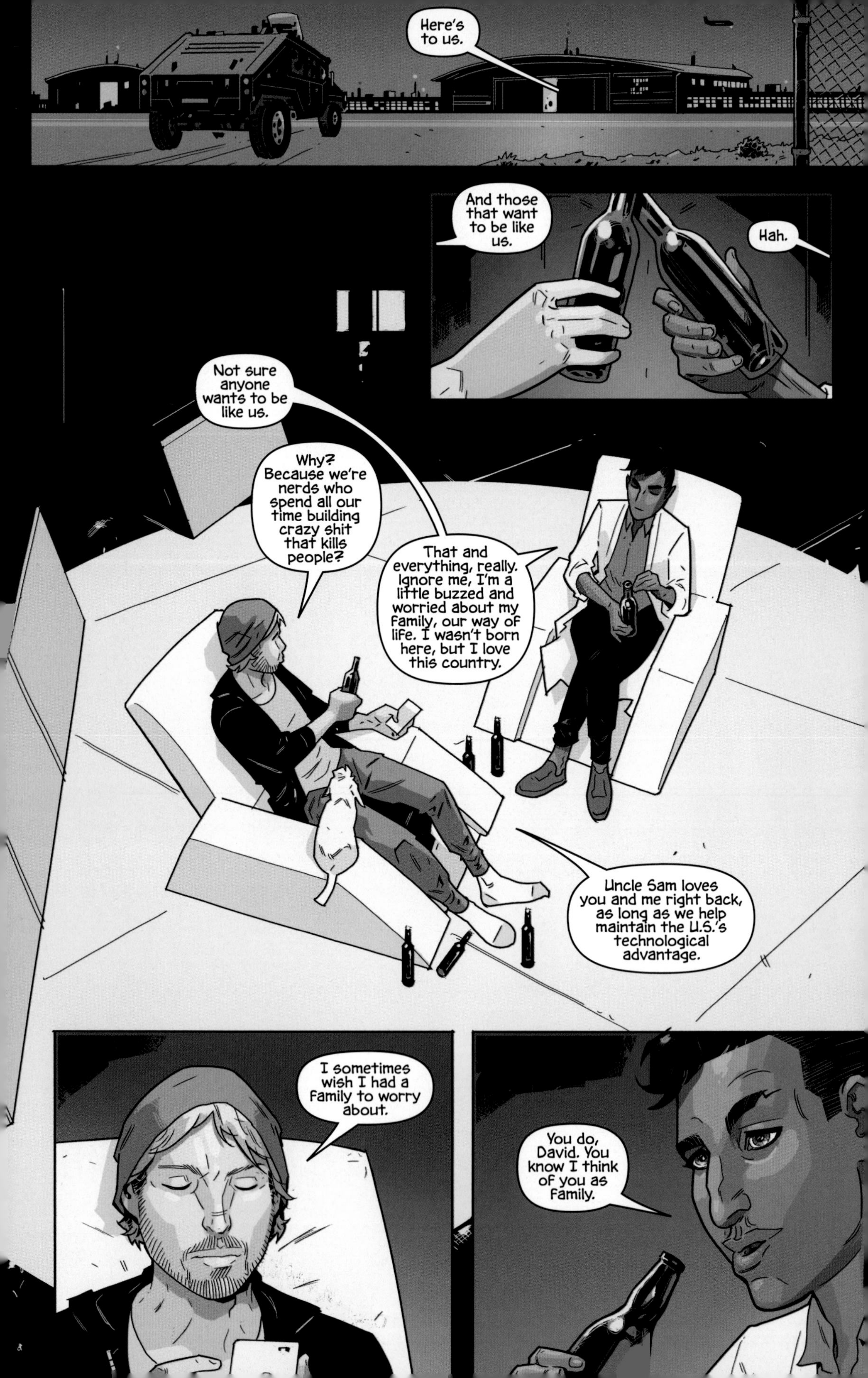
Here's to us.
And those that want to be like us.
Hah.
Not sure anyone wants to be like us.
Why? Because we're nerds who spend all our time building crazy shit that kills people?
That and everything, really. Ignore me, I'm a little buzzed and worried about my family, our way of life. I wasn't born here, but I love this country.
Uncle Sam loves you and me right back, as long as we help maintain the U.S.'s technological advantage.
I sometimes wish I had a family to worry about.
You do, David. You know I think of you as family.

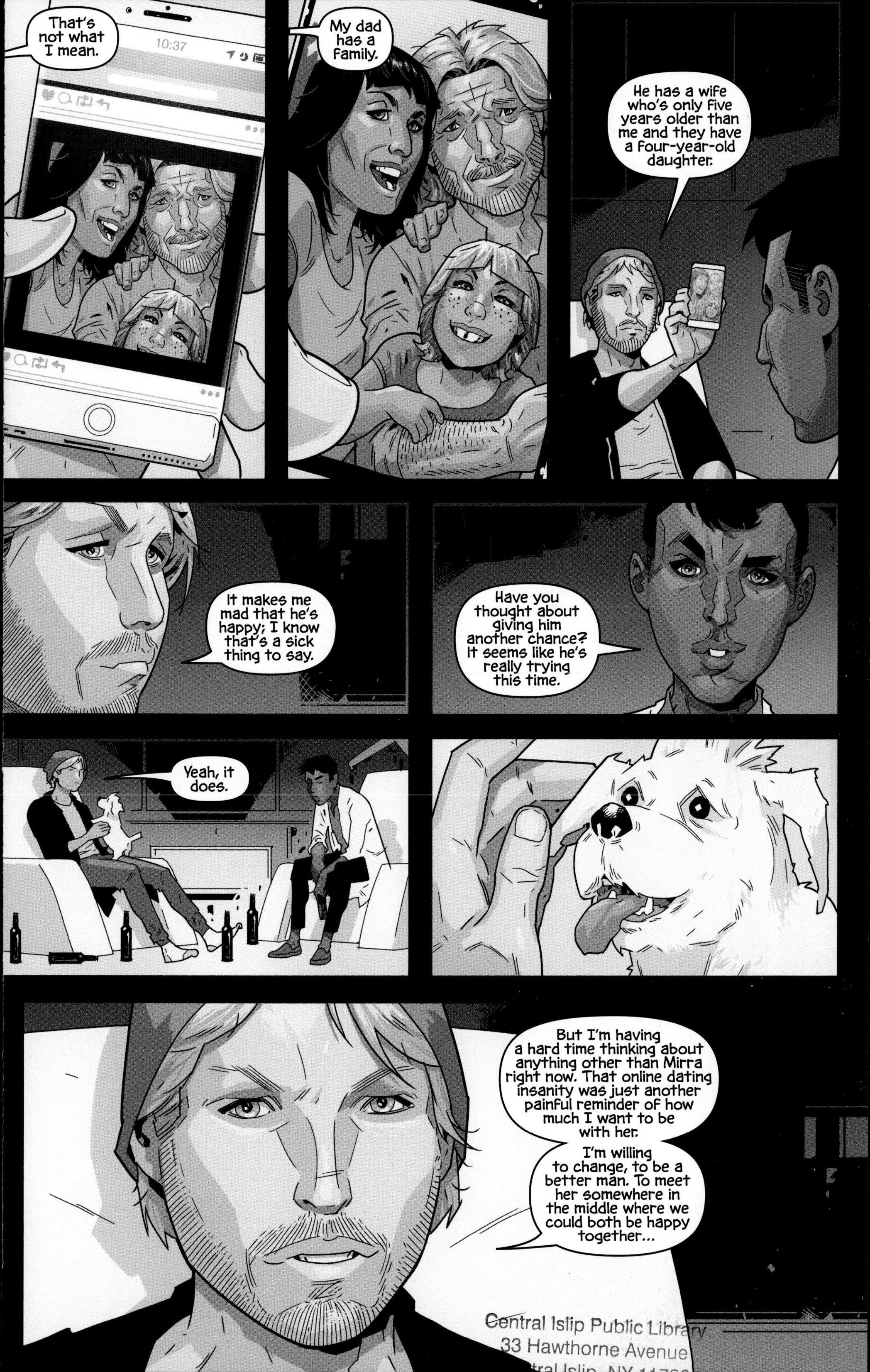
That's not what I mean.
10:37
My dad has a family.
He has a wife who's only five years older than me and they have a four-year-old daughter.
It makes me mad that he's happy; I know that's a sick thing to say.
Have you thought about giving him another chance? It seems like he's really trying this time.
Yeah, it does.
But I'm having a hard time thinking about anything other than Mirra right now. That online dating insanity was just another painful reminder of how much I want to be with her.
I'm willing to change, to be a better man. To meet her somewhere in the middle where we could both be happy together...

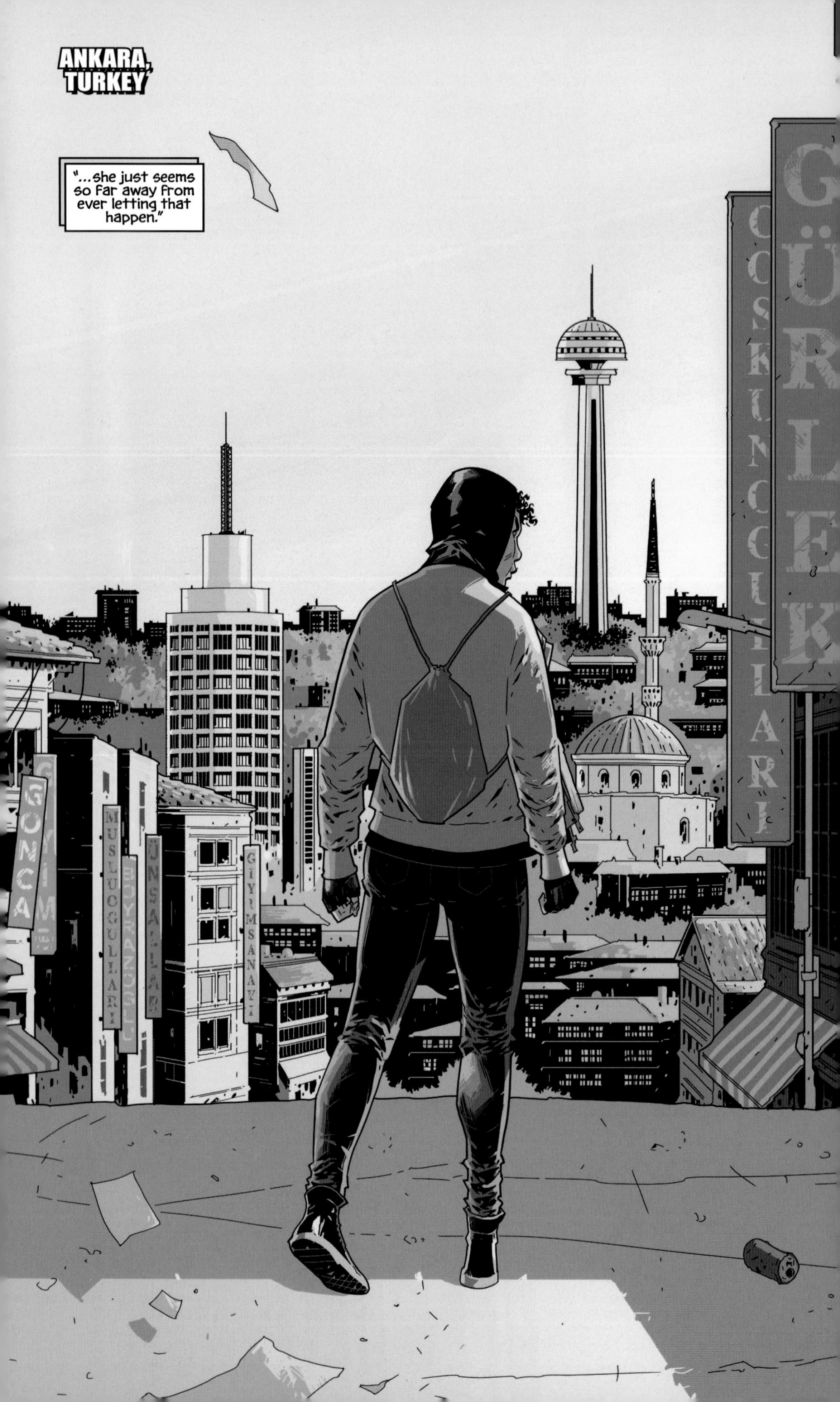
ANKARA, TURKEY
"...she just seems so far away from ever letting that happen."
GÜRLEK
GONCA
GIYIMSANAYI

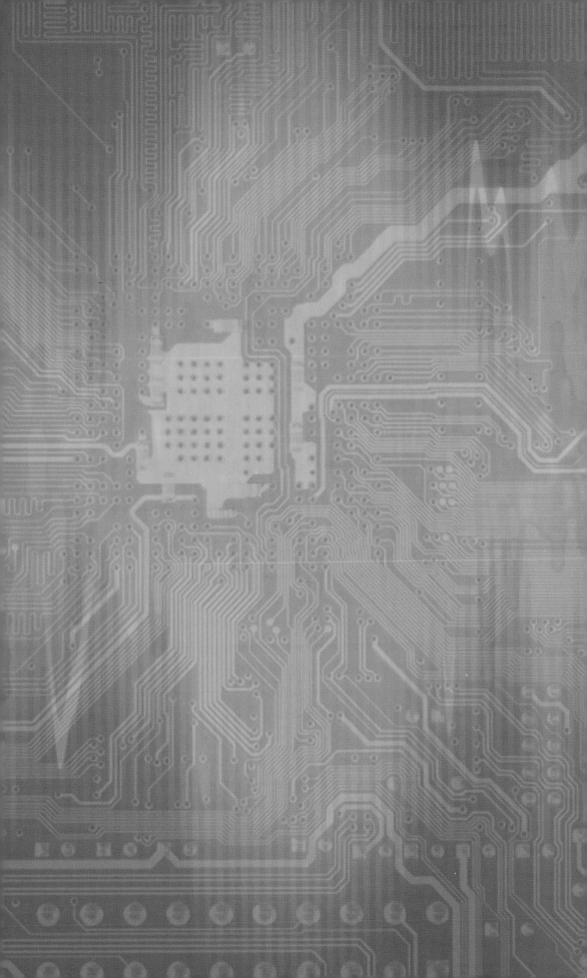

CHAPTER FOUR

THINK TANK

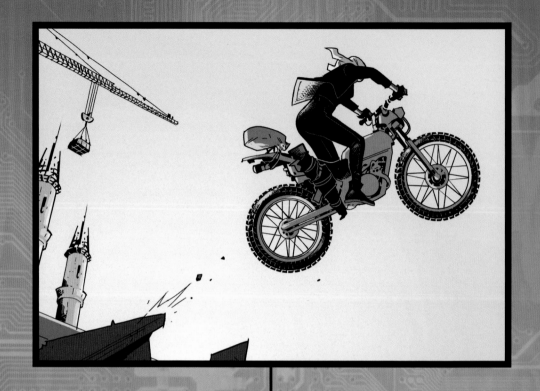

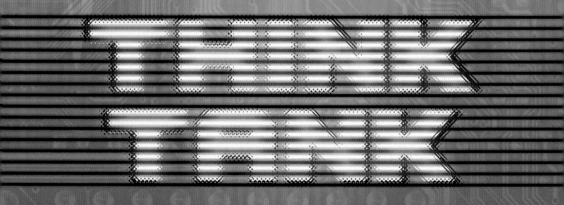

*" All good things
must come to an end."*

– Chaucer

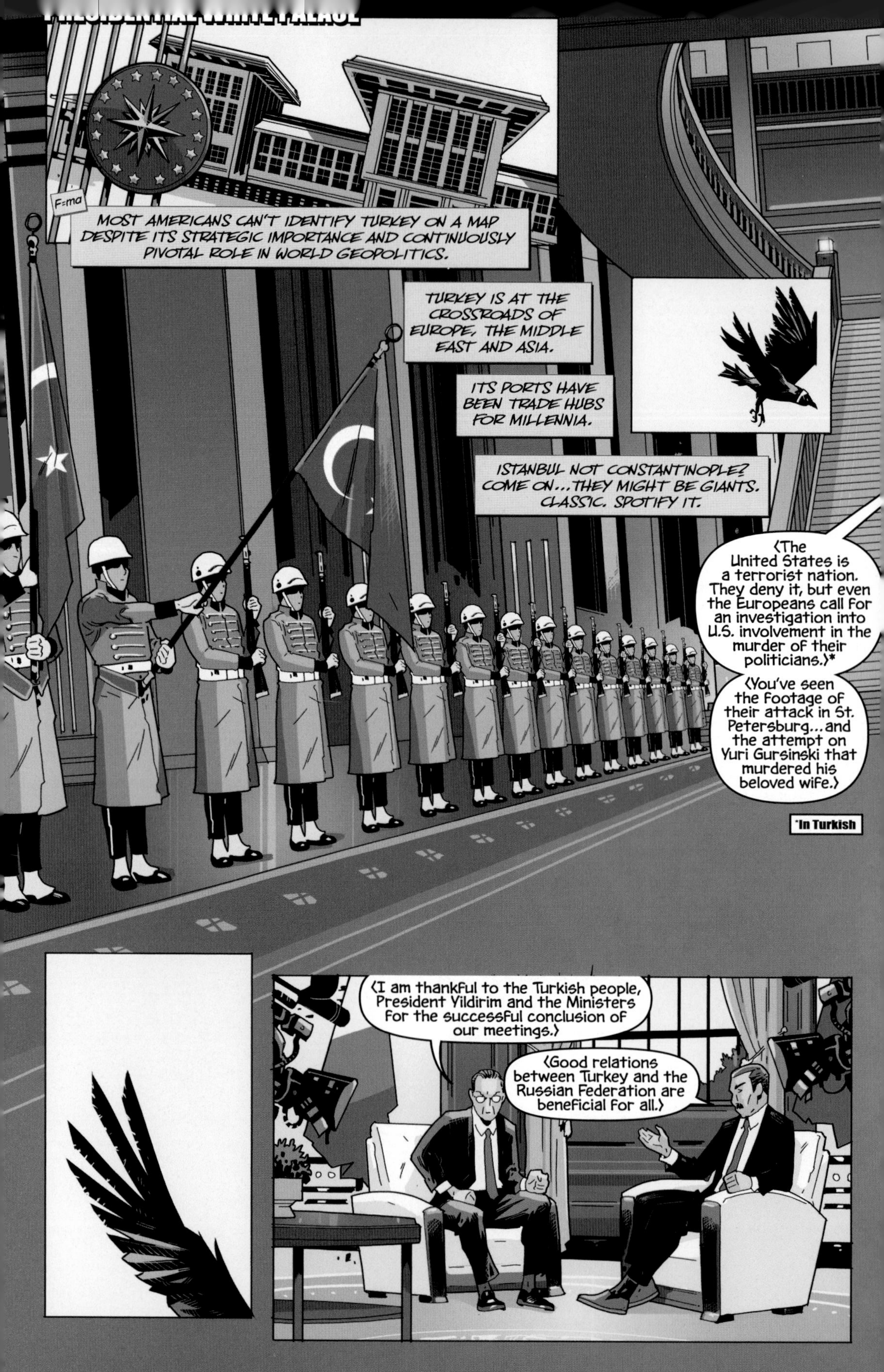
F=ma
MOST AMERICANS CAN'T IDENTIFY TURKEY ON A MAP DESPITE ITS STRATEGIC IMPORTANCE AND CONTINUOUSLY PIVOTAL ROLE IN WORLD GEOPOLITICS.
TURKEY IS AT THE CROSSROADS OF EUROPE, THE MIDDLE EAST AND ASIA.
ITS PORTS HAVE BEEN TRADE HUBS FOR MILLENNIA.
ISTANBUL NOT CONSTANTINOPLE? COME ON...THEY MIGHT BE GIANTS. CLASSIC. SPOTIFY IT.
‹The United States is a terrorist nation. They deny it, but even the Europeans call for an investigation into U.S. involvement in the murder of their politicians.›*
‹You've seen the footage of their attack in St. Petersburg...and the attempt on Yuri Gursinski that murdered his beloved wife.›
*In Turkish
‹I am thankful to the Turkish people, President Yildirim and the Ministers for the successful conclusion of our meetings.›
‹Good relations between Turkey and the Russian Federation are beneficial for all.›

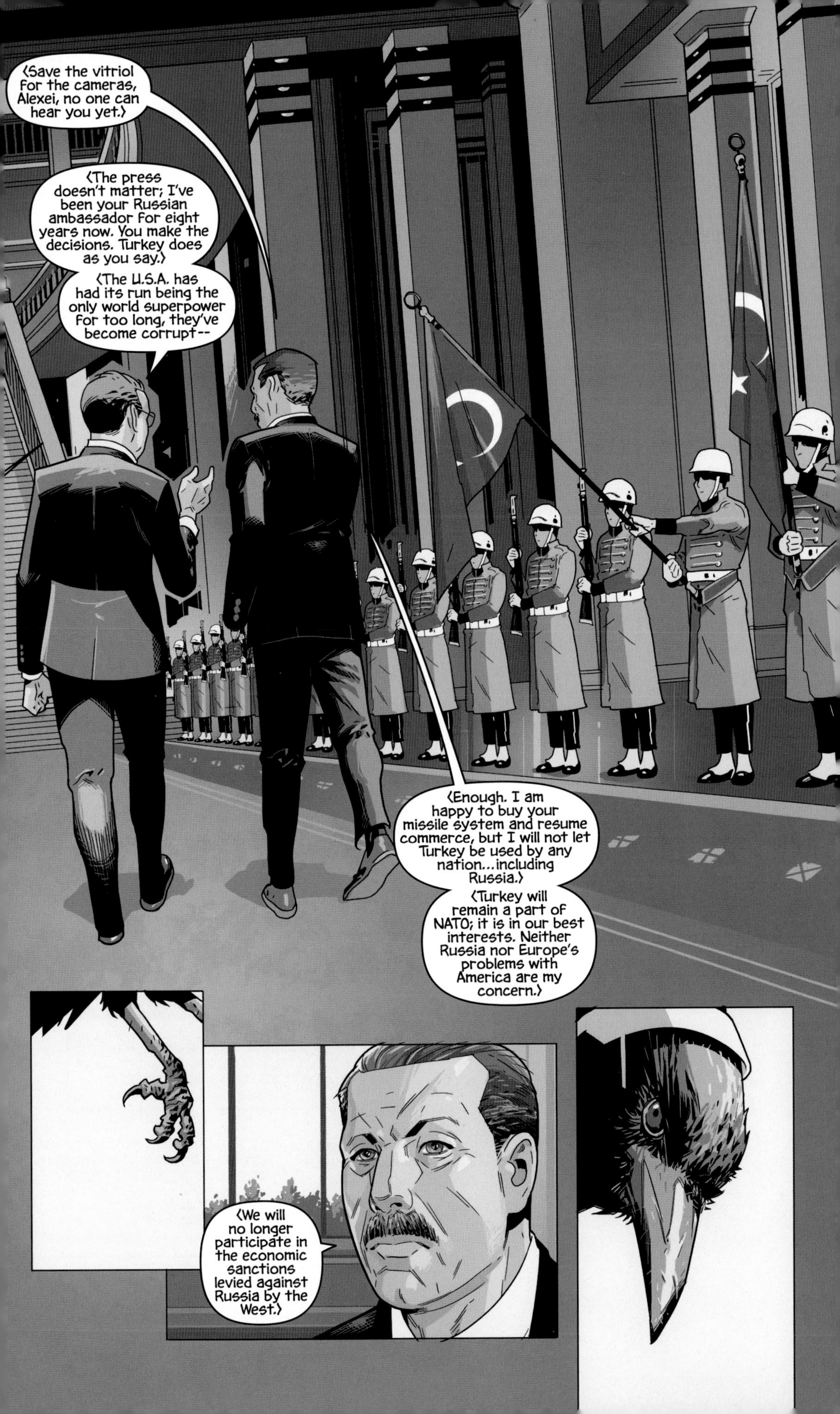
〈Save the vitriol for the cameras, Alexei, no one can hear you yet.〉
〈The press doesn't matter; I've been your Russian ambassador for eight years now. You make the decisions. Turkey does as you say.〉
〈The U.S.A. has had its run being the only world superpower for too long, they've become corrupt--
〈Enough. I am happy to buy your missile system and resume commerce, but I will not let Turkey be used by any nation...including Russia.〉
〈Turkey will remain a part of NATO; it is in our best interests. Neither Russia nor Europe's problems with America are my concern.〉
〈We will no longer participate in the economic sanctions levied against Russia by the West.〉

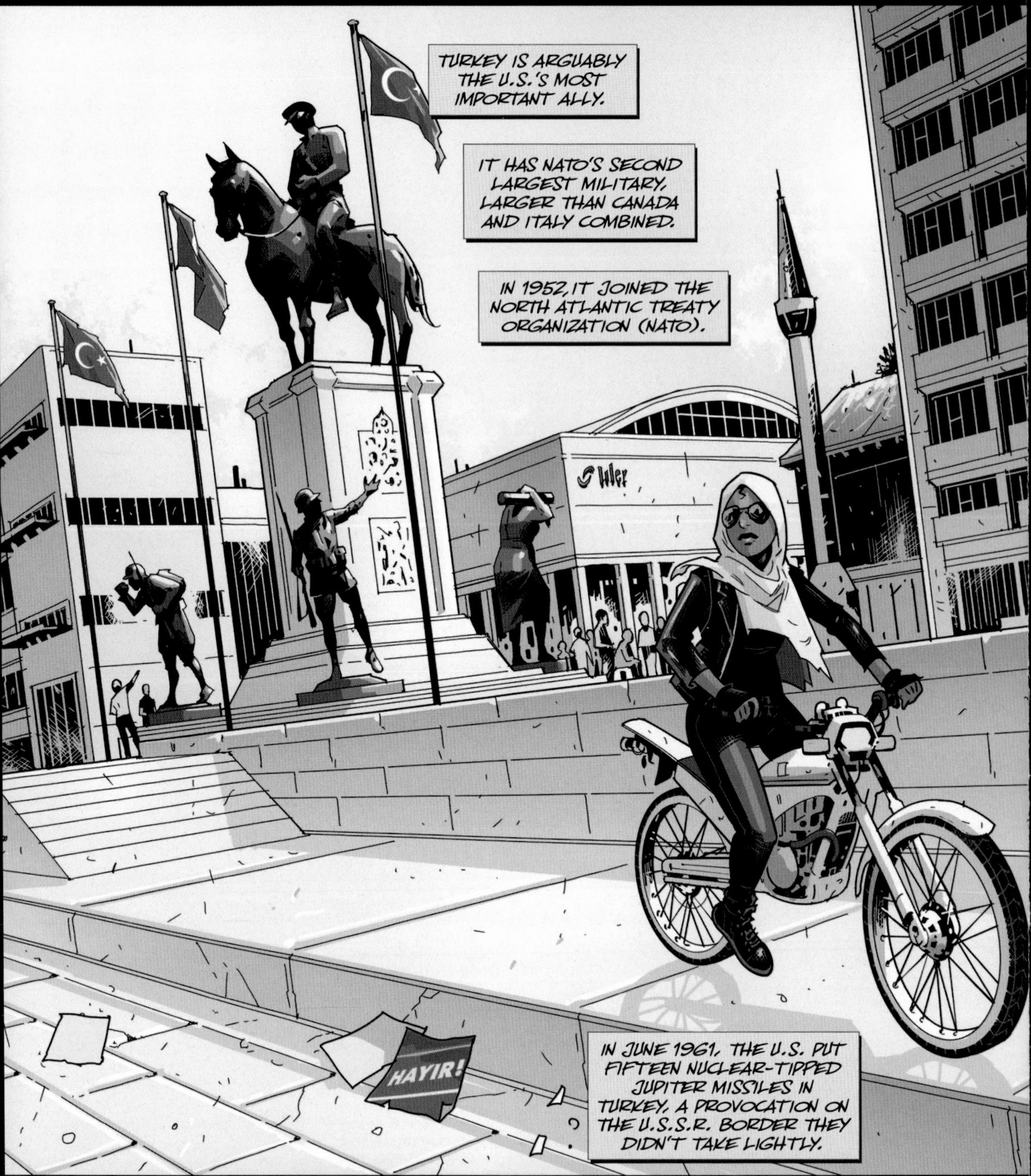
TURKEY IS ARGUABLY THE U.S.'S MOST IMPORTANT ALLY.
IT HAS NATO'S SECOND LARGEST MILITARY, LARGER THAN CANADA AND ITALY COMBINED.
IN 1952, IT JOINED THE NORTH ATLANTIC TREATY ORGANIZATION (NATO).
HAYIR!
IN JUNE 1961, THE U.S. PUT FIFTEEN NUCLEAR-TIPPED JUPITER MISSILES IN TURKEY, A PROVOCATION ON THE U.S.S.R. BORDER THEY DIDN'T TAKE LIGHTLY.

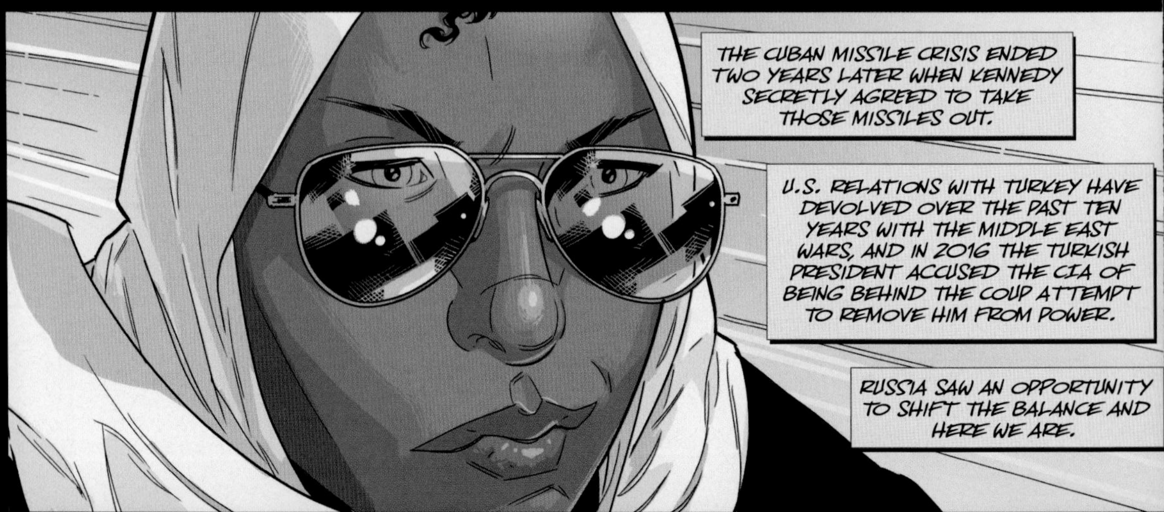
THE CUBAN MISSILE CRISIS ENDED TWO YEARS LATER WHEN KENNEDY SECRETLY AGREED TO TAKE THOSE MISSILES OUT.
U.S. RELATIONS WITH TURKEY HAVE DEVOLVED OVER THE PAST TEN YEARS WITH THE MIDDLE EAST WARS, AND IN 2016 THE TURKISH PRESIDENT ACCUSED THE CIA OF BEING BEHIND THE COUP ATTEMPT TO REMOVE HIM FROM POWER.
RUSSIA SAW AN OPPORTUNITY TO SHIFT THE BALANCE AND HERE WE ARE.

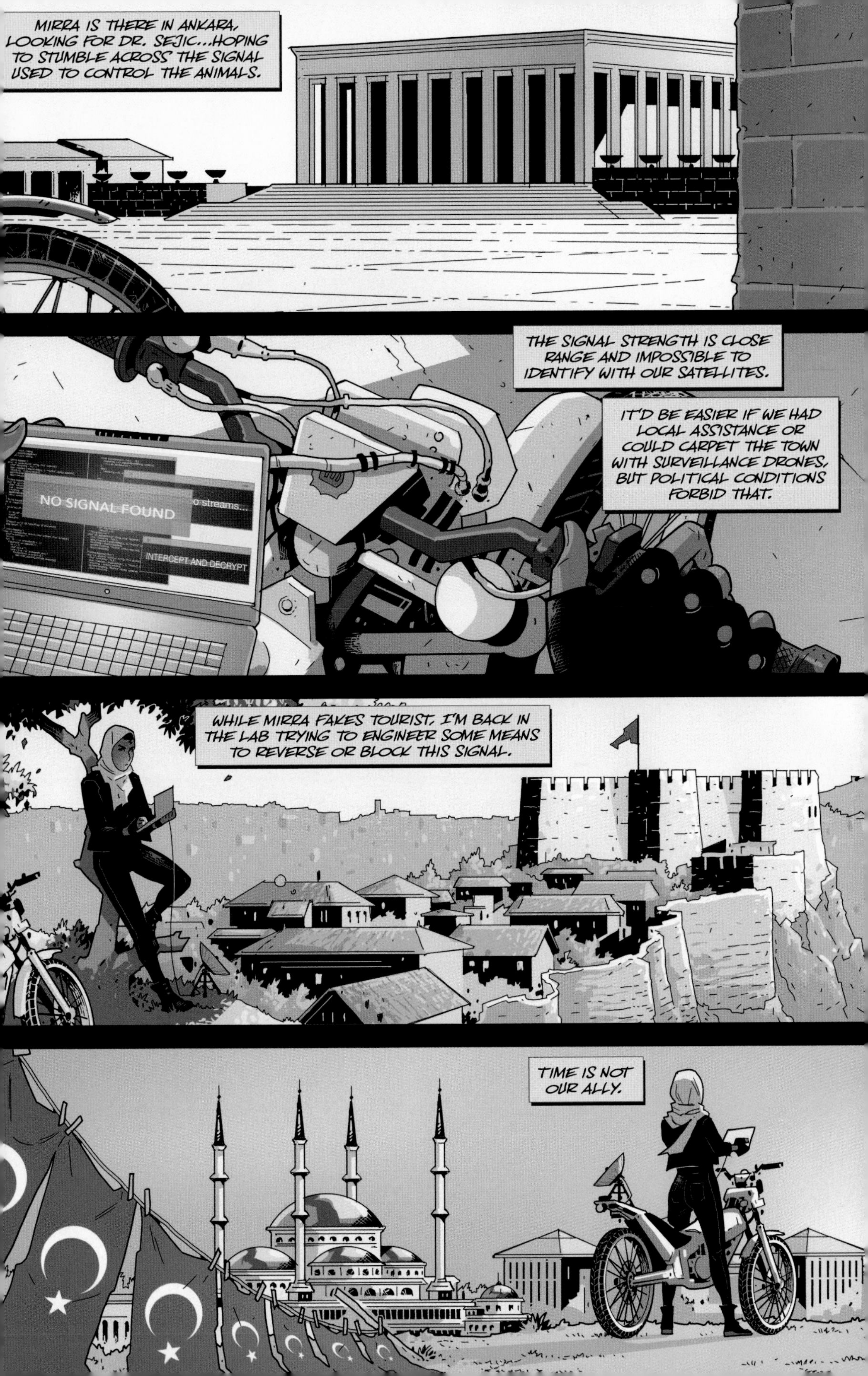
MIRRA IS THERE IN ANKARA, LOOKING FOR DR. SEJIC...HOPING TO STUMBLE ACROSS THE SIGNAL USED TO CONTROL THE ANIMALS.
THE SIGNAL STRENGTH IS CLOSE RANGE AND IMPOSSIBLE TO IDENTIFY WITH OUR SATELLITES.
IT'D BE EASIER IF WE HAD LOCAL ASSISTANCE OR COULD CARPET THE TOWN WITH SURVEILLANCE DRONES, BUT POLITICAL CONDITIONS FORBID THAT.
NO SIGNAL FOUND
o streams...
INTERCEPT AND DECRYPT
WHILE MIRRA FAKES TOURIST, I'M BACK IN THE LAB TRYING TO ENGINEER SOME MEANS TO REVERSE OR BLOCK THIS SIGNAL.
TIME IS NOT OUR ALLY.

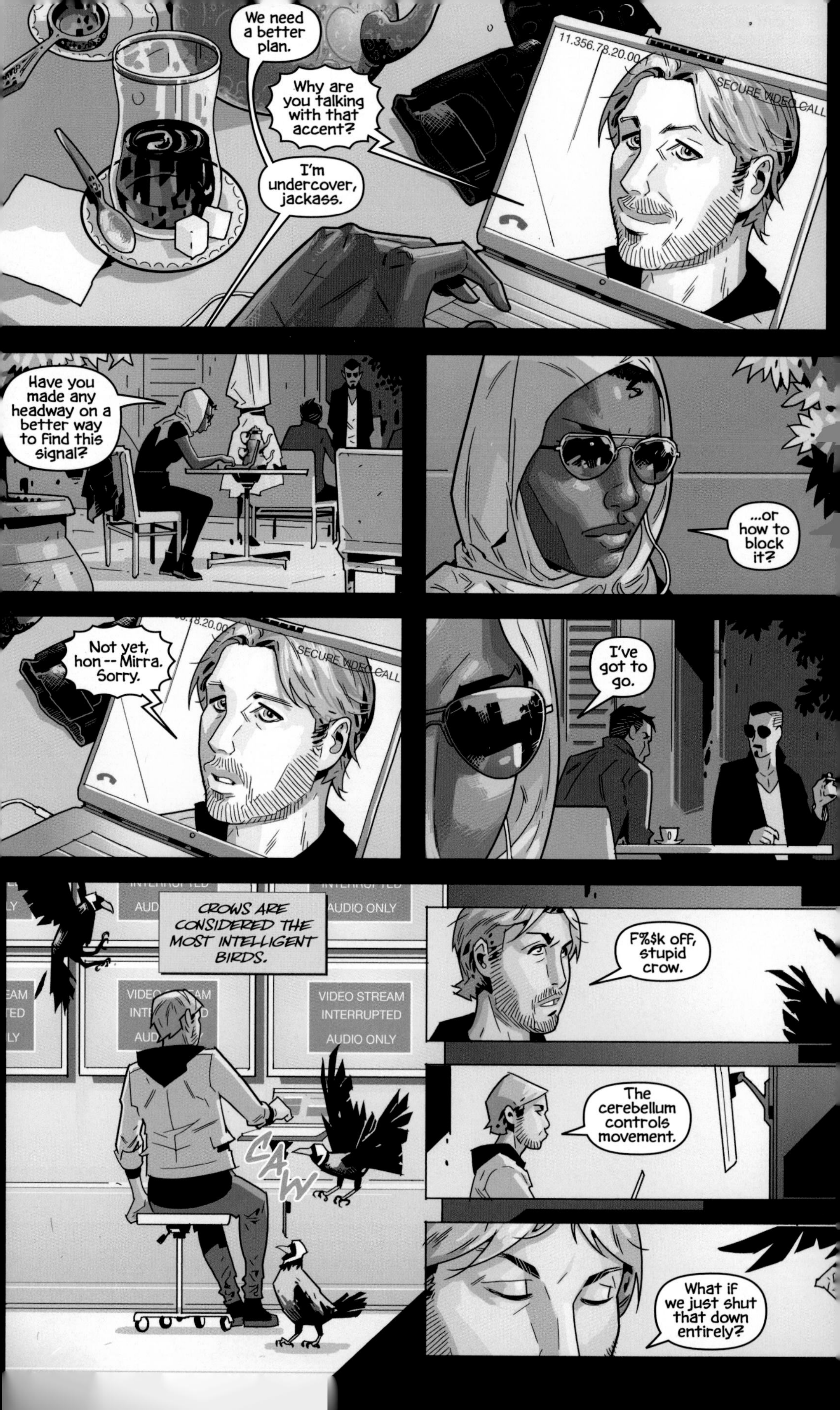

We need a better plan.
Why are you talking with that accent?
I'm undercover, jackass.
11.356.78.20.00
SECURE VIDEO CALL
Have you made any headway on a better way to find this signal?
...or how to block it?
Not yet, hon -- Mirra. Sorry.
SECURE VIDEO CALL
I've got to go.
CROWS ARE CONSIDERED THE MOST INTELLIGENT BIRDS.
AUDIO ONLY
VIDEO STREAM INTERRUPTED AUDIO ONLY
CAW
F%$k off, stupid crow.
The cerebellum controls movement.
What if we just shut that down entirely?

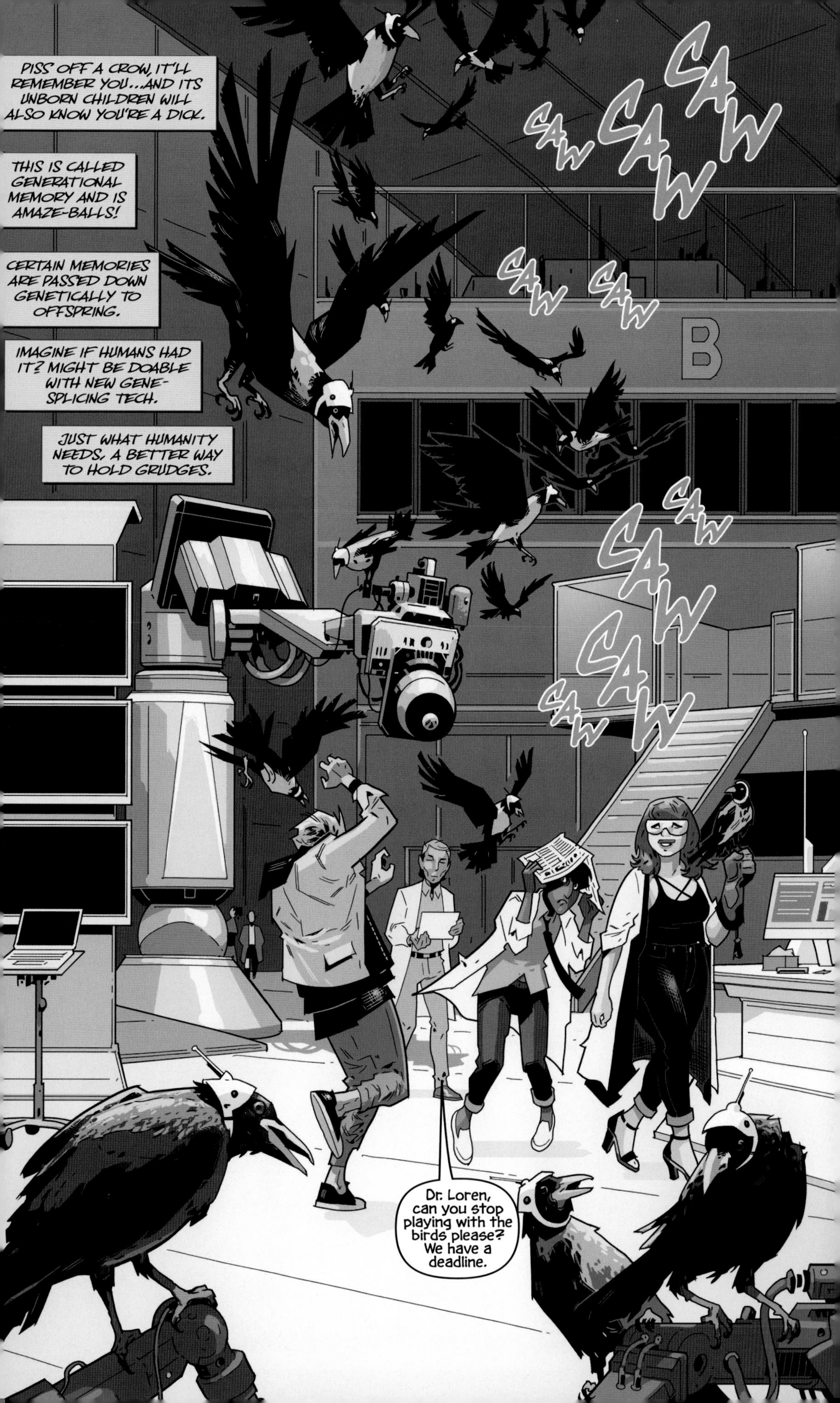
PISS OFF A CROW, IT'LL REMEMBER YOU...AND ITS UNBORN CHILDREN WILL ALSO KNOW YOU'RE A DICK.
THIS IS CALLED GENERATIONAL MEMORY AND IS AMAZE-BALLS!
CERTAIN MEMORIES ARE PASSED DOWN GENETICALLY TO OFFSPRING.
IMAGINE IF HUMANS HAD IT? MIGHT BE DOABLE WITH NEW GENE-SPLICING TECH.
JUST WHAT HUMANITY NEEDS, A BETTER WAY TO HOLD GRUDGES.
CAW CAW CAW
CAW CAW
B
CAW CAW CAW CAW
Dr. Loren, can you stop playing with the birds please? We have a deadline.

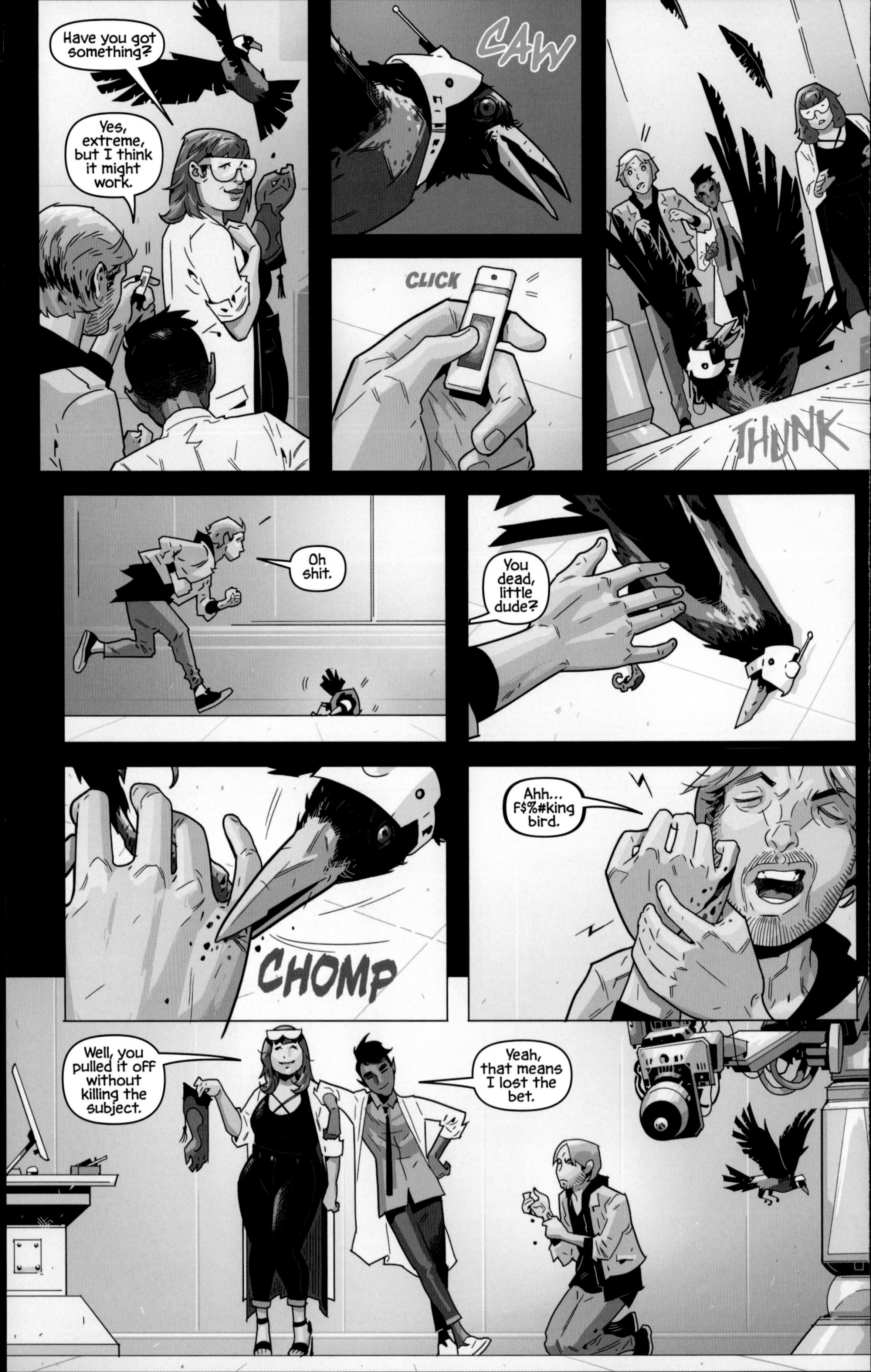
Have you got something?
Yes, extreme, but I think it might work.
CAW
CLICK
THUNK
Oh shit.
You dead, little dude?
CHOMP
Ahh... F$%#king bird.
Well, you pulled it off without killing the subject.
Yeah, that means I lost the bet.

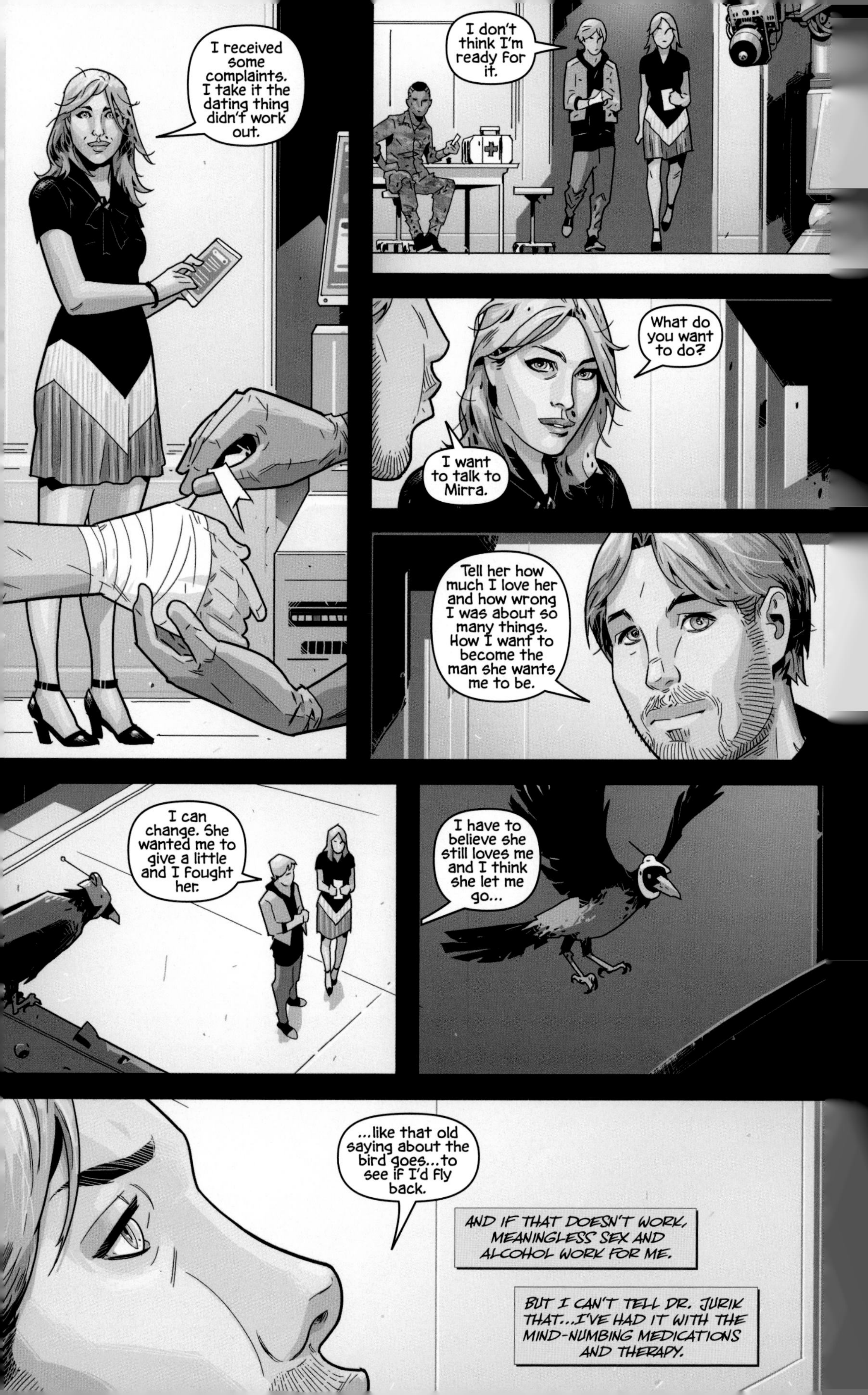
I received some complaints. I take it the dating thing didn't work out.
I don't think I'm ready for it.
What do you want to do?
I want to talk to Mirra.
Tell her how much I love her and how wrong I was about so many things. How I want to become the man she wants me to be.
I can change. She wanted me to give a little and I fought her.
I have to believe she still loves me and I think she let me go...
...like that old saying about the bird goes...to see if I'd fly back.
AND IF THAT DOESN'T WORK, MEANINGLESS SEX AND ALCOHOL WORK FOR ME.
BUT I CAN'T TELL DR. JURIK THAT...I'VE HAD IT WITH THE MIND-NUMBING MEDICATIONS AND THERAPY.

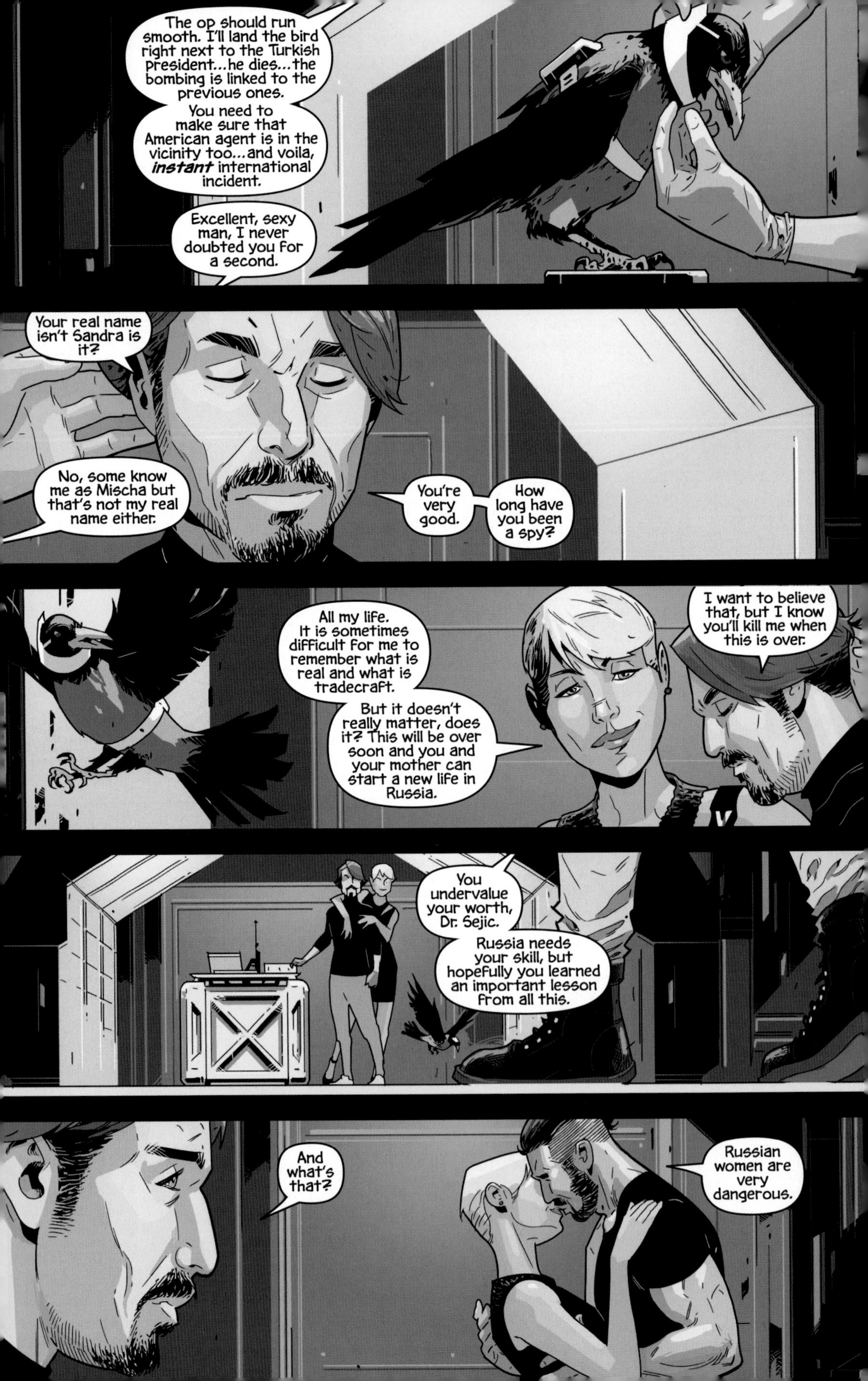

The op should run smooth. I'll land the bird right next to the Turkish president...he dies...the bombing is linked to the previous ones.
You need to make sure that American agent is in the vicinity too...and voila, *instant* international incident.
Excellent, sexy man, I never doubted you for a second.
Your real name isn't Sandra is it?
No, some know me as Mischa but that's not my real name either.
You're very good.
How long have you been a spy?
All my life. It is sometimes difficult for me to remember what is real and what is tradecraft.
But it doesn't really matter, does it? This will be over soon and you and your mother can start a new life in Russia.
I want to believe that, but I know you'll kill me when this is over.
You undervalue your worth, Dr. Sejic.
Russia needs your skill, but hopefully you learned an important lesson from all this.
And what's that?
Russian women are very dangerous.

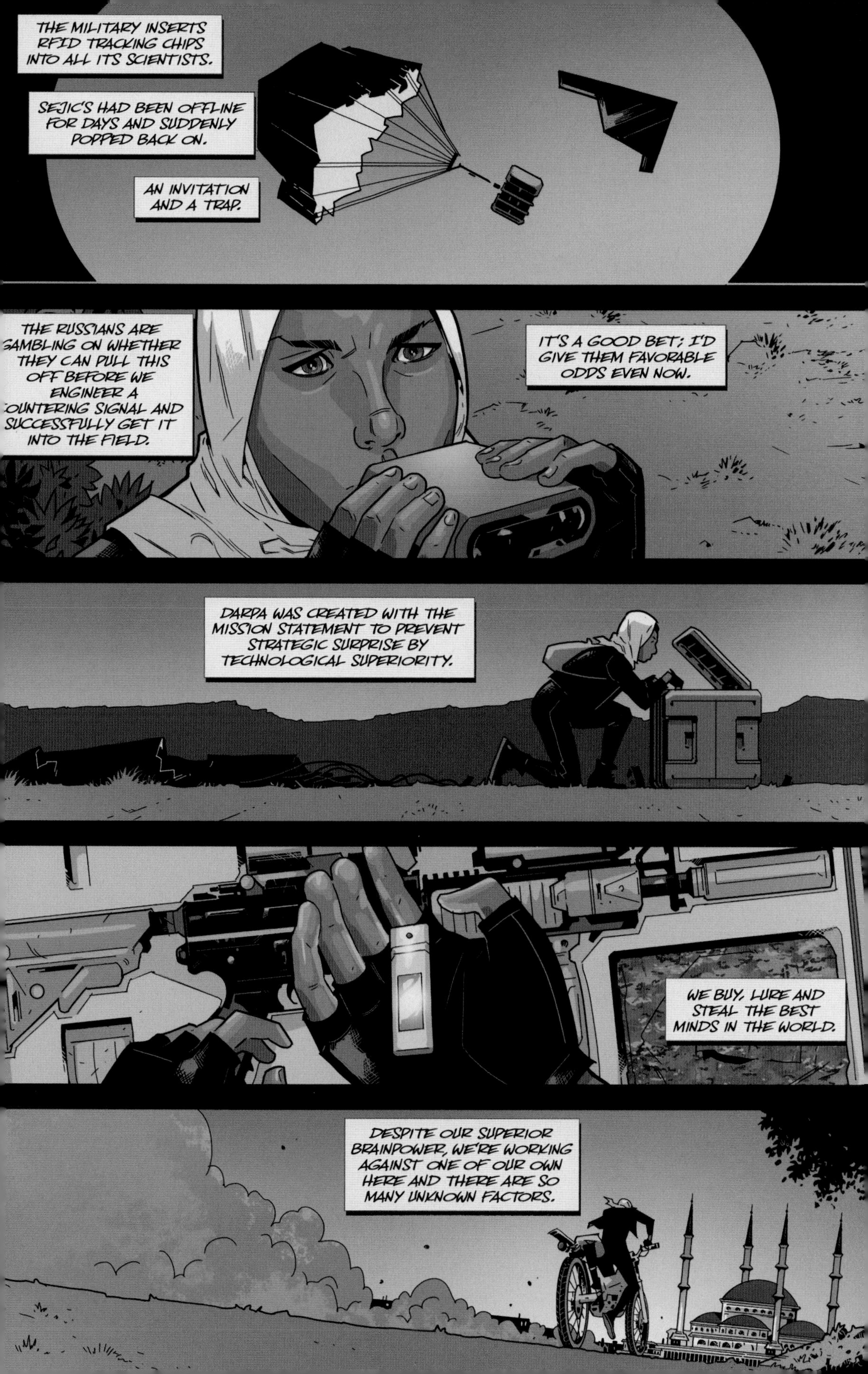
THE MILITARY INSERTS RFID TRACKING CHIPS INTO ALL ITS SCIENTISTS.
SEJIC'S HAD BEEN OFFLINE FOR DAYS AND SUDDENLY POPPED BACK ON.
AN INVITATION AND A TRAP.
THE RUSSIANS ARE GAMBLING ON WHETHER THEY CAN PULL THIS OFF BEFORE WE ENGINEER A COUNTERING SIGNAL AND SUCCESSFULLY GET IT INTO THE FIELD.
IT'S A GOOD BET; I'D GIVE THEM FAVORABLE ODDS EVEN NOW.
DARPA WAS CREATED WITH THE MISSION STATEMENT TO PREVENT STRATEGIC SURPRISE BY TECHNOLOGICAL SUPERIORITY.
WE BUY, LURE AND STEAL THE BEST MINDS IN THE WORLD.
DESPITE OUR SUPERIOR BRAINPOWER, WE'RE WORKING AGAINST ONE OF OUR OWN HERE AND THERE ARE SO MANY UNKNOWN FACTORS.

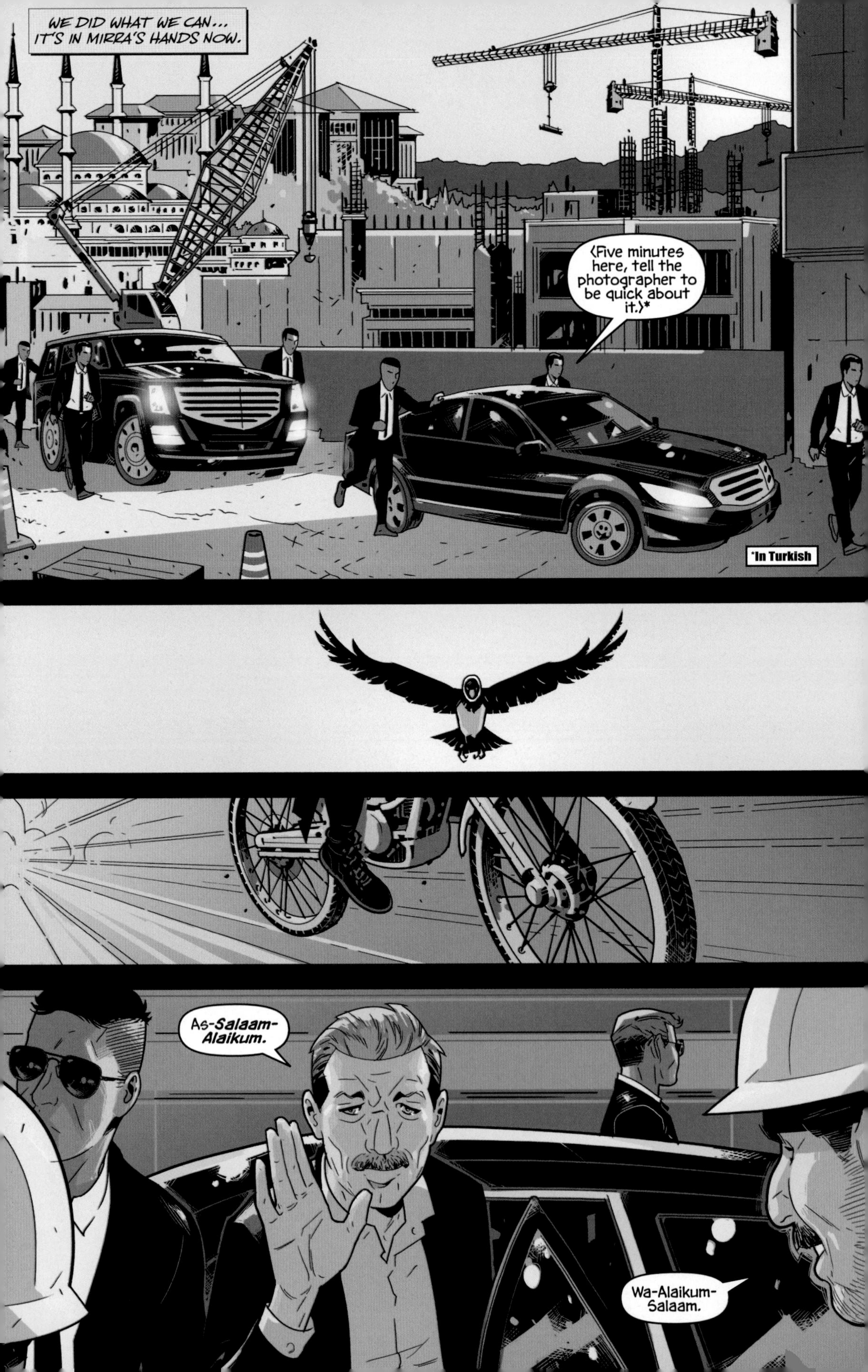
WE DID WHAT WE CAN... IT'S IN MIRRA'S HANDS NOW.
‹Five minutes here, tell the photographer to be quick about it.›*
*In Turkish
As-Salaam-Alaikum.
Wa-Alaikum-Salaam.

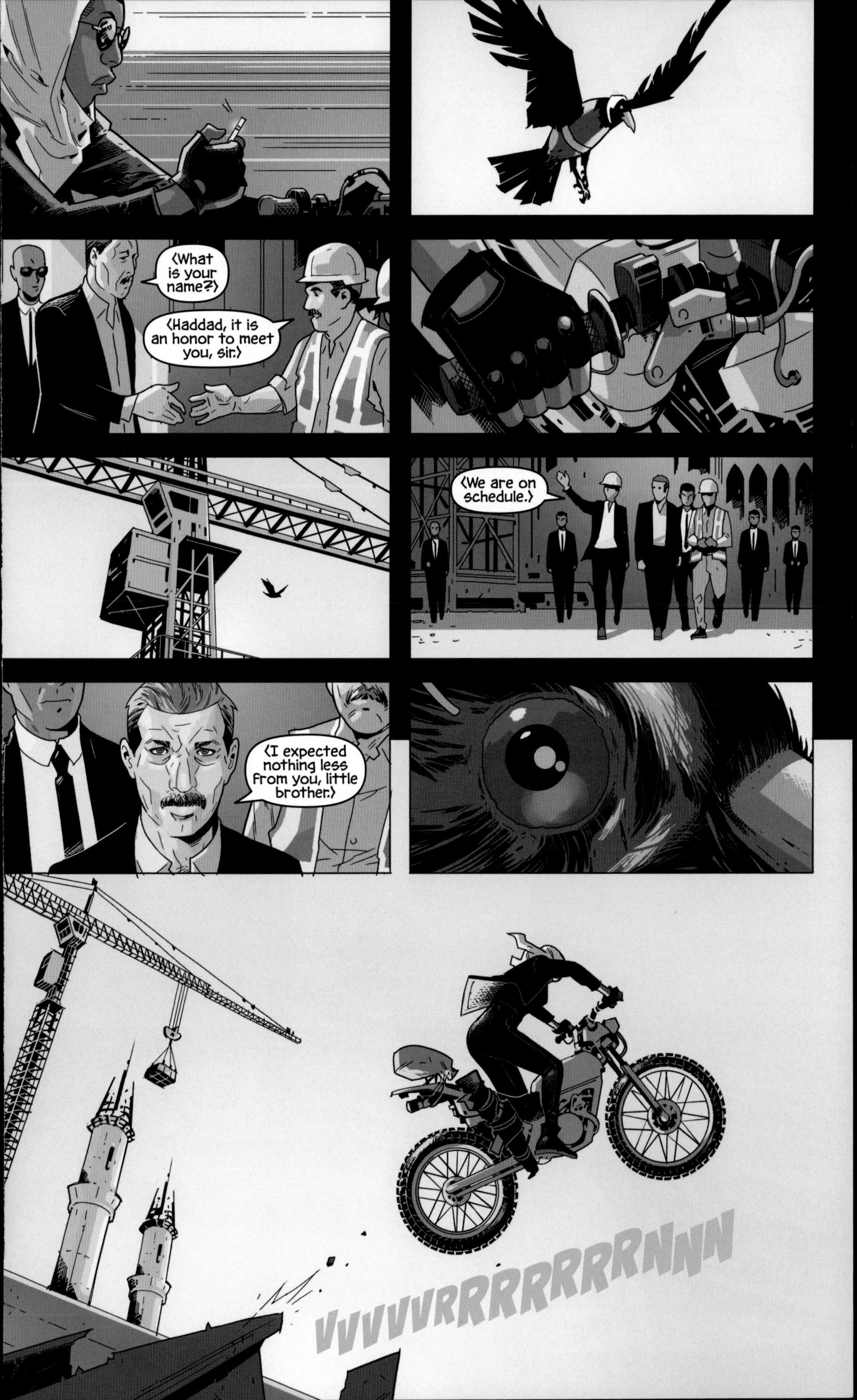

‹What is your name?›
‹Haddad, it is an honor to meet you, sir.›
‹We are on schedule.›
‹I expected nothing less from you, little brother.›
VVVVVRRRRRRRRNNN

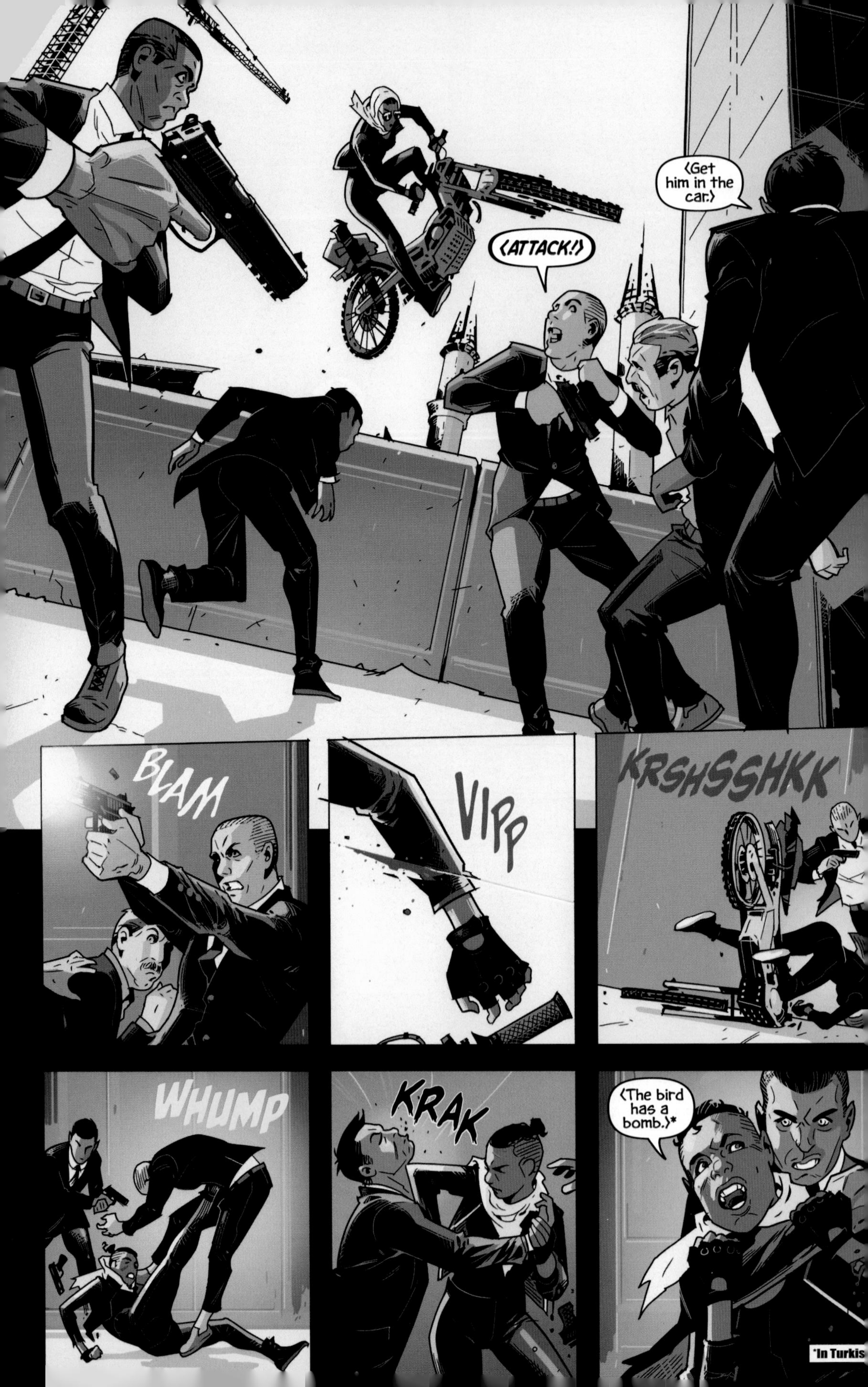
<Get him in the car.>
<ATTACK!>
BLAM
VIPP
KRSHSSHKK
WHUMP
KRAK
<The bird has a bomb.>*
*In Turkis

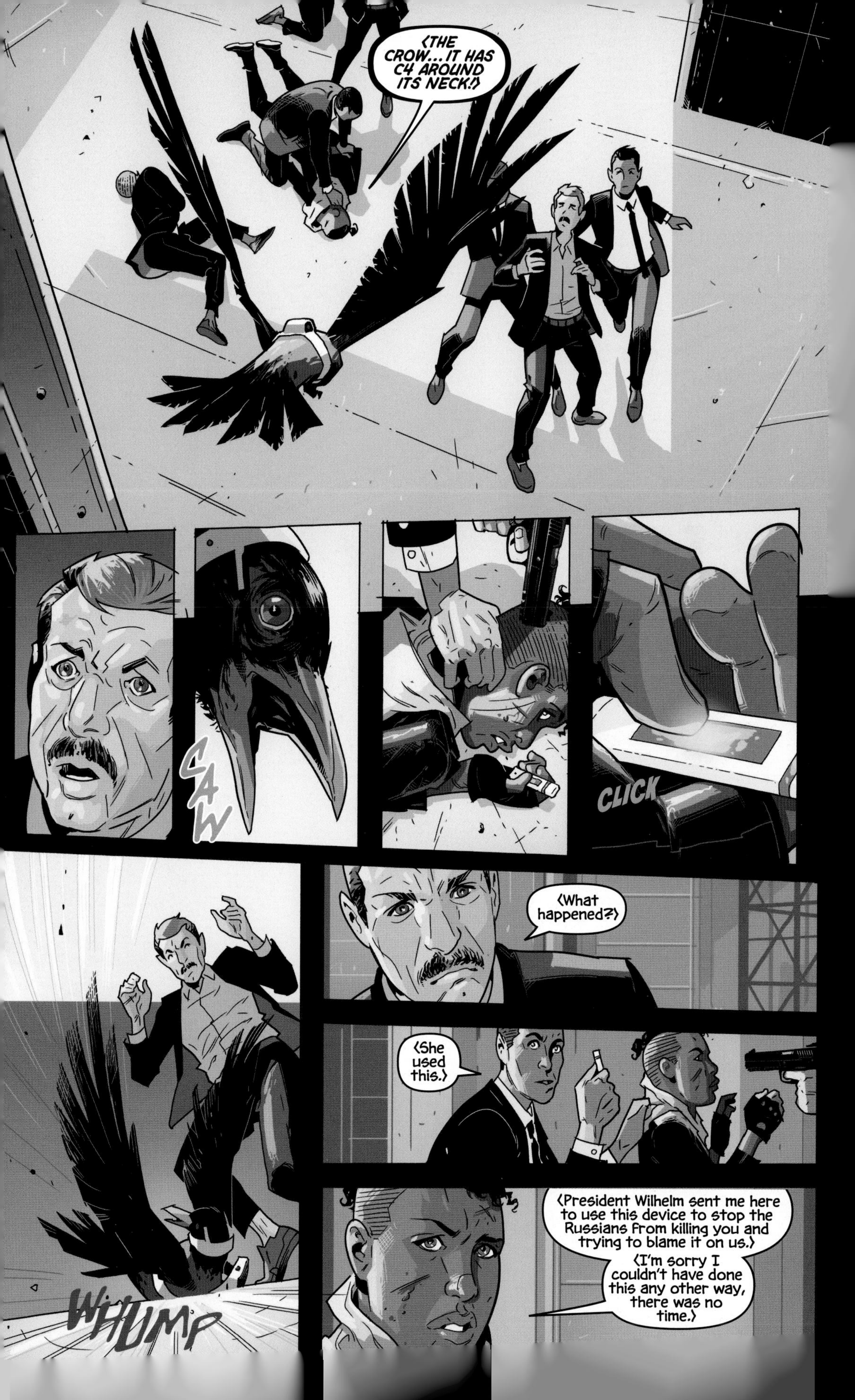

⟨THE CROW... IT HAS C4 AROUND ITS NECK!⟩
CAW
CLICK
WHUMP
⟨What happened?⟩
⟨She used this.⟩
⟨President Wilhelm sent me here to use this device to stop the Russians from killing you and trying to blame it on us.⟩
⟨I'm sorry I couldn't have done this any other way, there was no time.⟩

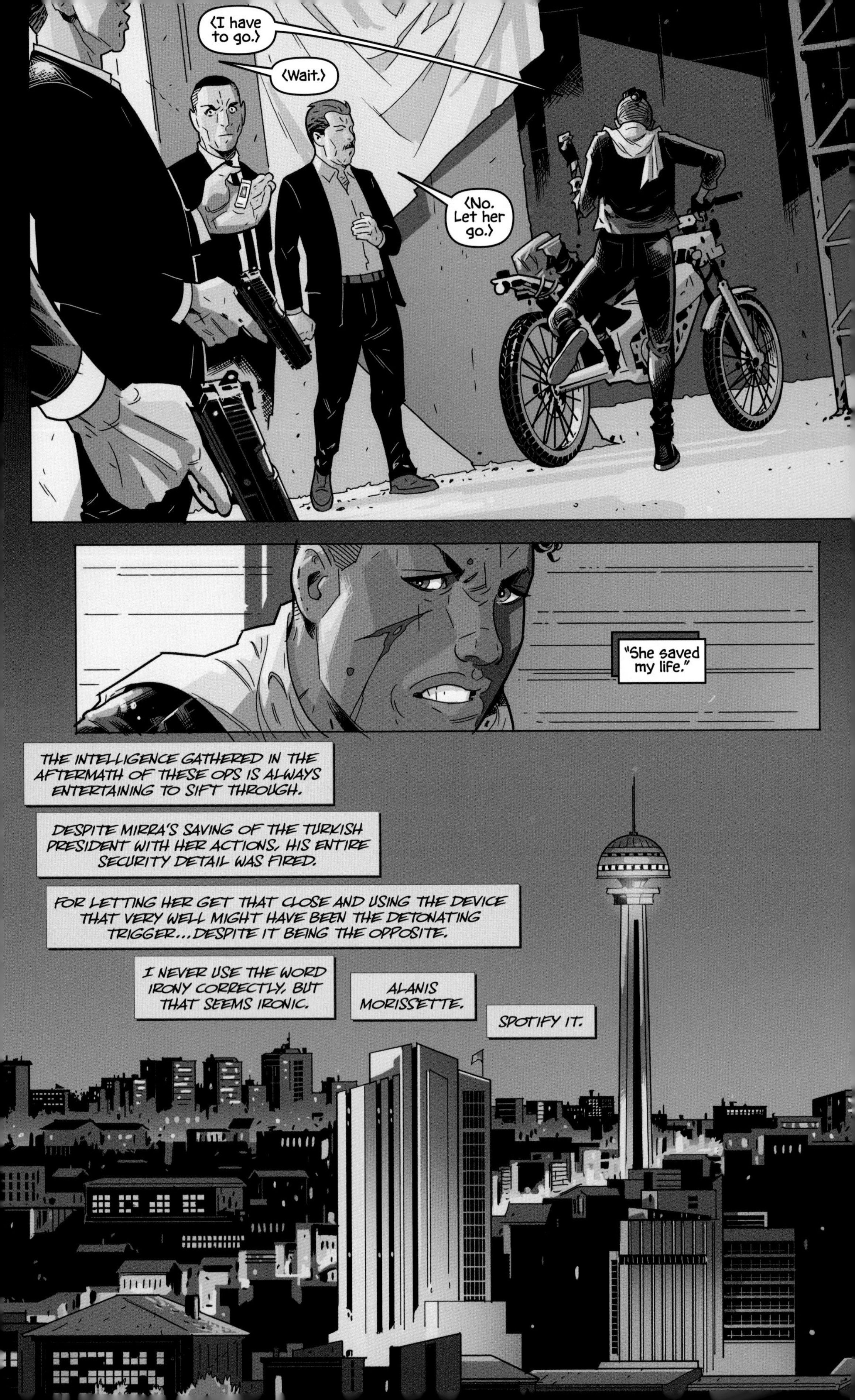

⟨I have to go.⟩
⟨Wait.⟩
⟨No. Let her go.⟩
"She saved my life."
THE INTELLIGENCE GATHERED IN THE AFTERMATH OF THESE OPS IS ALWAYS ENTERTAINING TO SIFT THROUGH.
DESPITE MIRRA'S SAVING OF THE TURKISH PRESIDENT WITH HER ACTIONS, HIS ENTIRE SECURITY DETAIL WAS FIRED.
FOR LETTING HER GET THAT CLOSE AND USING THE DEVICE THAT VERY WELL MIGHT HAVE BEEN THE DETONATING TRIGGER...DESPITE IT BEING THE OPPOSITE.
I NEVER USE THE WORD IRONY CORRECTLY, BUT THAT SEEMS IRONIC.
ALANIS MORISSETTE.
SPOTIFY IT.

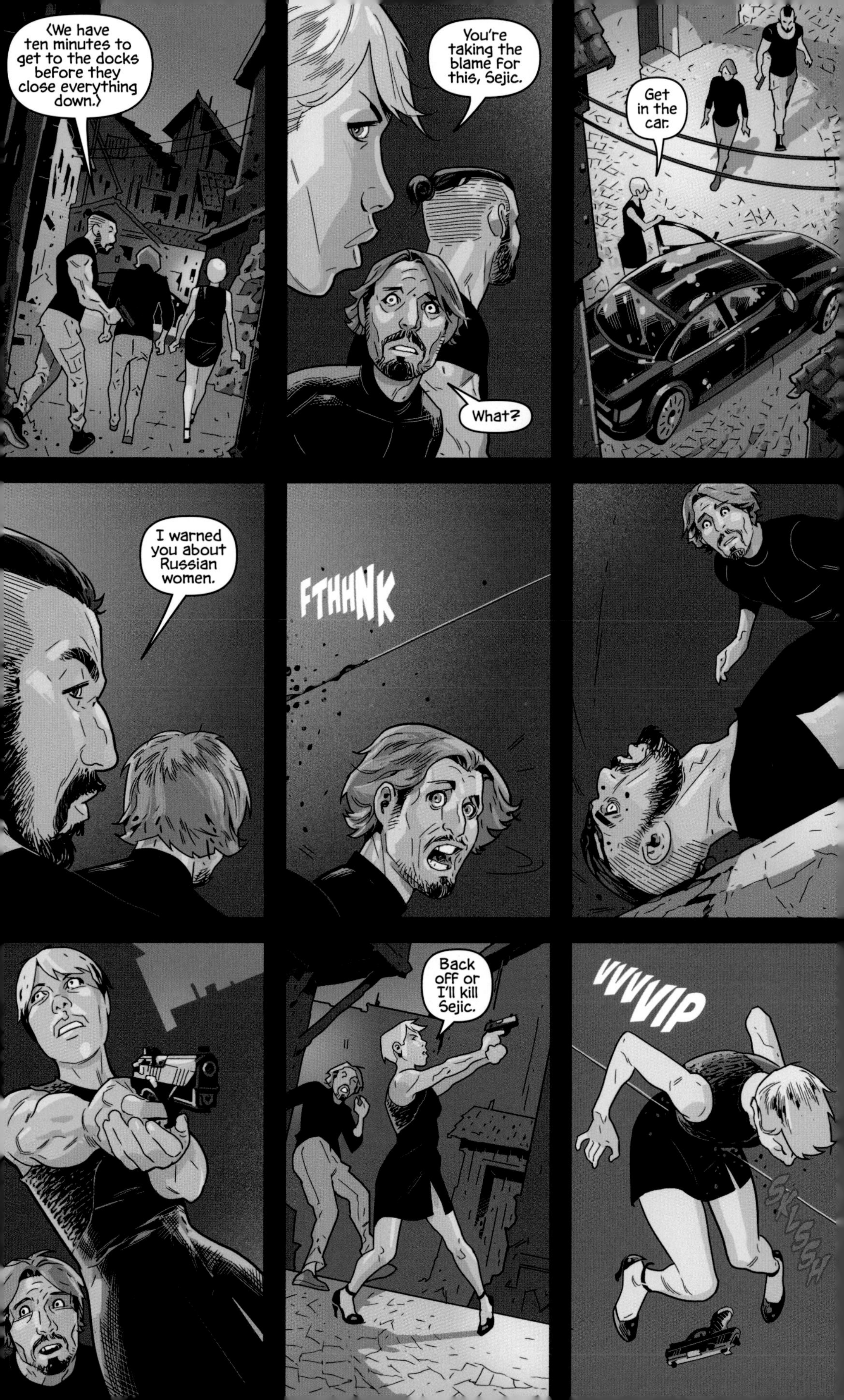

‹We have ten minutes to get to the docks before they close everything down.›
You're taking the blame for this, Sejic.
What?
Get in the car.
I warned you about Russian women.
FTHHNK
Back off or I'll kill Sejic.
VVVVIP
SKVSSH

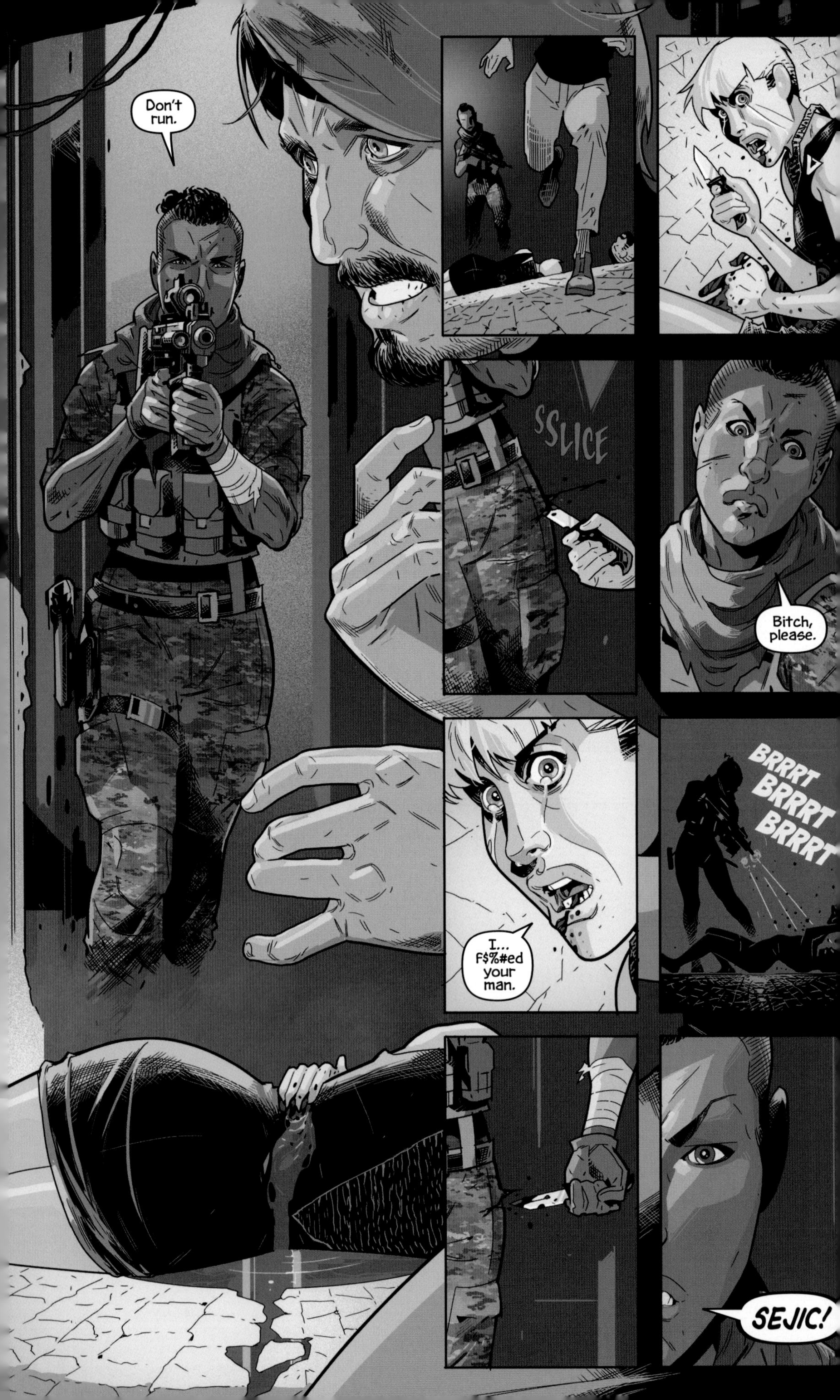
Don't run.
SSLICE
Bitch, please.
I... F$%#ed your man.
BRRRT BRRRT BRRRT
SEJIC!

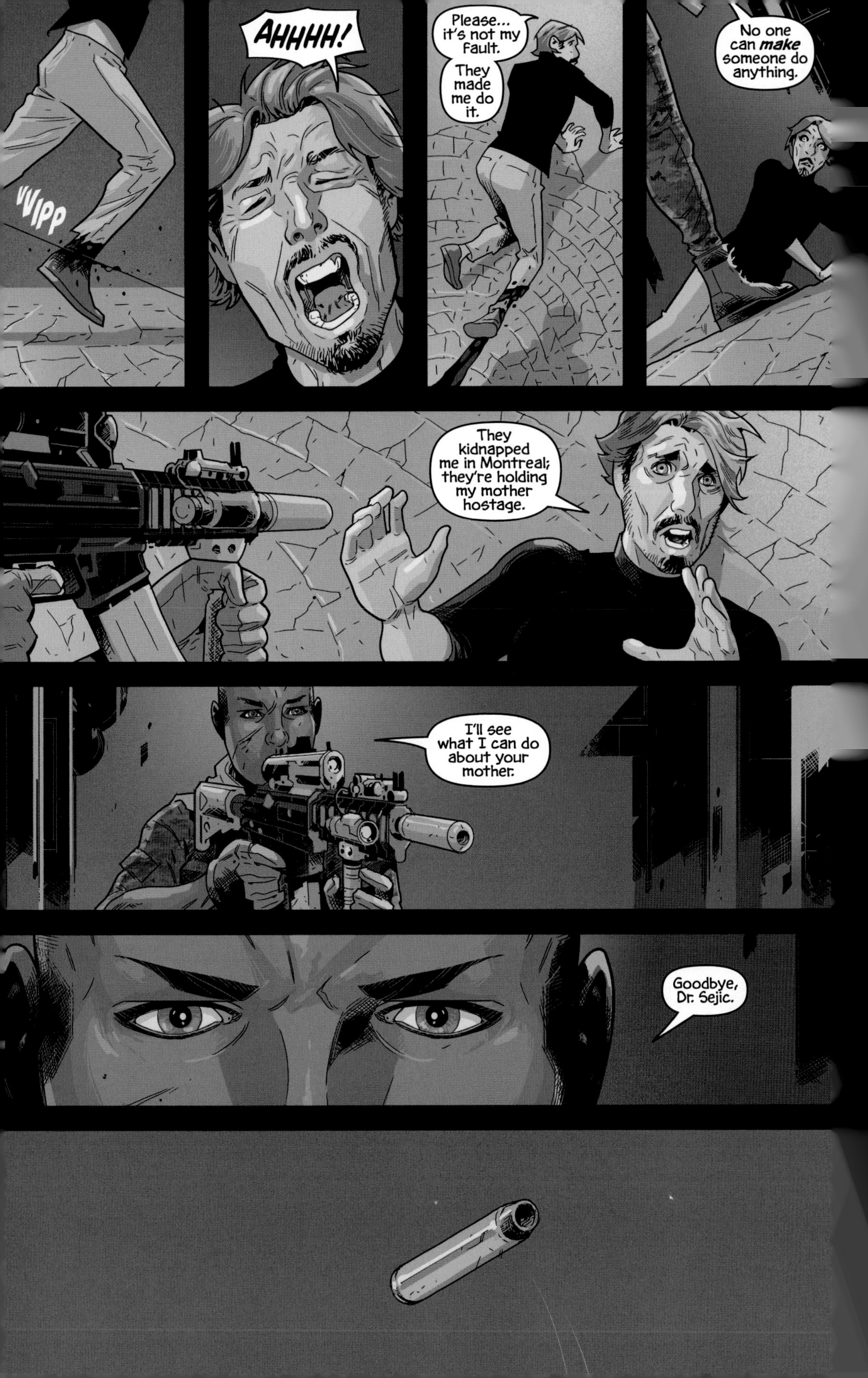
VVIPP
AHHHH!
Please... it's not my fault.
They made me do it.
No one can *make* someone do anything.
They kidnapped me in Montreal; they're holding my mother hostage.
I'll see what I can do about your mother.
Goodbye, Dr. Sejic.

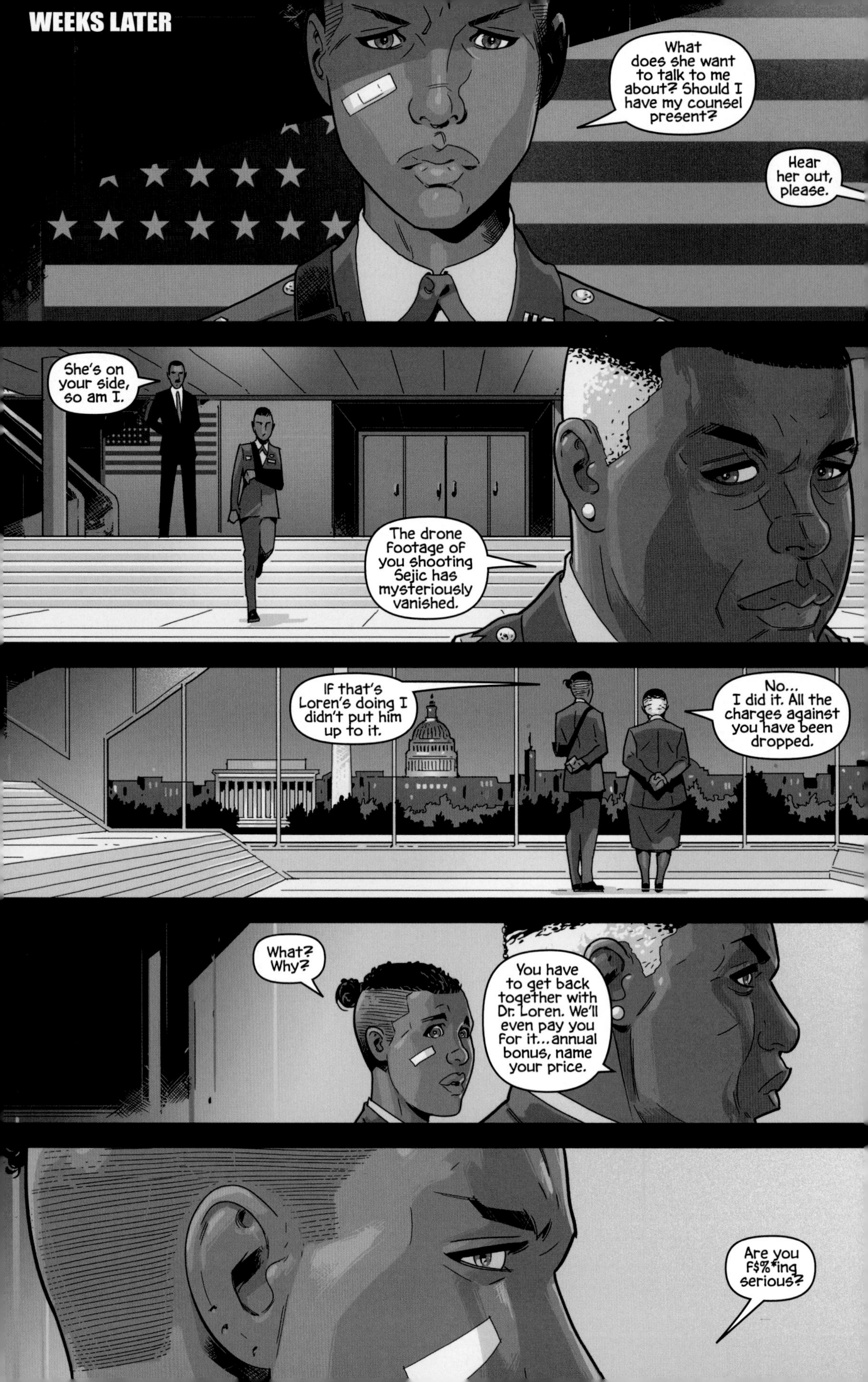
WEEKS LATER
What does she want to talk to me about? Should I have my counsel present?
Hear her out, please.
She's on your side, so am I.
The drone footage of you shooting Sejic has mysteriously vanished.
If that's Loren's doing I didn't put him up to it.
No... I did it. All the charges against you have been dropped.
What? Why?
You have to get back together with Dr. Loren. We'll even pay you for it... annual bonus, name your price.
Are you F$%*ing serious?

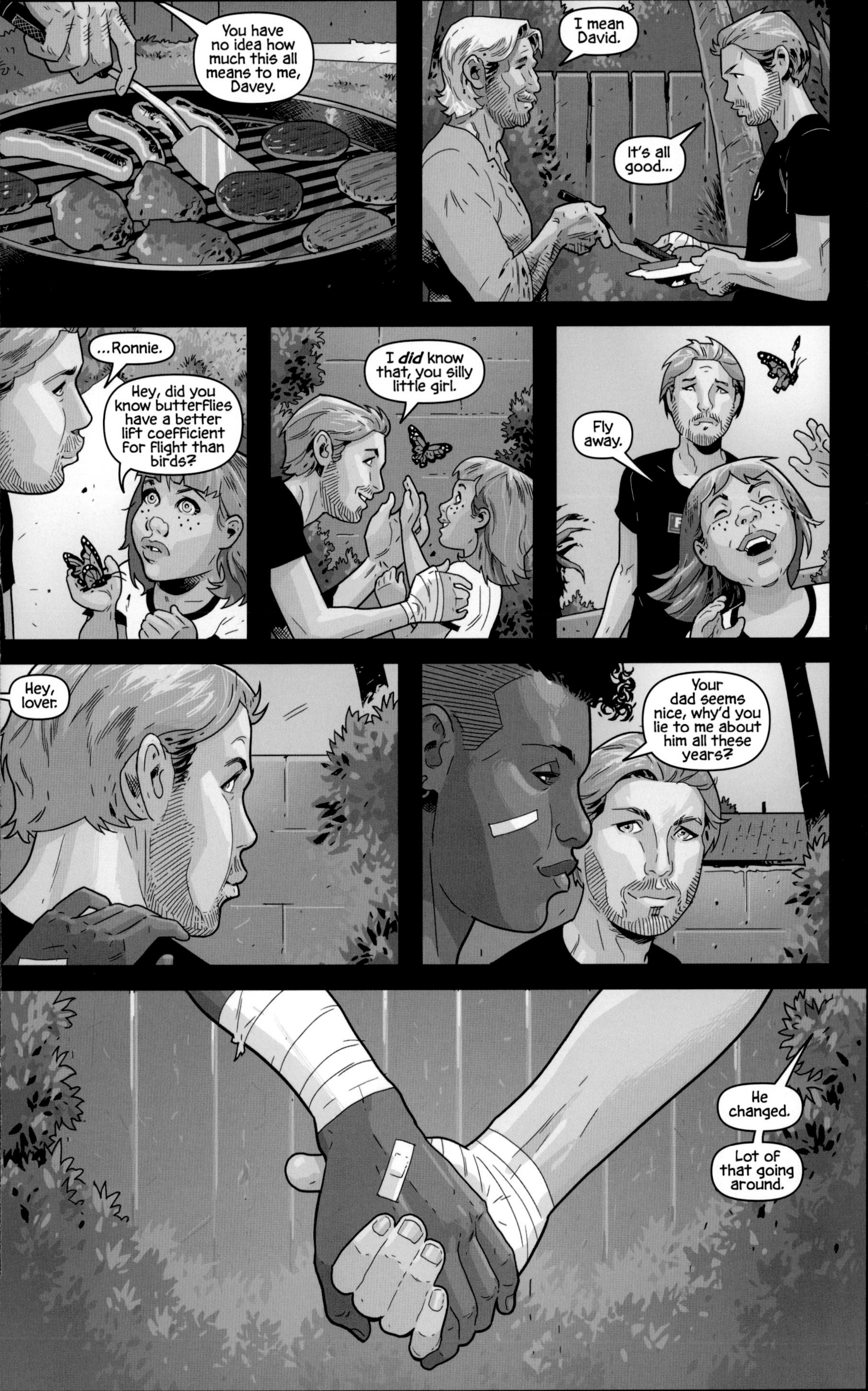
You have no idea how much this all means to me, Davey.
I mean David.
It's all good...
...Ronnie.
Hey, did you know butterflies have a better lift coefficient for flight than birds?
I *did* know that, you silly little girl.
Fly away.
Hey, lover.
Your dad seems nice, why'd you lie to me about him all these years?
He changed.
Lot of that going around.

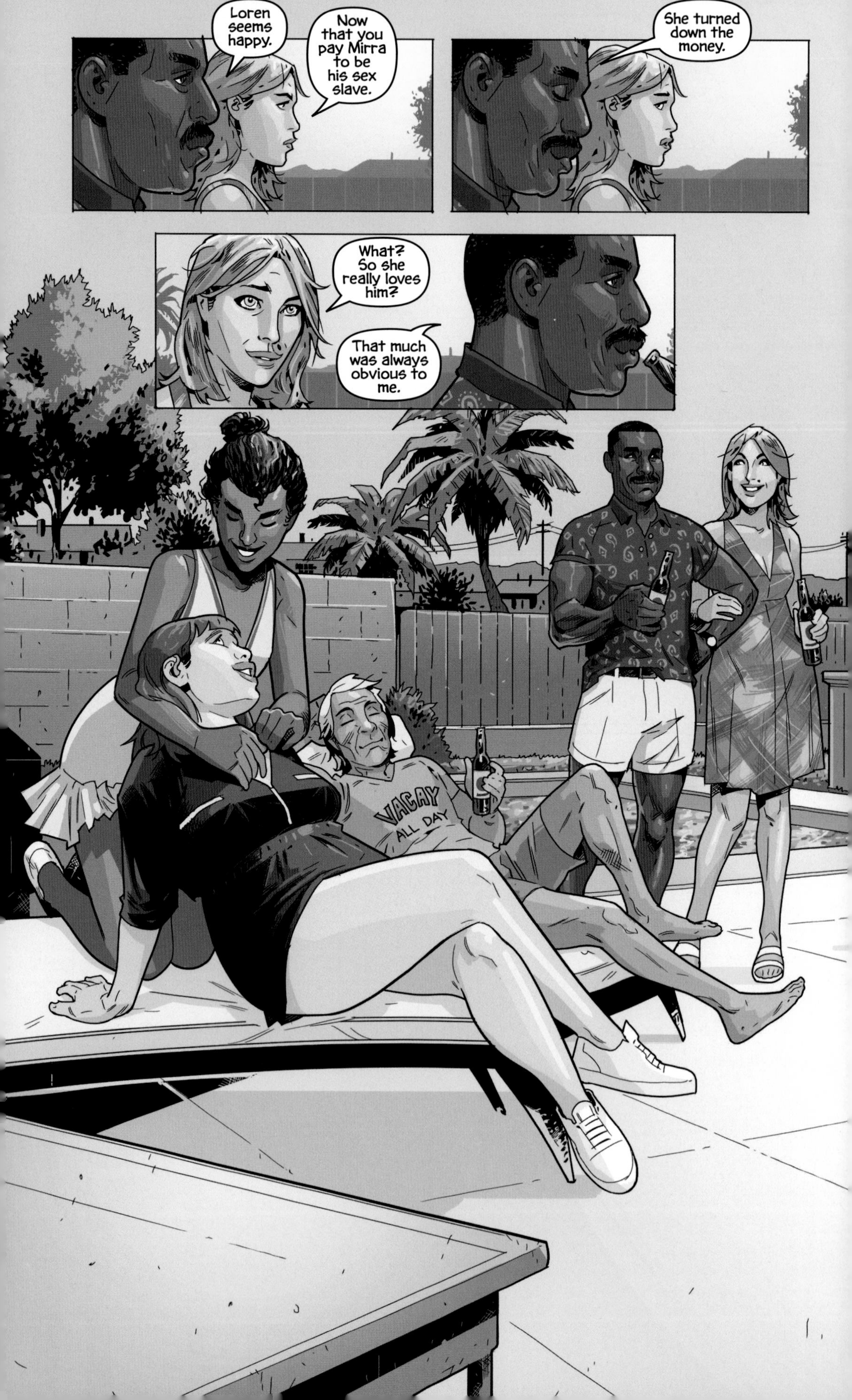
Loren seems happy.
Now that you pay Mirra to be his sex slave.
She turned down the money.
What? So she really loves him?
That much was always obvious to me.
VACAY ALL DAY

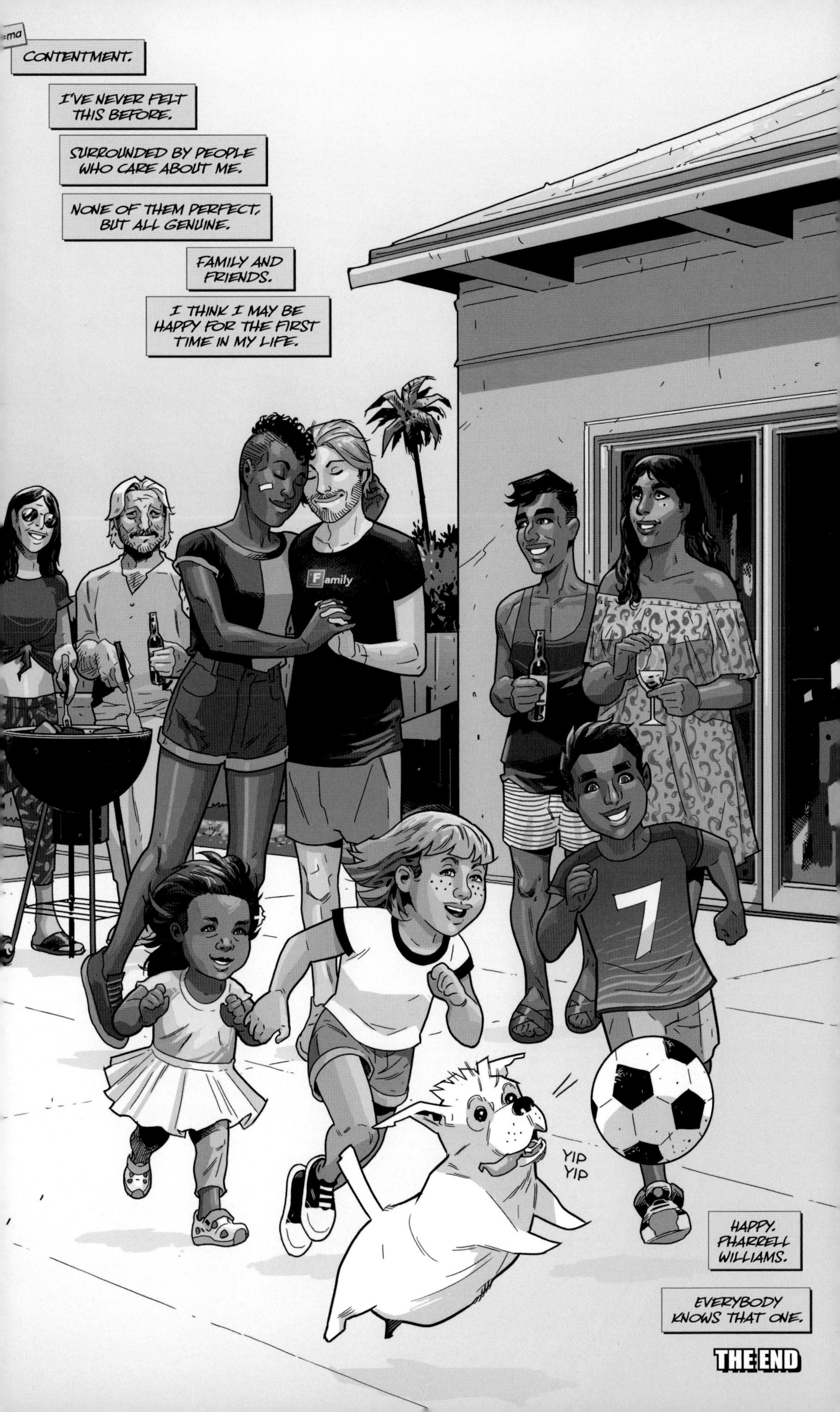
CONTENTMENT.
I'VE NEVER FELT THIS BEFORE.
SURROUNDED BY PEOPLE WHO CARE ABOUT ME.
NONE OF THEM PERFECT, BUT ALL GENUINE.
FAMILY AND FRIENDS.
I THINK I MAY BE HAPPY FOR THE FIRST TIME IN MY LIFE.
Family
7
YIP YIP
HAPPY. PHARRELL WILLIAMS.
EVERYBODY KNOWS THAT ONE.
THE END

COVER GALLERY

THINK TANK

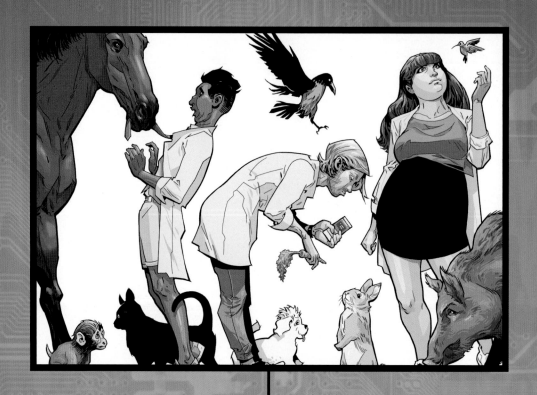

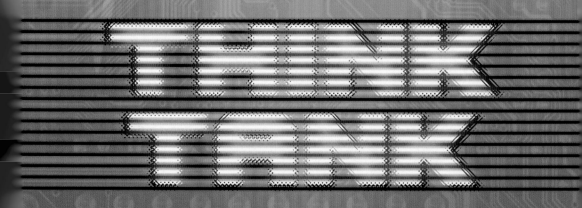

Think Tank: Animal #1 cover A art by **Rahsan Ekedal**

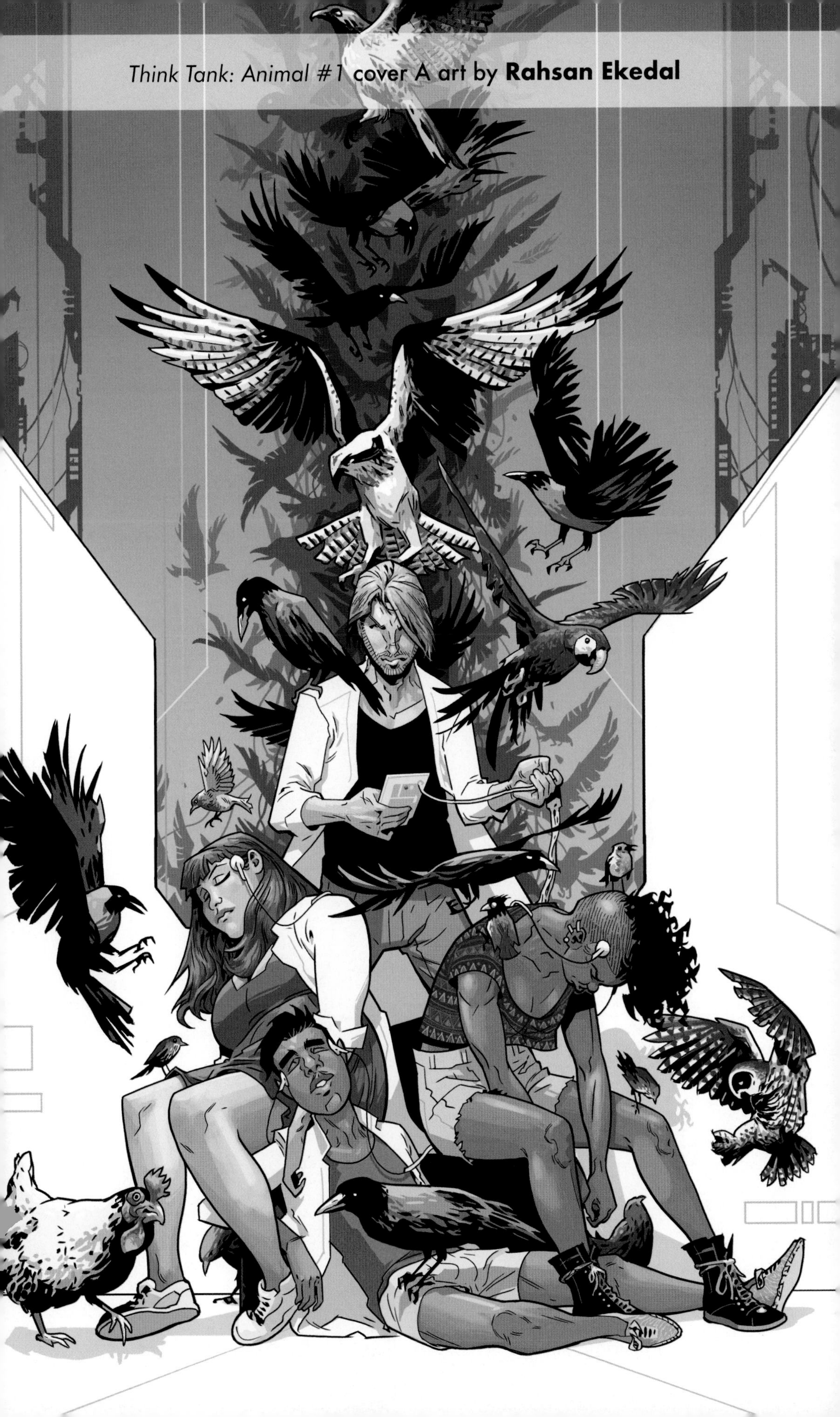

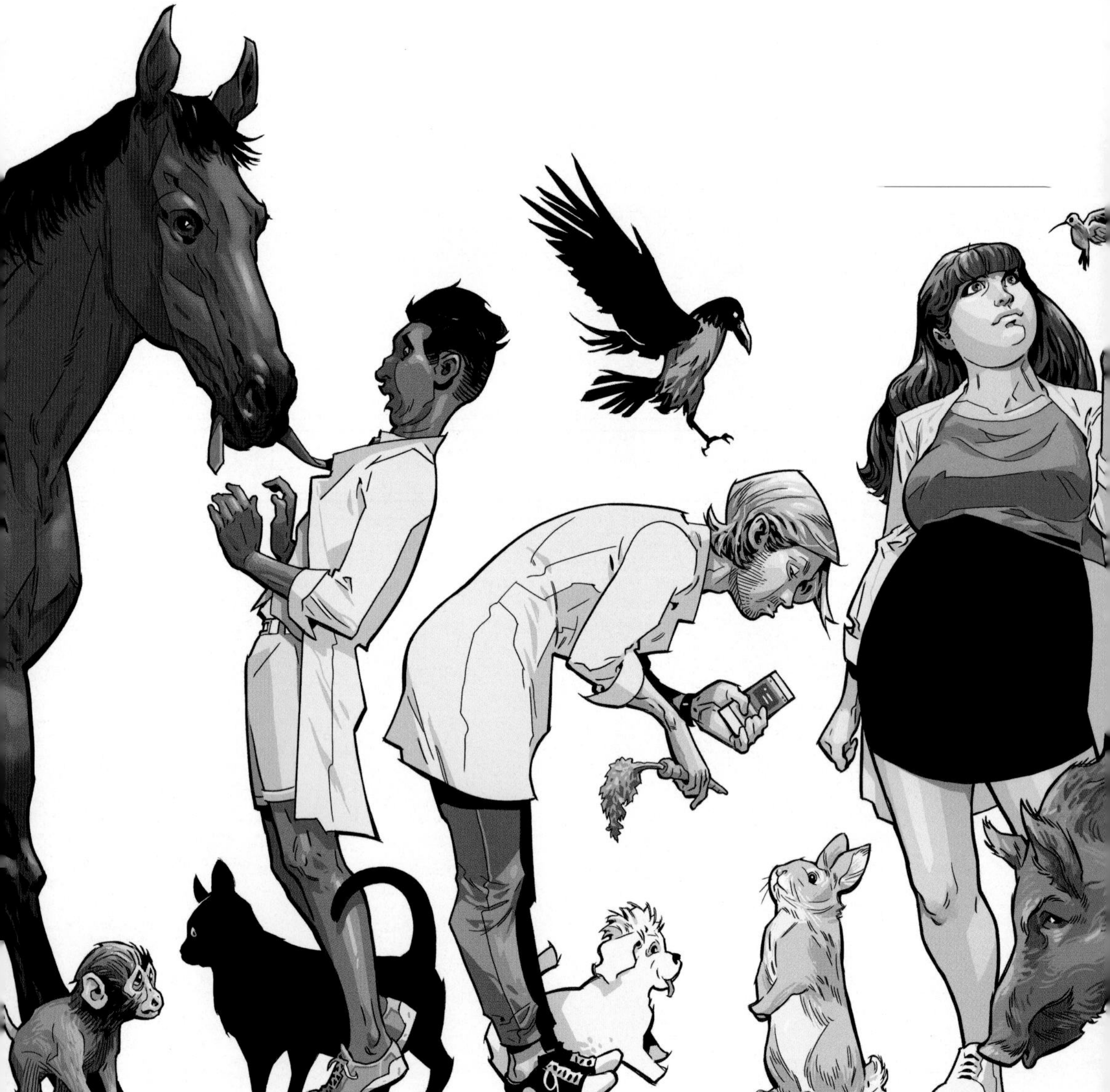

Think Tank: Animal #1 cover B art by **Rahsan Ekedal**

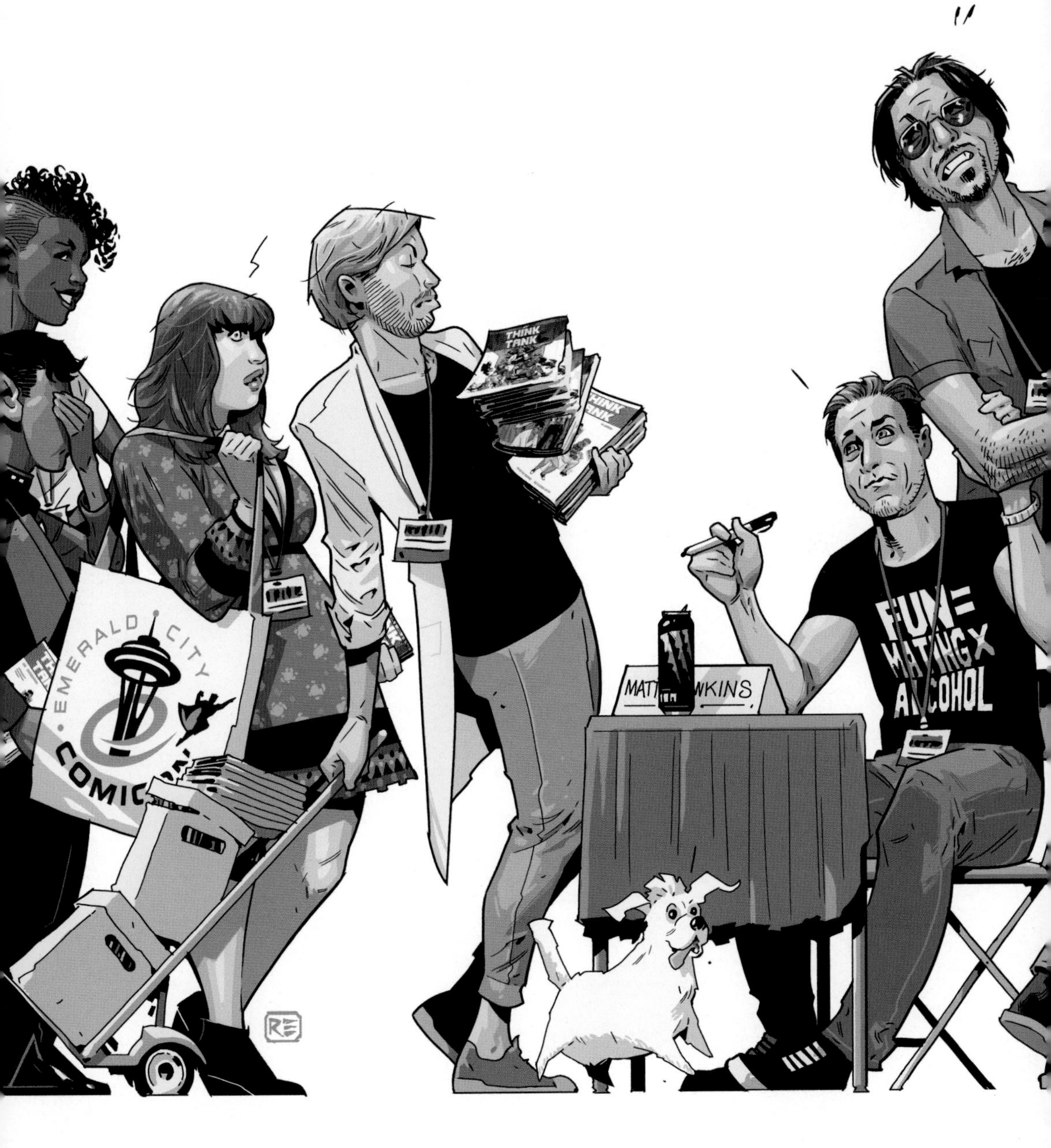

THINK TANK
EMERALD CITY
COMIC
MATT WKINS
FUN = MAKING X ALCOHOL

Think Tank: Animal #1 cover C art by **Rahsan Ekedal**

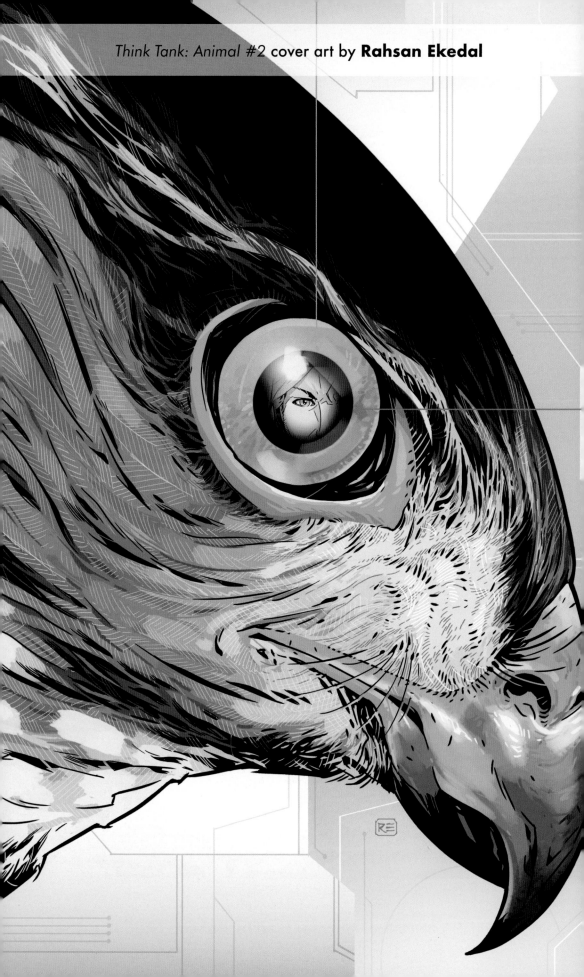

Think Tank: Animal #2 cover art by **Rahsan Ekedal**

Think Tank: Animal #3 cover art by **Rahsan Ekedal**

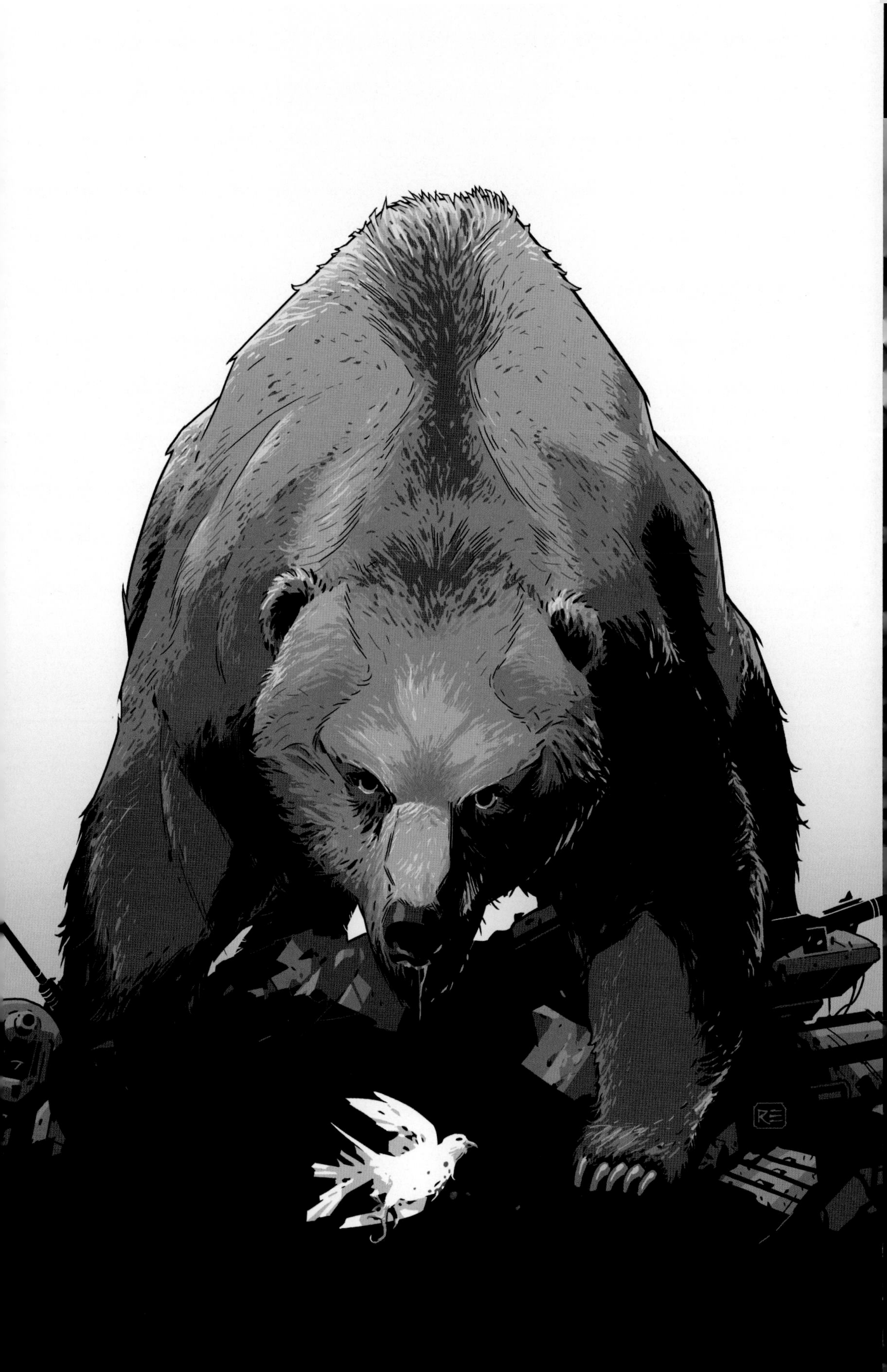

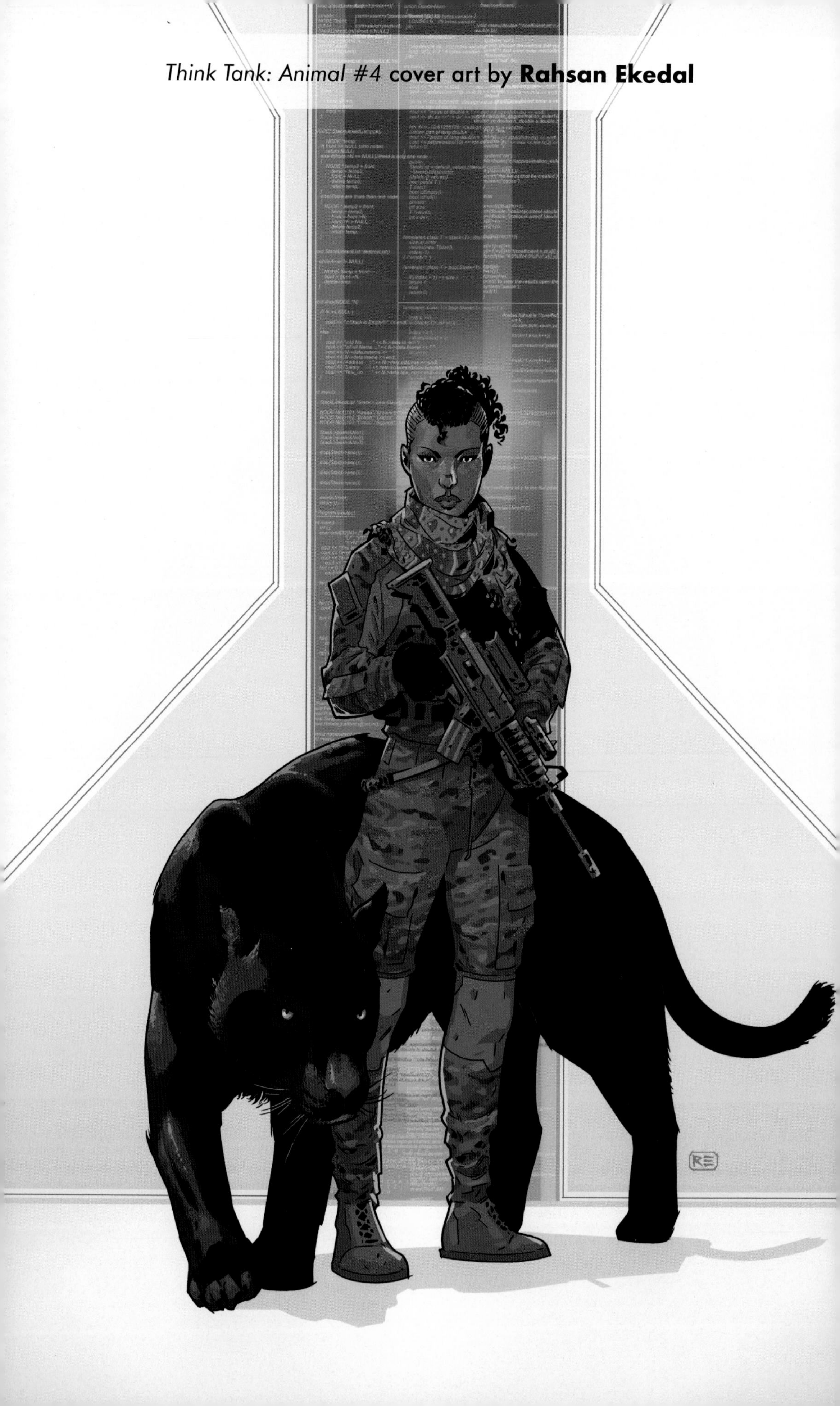

Think Tank: Animal #4 cover art by **Rahsan Ekedal**

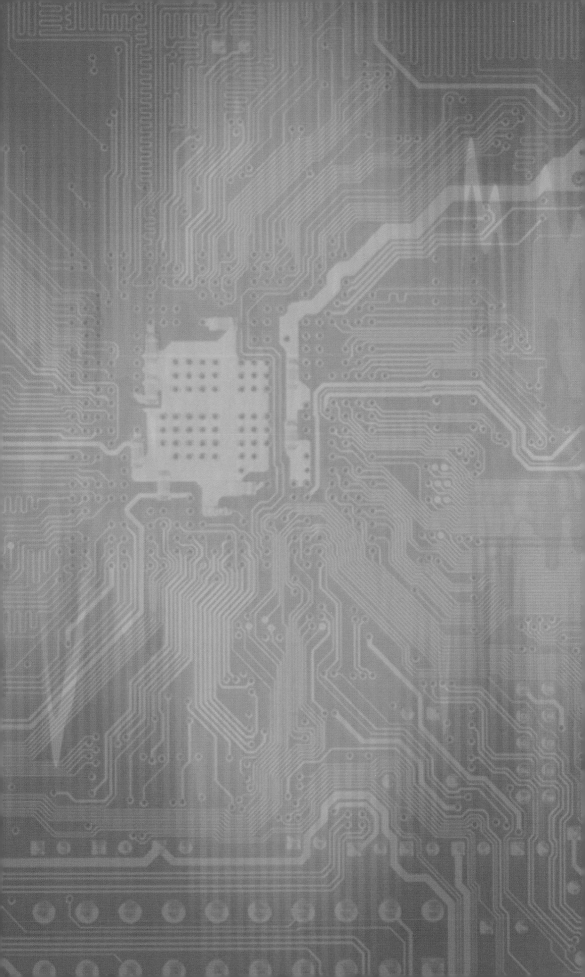

CONNECTION LOST
CONNECTION LOST
CONNECTION LOST
CONNECTION LOST
CONNECTION LOST
CONNECTION LOST
CONNECTION LOST

SCIENCE CLASS

THINK TANK

SCIENCE CLASS

Welcome to Volume 5 of *Think Tank*! Including the first four volumes and the standalone uncollected *Think Tank: Fun with PTSD* one-shot, this issue would be #21 in an ongoing series. If you missed the PTSD one-shot one you can download and read it for free here:

» *http://topcow.com/files/ThinkTank_FunwithPTSD01_reader.pdf*

Thank you for reading this book! It's a joy for Rahsan and I to do. We live in interesting times; a book like *Think Tank* feels prescient, scary and fun all at the same time. As always, I work hard to try and make the science as real as possible, if you're a scientist who specializes in any of the areas I cover and you feel I didn't do it justice, contact me on any of my feeds and I'll fix it when we reprint.

If you haven't figured out my pattern of storytelling with this book yet, there's always one geopolitical story, one technology story and one emotional relationship character story all coalescing into the over-all arcs.

As always, it's hard to get people to try a new comic, so we'd appreciate your recommendation to family and friends. It's the only way indie comics get tried, so we appreciate it!

ANIMALS IN COMBAT

I was reading about how the Danish were training birds to take out Drones and stumbled across some chatter about how the Russians were using crows for surveillance while I was writing *Think Tank Volume 4*. In an increasingly high-tech world, low-tech solutions seem to be the answer. For example, if you saw a Drone following you around you'd freak out yes? I would too. But would you give a second thought to seeing a crow? Would you even think about it being the same crow if you saw it several times in the same day? I wouldn't and neither would most people. Another example of the high-tech/low-tech solution is that the "drop" of written notes in intelligence has increased because of the ease of hacking. You can't hack a handwritten piece of paper. Back on point, I started researching animal use in the history of war and was shocked at how many animals have been used. We reflexively think of horses, dogs and maybe carrier pigeons, but would you consider war pigs, anti-tank dogs, bat/cat/rat bombs, death dolphins, pigeon guided missiles and landmine-seeking rodents? In almost all of these situations, these were suicide uses of the animal, none of them survived.

Not a huge surprise we have to be more careful about their uses in this modern era of social media and YouTube videos catching crazy shit like this on film. Can you imagine the backlash to our military strapping bombs to dogs and teaching them to suicide bomb tanks? There are whole books devoted to just the use of horses in combat, so this scratches the surface but here are a lot of links you can check out:

Here's the link for the Drone killers:

» http://www.theverge.com/2016/9/13/12900596/netherlands-drone-hunting-eagles

The CIA has been training animals for surveillance for decades:

» *http://www.smithsonianmag.com/history/the-cias-most-highly-trained-spies-werent-even-human-20149/*

Sixteen million animals were in service during WWI:

» http://www.iwm.org.uk/history/15-animals-that-went-to-war

» https://www.military-history.org/articles/war-culture-animals-of-war.htm

» http://www.livescience.com/15133-top-10-animal-recruits-war.html

» http://listverse.com/2013/02/05/10-creative-military-plans-to-use-animals-as-weapons/

» http://all-that-is-interesting.com/animals-as-weapons

BIOENGINEERED ANIMALS/INSECTS

We're also creating hybrid animals specifically to perform certain tasks. In an era of *CRISPR*, epigenetics and gene splicing, we're creating entire new species that could very well get out of hand. The implications are staggering to me. What happens if we create a smarter version of a great white shark that can walk and breathe air? That may be extreme, but there are thousands of examples.

DARPA in 2006 asked scientists "to develop technology to create insect-cyborgs" capable of carrying surveillance equipment or weapons. The agency quickly realized that tiny flying machines were impossible to build well — but that insects, already abundant in nature, were better than whatever humans might make. So *DARPA* changed its approach: In the past decade, the agency has encouraged and funded research into methods that can let humans control insects and mammals through electronic impulses to the brain, and through genetic modifications to the nervous systems of insects to make them easier to manipulate, with surprising success.

Read these following links if you want to sleep less at night:

» *http://foreignpolicy.com/2015/06/15/you-dont-have-to-watch-jurassic-world-to-see-bioengineered-animal-weapons/*

» *http://dujs.dartmouth.edu/2013/03/genetically-engineered-bioweapons-a-new-breed-of-weapons-for-modern-warfare/#.V2l6K5MrLVo*

Ethics of using animals:

» *http://www.animal-ethics.org/military-use-animals/*

CROWS

Crows are terrifyingly smart. They are able to remember people. They do hold grudges. They have been known to follow people for extended periods of time just out of curiosity. And they're easy to train to do complex tasks. If you feed a crow at a specific time of day, it'll return the next day and eventually it'll communicate that to its friends and they'll show up too (if there's enough food). One neuroscientist pegged them as equal to a seven-year-old human in cognitive ability.

I've become so fascinated by crows that I've completely reversed my prior resentment of their loud caws that sometimes wake me up in the morning. Now I find myself looking out the window at them wondering what they're thinking about. If you don't have respect for crows, watch this first YouTube link and then skim the following articles I've linked. The last YouTube video shows what a bird's vision looks like:

» https://www.youtube.com/watch?v=URZ_EciujrE

» http://nymag.com/scienceofus/2016/07/crows-continue-to-be-terrifyingly-intelligent.html

» https://cosmosmagazine.com/social-sciences/why-are-crows-so-smart

» https://www.youtube.com/watch?v=bG2y8dG2QIM

HORSES

I knew horses were smart, but I hadn't realized how much so until I started doing some of the research. Horses don't like most humans. They tolerate us. They will form bonds with specific individuals over periods of time and this is genuine attachment/affection, but even those horses will barely tolerate other people.

» ***http://www.horsetalk.co.nz/2012/10/11/understanding-horse-intelligence/#axzz4Who0ZKuy***

» ***http://blog.horze.com/how-intelligent-are-horses***

» ***http://www.globalanimal.org/2015/04/29/animal-iqs-which-is-the-smartest-animal/***

cerebellum
cerebral hemisphere
cerebellum
hind brain
dorsal view
hind brain
lateral view
cerebral cortex
cerebrum
nerve fibres joining right and left cerebral hemispheres
3rd ventricle
cerebellum
spinal cord
thalamus
hypothalamus
pons
medulla oblongata
pituitary gland

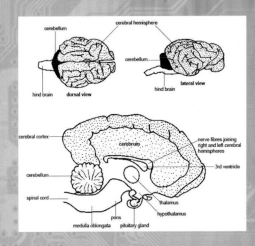

PIGS

Pigs are smarter than dogs. Let that sink in for a minute. I had zero clue what the difference between boar, pig and hog was so included that because I thought it was interesting. Pigs have been taught to play video games to get food, look at the first YouTube link. I like bacon, damn it's good, but I do find it kind of arbitrary what we pick as food animals and what we don't. I've been to a lot of foreign countries and actually seen a menu with a dog meat dish on it. I love all animals, I've tried a few times to go vegetarian but I've never been successful at it. The second I smell meat being cooked when I'm on a vegan bend, I crack…pathetic, I know.

» **https://www.youtube.com/watch?v=0dFwx95ufEk**

» **https://onekind.org/animal/pig/**

» **http://www.seeker.com/iq-tests-suggest-pigs-are-smart-as-dogs-chimps-1769934406.html**

» **http://www.nbcnews.com/id/24628983/ns/technology_and_science-science/t/smartest-animals/**

MIND CONTROL OF ANIMALS

Is this possible? Yes, and we are doing it now. Training a dog to perform tricks is a form of mind control in repeated behavior for reward, but that's not what I'm talking about. We are using light diodes to get mice to follow simple commands we pulse into their brains.

» **https://www.technologyreview.com/s/602695/how-network-neuroscience-is-creating-a-new-era-of-mind-control/**

» **http://www.livescience.com/48694-instant-brain-to-brain-communication.html**

» **https://www.technologyreview.com/s/513446/wireless-micro-leds-control-mouse-behavior/**

SURFACE-THOUGHT READER

I covered the science of this extensively in *Think Tank Volume 1*. When I started developing this arc, this came to me later that I could tie it back into the first tech in David's comic career. Seemed fun to link it all together and wasn't hard to figure out how to alter his original reader to transmit rather than receive. This is a bit science fiction, I fudged it a bit as I have no real research to correlate at this point, but I do believe that this is possible with today's tech and would be *SHOCKED* if someone hasn't done this already or is close to doing it.

BOLSHOI THEATER

This is a real place! It's on my bucket list of places to hit before I die. I've seen it many times on TV and have watched YouTube clips of some of the performances. I love how well Rahsan kills it showing real locations, so I wanted to highlight this place.

» **http://www.bolshoi.ru/en/**

RUSSIAN GEOPOLITICS

I try and keep this book somewhat relevant to the news at hand and the geopolitical story this arc centers on Russia and NATO. I always try and see every side of something, so I have researched why Russia does what it does. The greatest geopolitical disaster of the 20th century was the collapse of the Soviet Union (read the third link). A once proud, strong country became known for alcoholics, mafia and high-priced prostitutes to the rest of the world. This was unfair, but there was a negative, weak perception of Russia after the fall. Putin has rebuilt Russian pride and helped make Russia matter again on the modern global stage.

In George Friedman's amazing book *The Next 100 Years*, he details out how Russia will do exactly what they've done and how this is a short-term thing. I highly recommend this book; it will blow your mind. It talks about U.S./Chinese relations and how over the next 100 years, our biggest military problem will be with Mexico. It details out why and fascinates, so go get it now!

» **http://www.ecfr.eu/article/understanding_modern_russia_why_european_leaders_should_read_peter_pomerant**

» **https://news.virginia.edu/content/understand-modern-russia-j-term-students-review-1000-years-history**

» **https://www.thetrumpet.com/5976-the-key-to-understanding-russia**

2050: GLOBAL WAR BETWEEN U.S., TURKEY, POLAND, AND JAPAN—THE NEW GREAT POWERS
2100: MEXICO CHALLENGES U.S.
2020: CHINA FRAGMENTS
2080: SPACE-BASED ENERGY POWERS EARTH
THE NEXT 100 YEARS
A FORECAST for the 21st CENTURY

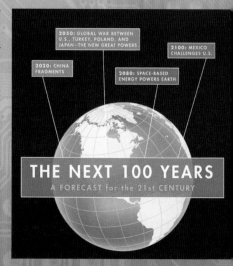

KFC IN RUSSIA

I'm always amazed when I travel internationally and see places I wouldn't expect. All throughout Tokyo I saw Denny's and AM/PMs. In Seoul, South Korea I kept seeing Taco Bells everywhere. KFC is legitimately huge in Russia; check the link.

» http://www.nytimes.com/2011/08/04/business/global/russia-becomes-a-magnet-for-american-fast-food-chains.html

RUSSIAN REFERENCE

From T-90 tanks, to Russian field uniforms, to their flag, here's where you can go see that Rahsan Ekedal strives for realistic portrayal of our subject matter!

» http://nationalinterest.org/blog/the-buzz/americas-mighty-m-1-abrams-tank-vs-russias-lethal-t-90-who-13919

» https://rusmilitary.wordpress.com/2013/12/26/russian-army-to-use-new-field-service-uniform/

» http://russianflag.facts.co/flagofrussia.php

COLD WAR

I grew up during the Cold War and lived on Air Force bases, so it was a real thing for me every day. The end of it came as a surprise, the reasoning was essentially that Gorbachev tried to make economic changes (Glasnost and Perestroika) and they simply did not work fast enough and the country imploded.

» http://history.stackexchange.com/questions/8084/are-there-ways-to-measure-how-much-power-did-russia-lose-when-the-soviet-union

» https://infogr.am/cold-war-statistics

RUSSIAN/BALTIC STATES RACISM

I was shocked to discover how overtly racist parts of the world are. We certainly have a lot of drama here in the USA, but read some of these links. Our NATO ally Estonia did ask NATO to stop sending black troops to protect them. There were people inside the government there that were horrified by this, including Estonian Air Force Supreme Commander Jaak Tarien who said: *"They are willing to give their lives for our freedom. Are you, petty patriotic racists, ready to give so much for our country?"*

» https://www.theguardian.com/world/2016/feb/15/black-in-the-ussr-whats-life-like-for-a-russian-of-colour

» http://observer.com/2016/02/estonia-wants-more-nato-troops-but-only-if-they-arent-black/

» https://sputniknews.com/europe/201510291029280282-estonia-nato-black-officers/

NAZIS, HITLER AND MISAPPROPRIATED QUOTES

I've used this quote many times: "If you tell a lie big enough and keep repeating it, people will eventually come to believe it." I've even used it in *Think Tank* on the quote page before. I was shocked to discover there's no real proof Goebbels ever said this. The quote I included in this issue came from *Mein Kampf* (My Struggle), which Hitler wrote and published in 1925. There are a LOT of quotes that seemingly have been made up for many famous people. Check the third link for a series of these from Churchill, Einstein and many more.

» https://www.quora.com/What-are-some-quotes-that-have-been-significantly-misused-abused-or-misinterpreted

» http://www.ihr.org/other/weber2011fakequotations.html

» http://paleofuture.gizmodo.com/9-quotes-from-winston-churchill-that-are-totally-fake-1790585636

PRESIDENTIAL SHIFT

So there were two things I wanted to include in the narrative of this issue to tie some things up for *Think Tank* and Edenverse, but ultimately left it out for space reasons and it felt too info-dumpy. For those of you also reading *Samaritan*, which takes place AFTER this volume of *Think Tank*, Senator Owen McKitrick becomes president between this volume and the *Samaritan* story. Ultimately, Wilhelm decided not to run and her VP ran instead for the Democrats and got defeated by McKitrick, who was sworn in as president. I've received many comments about the comparison of McKitrick to Trump and what I can say is that I wrote the outline for this series WELL before Trump even declared he was running for president. I based McKitrick on an evil version of Ted Cruz. Cruz is a religious ideologue, but McKitrick is NOT Cruz, it was just who in my head I took to the dark side and played with for fictional effect. I'm not a Cruz fan but I don't believe Cruz would do what McKitrick did in *Tithe* V2.

YURI GURSINSKI AND BOMBING AT THE BOLSHOI

Yuri Gursinski's wife was the one killed in the beginning of *Think Tank: Animal* #2 at the Bolshoi bombing. The first three bombings specifically targeted Euro-politicians, the Bolshoi was intended to show Russia under attack. These were all staged, and the Bolshoi one was intended as a win-win. Gursinski, as you can see from the dialogue, walks away at a key moment and lets his wife die. I had written this as a throwaway side plot that he wanted his wife dead anyway and was using this as an opportunity to take her out. I based this on a real thing that one of the Russian oligarchs had done to get rid of his wife so he'd keep all his money.

PLAUSIBILITY OF PLOT

In finalizing this last issue and reviewing the insanity that is our regular political and geopolitical world, I absolutely believe this is possible. People tend to believe what they want to depending on whether or not it conforms to their worldview and bias. The Turkish people are VERY wary of the US and our relations with them. I'll detail some specifics with links below. So you have a Muslim country with a population that believes we hate Islam. In the US we have a lot of access to media reports, and if you bother, you can filter through the fake news and figure out what's real…but this requires effort and access. A lot of other countries don't have access to the internet like we do and they can't READ English. Do you think the Arabic and Turkish language sites paint a positive view of the US? To be fair, some probably do (I don't know I can't read either), but I'd bet most of them do not. The tech stuff in this story is all accurate and in use now. The geopolitics is always tougher!

UNITED STATES AND TURKEY

We have a complicated relationship. Turkey is vitally important because of its geographic location and its democracy. "Turkey is in the middle of the four regions which are seen as predicament; Balkans, Caucasus, middle East and Gulf. This position puts Turkey as indispensable for the ones who have expedience in these regions. Turkey is located on the Anatolian peninsula, has three seas around: Black Sea, Mediterranean Sea and Aegean Sea." That's taken from the second link below. That link is worth reading because it's written by someone who lives in Turkey. The *TIME* one is written in the West and has our point-of-view. That *TIME* also explains WHY Turkey is so valuable to NATO. Before we built bases in Iraq and Afghanistan there was a US Air Force base in Turkey called Incirlik and it was one of the main bases used to attack at the beginning of those wars. Ironically, Germany was against these wars and we launched a LOT of sorties out of our Air Force base there. The third link listed is the Air Force's accounting of Incirlik but it's under Turkish control now. That fourth link talks specifically about US and Turkey relations over the years and has a flowchart timeline.

» http://time.com/4457369/the-u-s-and-nato-need-turkey/

» http://mensur-boydas.blogcu.com/strategic-importance-of-turkey/7861648

» http://www.incirlik.af.mil/

» https://www.nationalreview.com/magazine/2017-06-11-2050/turkeys-us-relations-erdogan

TURKISH COUP ATTEMPT

On July 15, 2016, part of the Turkish military tried to take over the country and unseat Turkish President Recep Tayyip Erdoğan who was elected democratically. This coup failed in dramatic fashion as the people rose up and struck the military down, you can see a timeline and some fascinating videos here:

» http://www.aljazeera.com/news/2016/07/turkey-timeline-coup-attempt-unfolded-160716004455515.html

President Erdoğan accused the CIA of being behind the coup. There are politicians in the US who want to kick Turkey out of NATO and Turkey has threatened to leave NATO because of stuff like this, but the reality is Turkey and the US really need each other for a lot of complicated reasons. Things could change, but I don't see them leaving. Part of my story was trying to figure out given this tenuous balance what would cause Turkey to leave NATO. Killing off the president and it being blamed at least partially on the US and then having a more religious ideologue Muslim leader coming into power there would do it in a heartbeat. The Russians were prepared to back a new candidate financially to get him in and VOILA no more NATO.

» https://www.voanews.com/a/timeline-turkey-attempted-coup/3420876.html

» http://www.mirror.co.uk/news/world-news/what-happened-turkey-attempted-coup-8432395

TURKEY/RUSSIAN RELATIONS

Their relations are equally complicated and have a longer history than the US has even been a nation. Turkey borders Georgia, which used to be part of the USSR so they shared a border for a long time during the Cold War. The Jupiter missiles I talk about in the story partially caused and helped resolve the Cuban Missile Crisis.

» *http://www.bbc.com/news/world-middle-east-34912581*

» *https://www.economist.com/news/europe/21717080-putin-and-erdogan-expect-different-and-contradictory-things-their-relationship-turkeys*

TURKEY DID RECENTLY BUY MISSILES FROM RUSSIA

I have this in the beginning of the story in this issue, but this was straight out of the headlines. How this impacts Russia/US/Turkey relations hasn't fully shaken out yet, but it's fascinating to read about.

» *https://www.economist.com/news/europe/21721665-their-friendship-should-worry-nato-turkey-and-russia-cosy-up-over-missiles*

NATO ARTICLE 5

I've talked about NATO in previous *Think Tank* Science Classes so won't go into detail here but the Article 5 I refer to is simply a clause to provide for the collective defense. Any NATO member attacked, the rest of the membership is required to respond as if they'd been attacked themselves. You can read the charter and this clause at the link below.

» **http://www.nato.int/cps/cn/natohq/topics_110496.htm**

TURKEY'S WEAPONS PROGRAMS

Turkey has the second largest army in NATO. That surprises most people when people realize that. Another interesting fact is that Turkey has now started exporting its own weapons around the world, just like the US, China and Russia do. The catalog to buy Turkish weapons is below at the link. If you buy two tanks, you get a free VCR (that's a joke).

» **http://www.ssm.gov.tr/urunkatalog/data/ekatalog/eng/index.html#20**

COMPARISON OF USA AND TURKEY

If Turkey were your home instead of The United States you would "die 6.27 years sooner, be 3.5 times more likely to die in infancy, be 27.4% more likely to be unemployed, make 71.02% less money, spend 92.53% less money on health care, consume 85.28% less oil, use 82.87% less electricity, be 69.63% less likely to be in prison…" Stats from the link, I love this site:

» **http://www.ifitweremyhome.com/compare/US/TR**

CROW CEREBELLUM AND MOVEMENT

» **https://www.ncbi.nlm.nih.gov/pubmed/17786812**

THE END?

To be determined. I hope not. I'm writing a *Think Tank* prose novel that will be out in late 2018. I'm actively working on trying to get it set up as a TV series like we did with *Postal*. If this is it, I'd like to thank all of you who've read the series and been so kind. I'll see you on the convention circuit.

Carpe Diem,

Matt Hawkins
7/10/2017 Los Angeles
Twitter: @topcowmatt | http://www.facebook.com/selfloathingnarcissist

MATT HAWKINS

A veteran of the initial Image Comics launch, Matt started his career in comic book publishing in 1993 and has been working with Image as a creator, writer and executive for over 20 years. President/COO of Top Cow since 1998, Matt has created and written over 30 new franchises for Top Cow and Image including *Think Tank*, *The Tithe*, *Necromancer*, *VICE*, *Lady Pendragon*, *Aphrodite IX*, and *Tales of Honor*, as well as handling the company's business affairs.

RAHSAN EKEDAL

Rahsan Ekedal is an artist best known for his work on *Think Tank*, and the Harvey Award-nominated graphic novel *Echoes*. He has illustrated a variety of titles such as *Solomon Kane*, *Creepy Comics*, *The Cleaners*, and *Warhammer*, and worked with many publishers including Top Cow, Dark Horse, DC/Vertigo and Boom! Studios. He was born in California and educated at the School of the Arts High School and the Academy of Art University, both in San Francisco. Rahsan currently lives in Berlin, Germany, with his wife, Shannon, and their big black cat, Flash.

OTHER BOOKS WRITTEN BY ME AND RAHSAN EKEDAL

The Tithe vol. 1
ISBN: 978-1632153241
Written by Matt Hawkins
Art by Rahsan Ekedal
A heist story like no other, with fraudalent megachurches pitted against Robin Hood hackers.

Symmetry vol. 1
ISBN: 978-1632156990
Written by Matt Hawkins
Art by Raffaele Ienco
Unlikely love sparks a dangerous revolution in a Utopian future!

Echoes vol. 1
ISBN: 978-1632156600
Written by Joshua Fialkov
Art by Rahsan Ekedal
A young man stricken with schizophrenia discovers his abusive father's horrifying legacy.

Wildfire vol. 1
ISBN: 978-1632150240
Written by Matt Hawkins
Art by Linda Sejic
In this GMO conspiracy thriller, a plant growth formula leads to the destruction of Los Angeles.

Read **Think Tank #1** for FREE!   *http://topcow.com/files/Think_Tank_01_Digital.pdf*

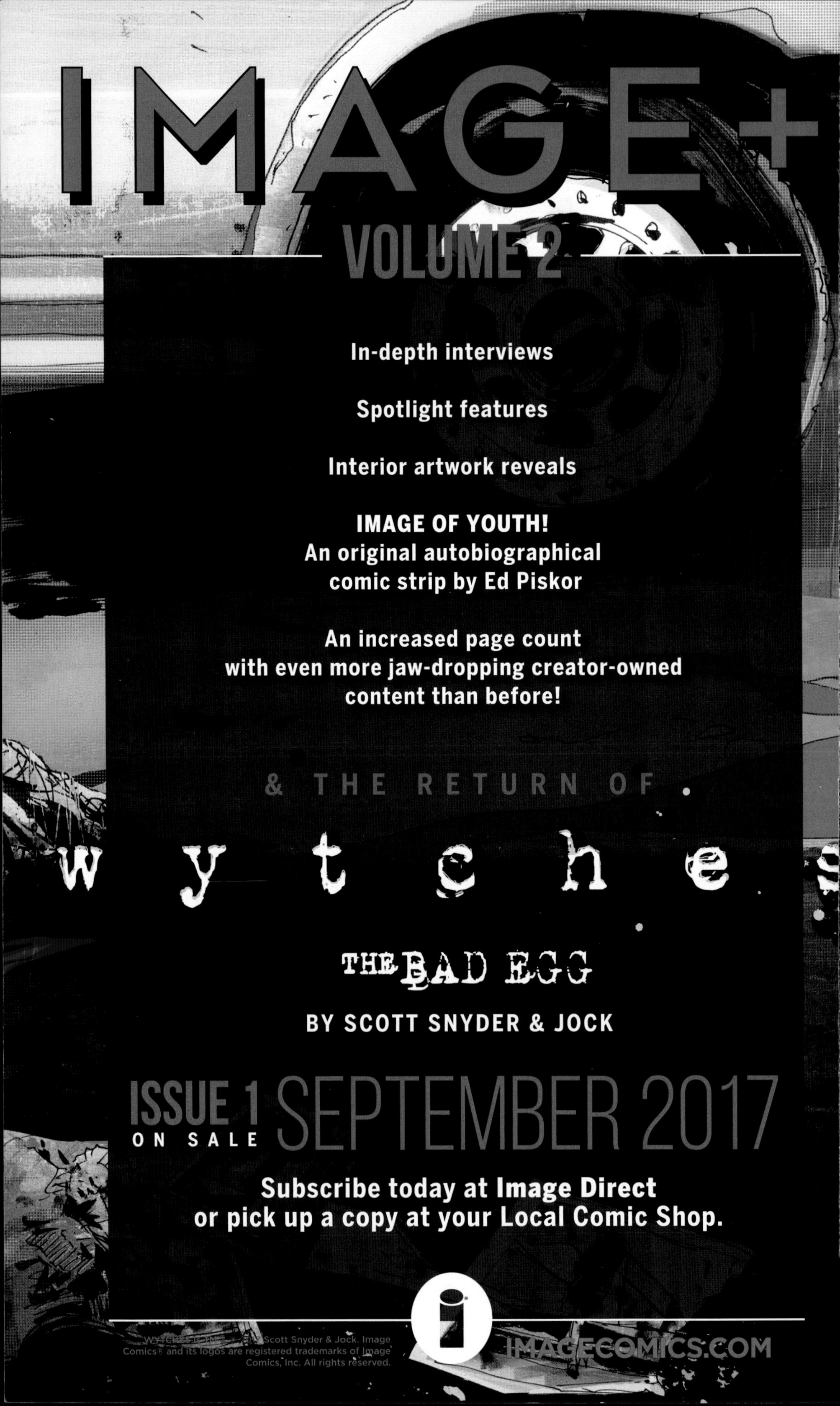
IMAGE+
VOLUME 2
In-depth interviews
Spotlight features
Interior artwork reveals
IMAGE OF YOUTH!
An original autobiographical
comic strip by Ed Piskor
An increased page count
with even more jaw-dropping creator-owned
content than before!
& THE RETURN OF
wytches
THE BAD EGG
BY SCOTT SNYDER & JOCK
ISSUE 1
ON SALE
SEPTEMBER 2017
Subscribe today at Image Direct
or pick up a copy at your Local Comic Shop.
Scott Snyder & Jock. Image
Comics® and its logos are registered trademarks of Image
Comics, Inc. All rights reserved.
IMAGECOMICS.COM

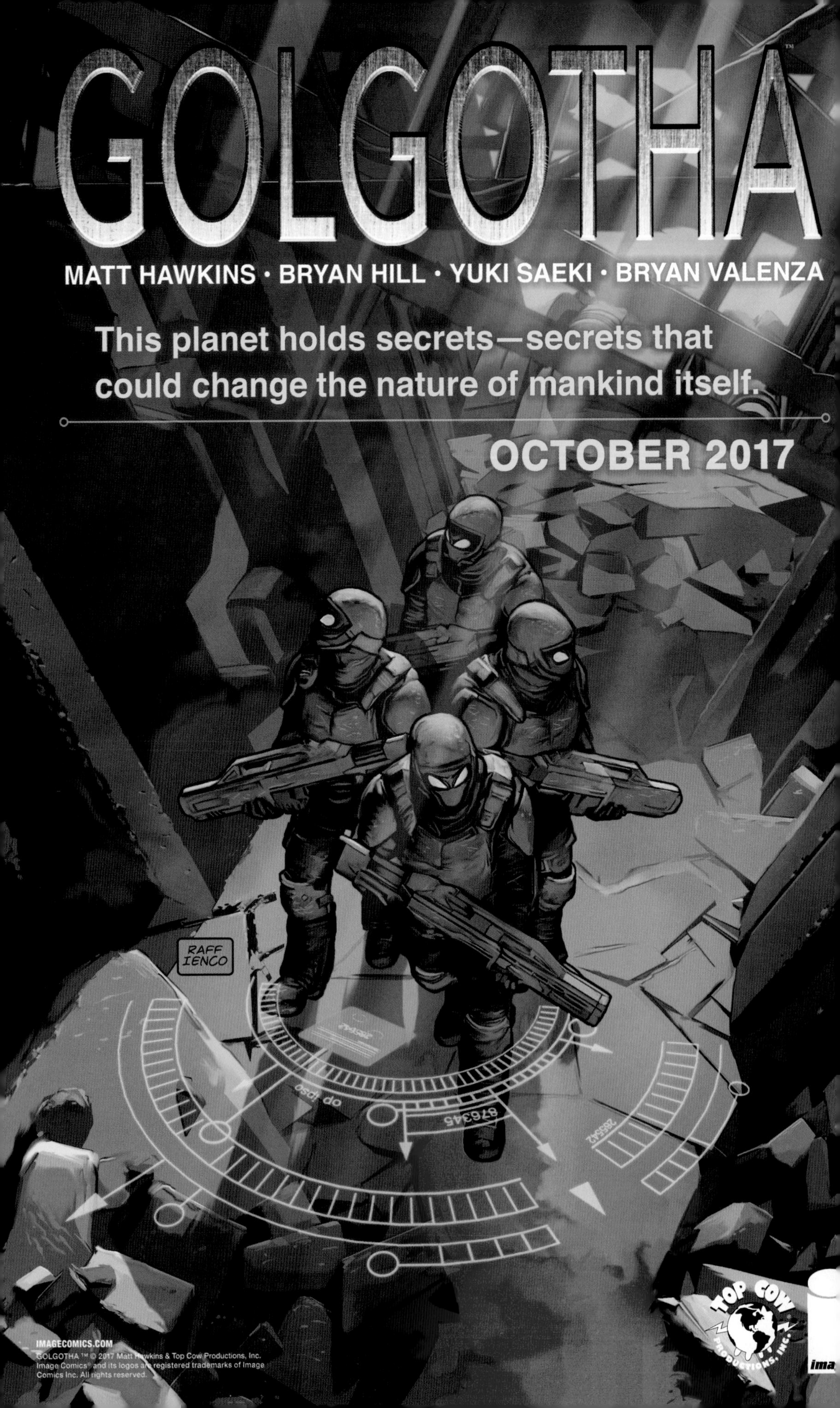
GOLGOTHA™
MATT HAWKINS · BRYAN HILL · YUKI SAEKI · BRYAN VALENZA
This planet holds secrets—secrets that could change the nature of mankind itself.
OCTOBER 2017
RAFF IENCO
IMAGECOMICS.COM
GOLGOTHA ™ © 2017 Matt Hawkins & Top Cow Productions, Inc. Image Comics® and its logos are registered trademarks of Image Comics Inc. All rights reserved.
TOP COW PRODUCTIONS, INC.

The Top Cow essentials checklist:

For more ISBN and ordering information on our latest collections go to:
www.topcow.com
Ask your retailer about our catalogue of collected editions,
digests, and hard covers or check the listings at:
Barnes and Noble, Amazon.com,
and other fine retailers.

To find your nearest comic shop go to:
www.comicshoplocator.com

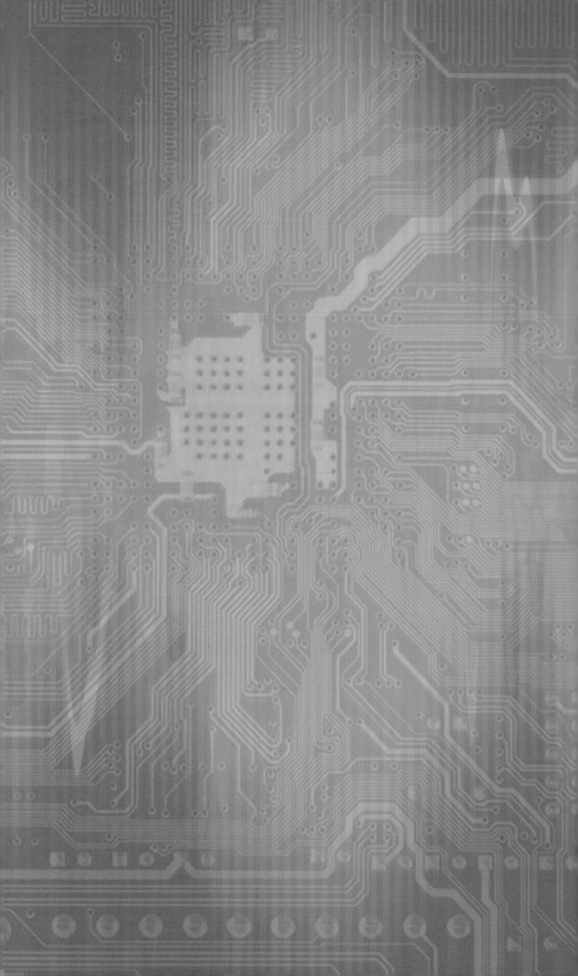